# W.H. Crossland

# W.H. Crossland

## An Architectural Biography

Sheila Binns

Ⓛ

The Lutterworth Press

**The Lutterworth Press**
P.O. Box 60
Cambridge
CB1 2NT
United Kingdom

www.lutterworth.com
publishing@lutterworth.com

Paperback ISBN: 978 0 7188 9548 8
PDF ISBN: 978 0 7188 4802 6
ePub ISBN: 978 0 7188 4803 3
Kindle ISBN: 978 0 7188 4804 0

*British Library Cataloguing in Publication Data*
A record is available from the British Library

First published by The Lutterworth Press, 2020

This book is published
with the generous assistance of grants
from the Marc Fitch Fund and
Isobel Thornley's Bequest to the University of London

# Contents

Opposite page:
(top) Rochdale Town Hall by Edward Walker, 1875.
(middle) Virginia Park, previously the Holloway Sanatorium.
(bottom) Royal Holloway, University of London.

# List of illustrations and credits

Images marked with an asterisk (*) are property of the author.

*Note:* The Holloway Sanatorium, now private housing, has been renamed Virginia Park. Holloway College was renamed Royal Holloway College at its opening in 1886 and is now Royal Holloway, University of London.

# Acknowledgements

My first acknowledgement must be to the extraordinary building that is Founder's Building at Royal Holloway, University of London. I have both worked and enjoyed being a mature student at Royal Holloway, and the flamboyant architecture of the building never ceased to draw my attention. It seemed that every time I walked past, something new enticed me to look closer. The interior is also fascinating, and yet, when I asked about the architect of this stupendous building, few people knew anything about him. An invisible finger seemed to point to me to find out about the person who designed this unique edifice.

With no core repository of his work to draw on, piecing together the life of W.H. Crossland and writing this biography has been a long process. I sincerely thank everyone who has helped me along the way. I am indebted to L.J. Whitaker and Edward Law for their earlier work on Crossland, which gave me a considerable start in my research. I am grateful to numerous people for their assistance and encouragement, not least the archivists and librarians who have helped me uncover material about him. I owe thanks to Janet Douglas for welcoming me to the event that really began my research on Crossland. This was the study weekend entitled 'Stanhope Country' run by the Victorian Society's West Yorkshire Group in 2012, when I was privileged to share some of her knowledge of Crossland and visit a few of Crossland's Yorkshire churches. I thank Ian Dungavell for his help and support, as well as friends at The Victorian Society's London headquarters for their interest and encouragement. I say *merci* to Danièle Meune for helping me to understand the account of the death of Crossland's wife. I am particularly grateful to Steven Brindle for proofreading my work and for his advice and invaluable suggestions.

Above all, I am grateful to Peter, my husband, for his constant support. He has made suggestions, given me ideas, encouraged me in my numerous visits to archives and has usually acted as the driver for expeditions to visit

Crossland's buildings. He discovered the Crossland connection with the church in Kildwick, West Yorkshire, when he joined the bell ringers for their regular practice one evening and afterwards joked that it was the reason for his promotion from research assistant to assistant researcher. Peter's Yorkshire roots meant that we visited West Yorkshire often, which provided perfect opportunities to find out about Crossland in Yorkshire.

I have tried always to check source material carefully, but if any errors or misinterpretations have slipped through, I apologise, as they are my fault alone.

Sheila Binns
2020

# Crossland: a note on the name

The name 'Crossland' pinpoints very precisely the origins of William Henry Crossland.[1] Crosland (one 's') is a Huddersfield name that derives from Crosland Moor, an area to the south-west of the town. The 1881 census results show those having the name mostly limited to the Huddersfield area, with a few in Leeds, but no significant numbers anywhere else in the country. It comes as a surprise that, although sometimes recorded with only one 's', W.H. Crossland's family generally used a double 's' in their name. So unusual was this spelling in the Huddersfield area that a report in a local paper describing Crossland's first work made a reasonable assumption and spelled the name with one 's'.[2] It was also spelled with only one 's' on some official documents such as census entries.

The name spelled with a double 's' is also a localised name in the West Riding of Yorkshire. In 1881, it was used predominantly nearby in the Wakefield area, but spreading over Halifax, Sheffield, Leeds, Bradford and Huddersfield. Crossland's father spelled his name with a double 's', suggesting that previous generations of his family may have moved from Huddersfield to one of the neighbouring towns and adopted the local spelling of the name, which was then retained by a later generation on moving back to Huddersfield. This would account for the unfamiliar spelling among the Croslands of Huddersfield. As if to emphasise the difference in the spelling of his name from the more usual single 's' in the Huddersfield area, early in his career William Henry sometimes used the β symbol for the double 's' in his name.

His name would undoubtedly have been an advantage as the young architect began to make his way professionally. Crossland's early work kept him almost exclusively in the West Riding, where, whether his name was

---

1. http://gbnames.publicprofiler.org/ (accessed 30 November 2015).
2. *The Huddersfield Chronicle and West Yorkshire Advertiser,* 29 March 1856, Issue 315, p. 6.

spelled with a single or double 's', he would have been recognised as a
local man, even before potential clients met him, inspiring confidence and
a reassurance that he would instinctively understand how best to design
buildings suitable for the West Riding.

W.H. Crossland's usual signature.

William Henry Crossland.

# Introduction

At the lavish opening ceremony of the Royal Holloway College in 1886, William Henry Crossland presented Queen Victoria with an album of his drawings of Royal Holloway College – the phantasmagoria of a building he had created for Thomas Holloway in Egham, Surrey. This, Crossland must have reflected, was truly the high point of his life and of his career and a long way from the Huddersfield quarry business where he had grown up. A well-known and much-praised architect, he proudly offered the Queen his own work in a gesture that underlined the extent of his success. As he gloried in the admiration of his College – a highly successful architect at the peak of his career – he could never have foreseen that in just a few years, he would have fallen from this peak into obscurity.

W.H. Crossland is often described using terms such as 'maverick', 'enigma' and 'mysterious'. Indeed, among the architects of the second half of the nineteenth century who have left great buildings for posterity, Crossland has remained a shadowy figure, although he has also been described as one of the finest architects of the day.[1] In addition to the Royal Holloway College, his portfolio includes two more glorious buildings now listed as Grade I, as well as a collection of more than twenty other listed buildings[2], that does not include his restoration work on ancient churches (several of which are also listed at Grade 1). He is known to have built seventeen churches and to have restored or rebuilt another thirteen, but there may be more of his work that is still unknown. He also designed many secular buildings. It has been said of him that his 'versatility in adapting historical styles was astonishing, even among Victorian architects'.[3] Yet, despite most of his buildings surviving to

---

1. *Huddersfield Daily Examiner*, 10 May 1985.
2. https://historicengland.org.uk/listing/the-list/list-entry/1415452 (accessed 21 November 2016).
3. Williams, Elizabeth, 'An Architectural History of Royal Holloway College, Egham, 1876-87' in *Surrey Archaeological Society Journal*, 1986, p. 95.

the present day, little is known of him and almost nothing is known of the last few years of his life. No obituary was written for him and his burial or cremation place is a secret still waiting to be discovered.

Several people, including Sir John Betjeman, have tried hard to uncover Crossland's secrets, but have always come across gaps in information, loose ends and big question marks. So far as is known, he left no diaries, logbooks or other records of his work, and, towards the end of his life, he destroyed all the work he had in his possession. His work was documented in architectural journals, but the only substantial piece of writing linked directly to him is the record of an address he gave to the Royal Institute of British Architects in 1887, the year after the formal opening of the College. This address is preserved among the Transactions of the R.I.B.A.. Copies of plans of some of his buildings, a few letters and a small number of other documents are scattered thinly over several archives, but these sources paint only a partial picture.

Much of what little is known about Crossland is by way of short accounts, with surprisingly little connection made between his work in the north of England and his work in the south. The most substantial pieces of work on Crossland, so far, are a master's degree thesis by L.J. Whitaker, submitted in 1984 and held by Manchester University, and an account by Edward Law, dated 1992 and published on the internet.[4] However, recently available digitised material has provided information that was unavailable to earlier researchers, filling some of the gaps, tying off some of the loose ends and providing some answers regarding Crossland's life and career. In particular, the nineteenth-century newspapers digital archive[5] and online archive catalogues proved to be rich resources.

It is clear that Crossland had a good, even privileged, start in life. His architectural training was under George Gilbert Scott, which gave him a certain status, and he went on to seek out and grasp opportunities. He ran a busy practice in the West Riding of Yorkshire mostly designing and building churches, for which he established a good reputation. He also designed numerous secular buildings, particularly in his home town of

4. Edward Law's work, *William Henry Crossland, Architect, 1835-1908*, http://homepage.eircom.net/~lawedd/WHC1.htm, is divided into seven Parts. Each Part is presented as one extended page. Footnotes therefore refer to the relevant Part.

5. All material from newspapers (except *The Times*) was sourced from the online databases *19th Century British Library Newspapers: Part 1 and Part II: 1800-1900* (British Library Newspapers/Gale Digital Collections). *The Times* was sourced from *The Times Digital Archive*. For the sake of brevity, references cite the newspapers only. In the instances of some material sourced online, particularly from classified advertisements, only the newspaper issue number is cited, as no page number is provided in the online source.

Huddersfield, but also nearby in Elland, Halifax, Dewsbury and Leeds. Only a few of his Yorkshire projects took him further afield. He travelled abroad several times during his life, visiting France and Belgium, and, according to Edward Law, he went to Switzerland when he was working on Rochdale Town Hall. He also spent time in Canada.

Little is known of the office support that Crossland had. He mentioned 'assistants' and 'clerks' occasionally in some of his letters, and from around 1867 his Chief Assistant was essential to the success of many of Crossland's projects. This was Mr A.J. Taylor, who worked for Crossland for more than a decade. He may also have employed the architect William Bakewell for a while at the end of the 1860s.[6] It would have been normal practice to take on architectural pupils both for the fees such training would provide and because routine drafting tasks could have been given to pupils, allowing Crossland to pursue more strategic obligations. However, details of pupils, if any, remain unknown.

Few images of Crossland remain and almost nothing is known of his personality, although the designer C.R. Ashbee said of him: 'I like him – he is a fine quiet man with a dreamlike dignity in him.'[7] He won the long-term confidence of wealthy patrons, suggesting reliability, honesty, integrity, hard work, fairness and the ability to work to schedules and deadlines. This confidence in him was to yield large dividends.

Alongside his architectural skills, Crossland was also a talented artist. He sketched and painted, mentioning his sketches in his report preceding the restoration of Almondbury Church.[8] He exhibited at the Royal Academy first in 1855 and then from 1869 (when he moved his office to London) for the next fifteen years.[9] Little of his artwork remains, but the Royal Holloway archive holds a charcoal cartoon by him showing the interior of the chapel. He understood the precarious role of artists, and in his address to the R.I.B.A. in 1887, he devoted a considerable part of his speech to a plea for sculptors to be better recognised and supported.

Until he moved south, his work held almost entirely to the tenets of the Gothic revival and his churches show a clear understanding of Gothic forms[10], revealing him as a true disciple of his master, George Gilbert Scott, and of the principles of Augustus Pugin that Scott so thoroughly absorbed.

6. Douglas, Janet, correspondence 2017.
7. Quoted in Saint, Andrew and Richard Holder, 'Holloway Sanatorium: A Conservation Nightmare', *The Victorian Society Annual*, 1993, p. 25, citing the Ashbee Journals.
8. West Yorkshire Archive Service Kirklees, DD/RA/C/box 36, Crossland, W.H., *Report of the Proposed Restoration of the Parish Church Almondbury*, Copy, 1872.
9. Law, Edward, *William Henry Crossland, Architect, 1835-1908*, 1992, Part 1.
10. Whitaker, L.J., *W.H. Crossland* (master's degree thesis), University of Manchester, 1984, p. 245.

His style was generally based on the Decorated or 'Second Pointed' style, but included elements from earlier periods, which he combined with confidence. It was not until much later in his career that he showed any interest in other architectural styles, and even in his later work elements of Gothic are often evident. Some consider that his buildings in Huddersfield have been undeservedly overlooked nationally in favour of his three magnificent buildings that are now listed at Grade 1.[11]

Crossland designed churches only for the Church of England. He was a member of the Ecclesiological Society and subscribed to their journal, *The Ecclesiologist*.[12] He was therefore well aware of the Society's design guidelines for new churches and restorations, and he designed with its principles in mind, several of his designs being reviewed in the journal. His early church buildings were mostly in Huddersfield or within a few miles of that town and all were built of stone, as there was a plentiful supply from the quarries in the locality. He understood how decorative stone and wood carving could bring a building alive and, depending on the funds available, used it as much possible, favouring a local Yorkshire sculptor by the name of Samuel Ruddock to work on several of his Yorkshire churches. As Whitaker observed, 'His largest and most important churches show Crossland to be aware of the ideas prevalent in contemporary church architecture and also to be capable of originality and experiment.'[13]

Throughout the 1860s, church-building provided Crossland's main income. The character of his church designs depended on the funding available, and there was a great difference between, for instance, St Stephen the Martyr, Copley, near Halifax (1865), which had the support of a wealthy patron, and St James the Great, Flockton (1869), which was built with limited funds. He also designed shops, houses, lodges, schools and offices and attempted to secure larger projects by entering architectural competitions. The number of commercial and other non-church commissions increased as he established his reputation as a talented architect, and the major buildings of his career amply demonstrate his outstanding architectural ability.

This book sets out to place William Henry Crossland in his rightful position in the pantheon of great Victorian architects. Drawing on recently available material, as well as the work of earlier researchers, it attempts to provide a more detailed picture than has previously been available of a man

---

11. Gibson, Keith and Albert Booth, *The Buildings of Huddersfield* (Stroud 2005, reprinted 2009), p. 98.
12. Douglas, Janet, *William Henry Crossland*, unpublished notes of lecture delivered at Cannon Hall, Cawthorne, South Yorkshire, 21 April 2012.
13. Whitaker, p. 65.

who wrote of himself, 'I found myself leading a life we architects read about but few experience.'[14] The narrative is chronological with glimpses of his private life and discussion of his building projects as he worked on them. Some of his works were completed quickly and some needed a protracted period of development so that, at any one time, he was managing several projects at varying stages of maturity, including both new buildings and restorations. A hectic work programme becomes evident, as these projects, particularly later in his career, could be some 200 miles apart at a time when transport was limited.

This is the first account of Crossland's life that places him at the centre of the narrative, unravelling some of the mysteries in his history and enabling, for the first time, an appreciation and understanding of his life and work. It is supported by new photographs and contemporary images.

14. Crossland, W.H., 'The Royal Holloway College', *R.I.B.A. Transactions*, Second series, Vol 3, 1886-67, p. 145.

*Chapter 1*

# Early years

William Henry Crossland was born into a prosperous family of working-class origins in 1835 in Elland, near Halifax in the West Riding of Yorkshire. He was baptised in the ancient parish church of St Mary in Elland on 10 May 1835.[1] His parents were Henry Crossland (1806-77) and Ellen (née Wilkinson, 1812-67).

His father's birthplace was Halifax[2], and Ellen was born in Lindley, a village in the parish of Halifax.[3] They both seem to have moved to Huddersfield before their wedding, as when they were married on 19 August 1832 at Huddersfield Parish Church, they were both stated to be of that parish. Henry signed the register and Ellen made her mark, implying she was not literate. William Henry had one elder brother, James, who was born in Huddersfield in 1833 and who, by 1851, was employed as a clerk in a woollen mill. Their father was described as a mason on William Henry's birth certificate.[4] During the 1850s and 1860s, he was also a churchwarden at the nearby church of St. John's, Bay Hall, suggesting that the brothers were brought up in an active Anglican family.

William Henry's childhood home was Longwood House, Netheroyd Hill, some three miles north of the centre of Huddersfield[5], rented by his father from the Thornhill family of Fixby Hall, Huddersfield.

This was a substantial house, indicating his father's business standing. It was in a rural area where the natural landscape was scarred by quarries. Nearby were the woodlands of Fixby Hall and Bradley Park, possibly part of the long wood from which the house took its name.[6] The 1841 census

---

1. https://www.ancestryinstitution.com.
2. https://www.ancestryinstitution.com.
3. Law, Edward, *William Henry Crossland, Architect, 1835-1908*, (homepage.eircom. net/,1992), Part 1.
4. https://www.ancestryinstitution.com.
5. https://www.ancestryinstitution.com.
6. Law, Part 1.

1.1 Longwood House, Crossland's childhood home.
Photograph taken in January 2017, when the house
was undergoing restoration.

described Henry Crossland ungenerously as a stone delver – or an ordinary quarryman. In fact, Crossland's father was the manager of a stone quarry – a 'quarry master' and a 'respectable stone merchant', according to the agent of the local estate, writing to his superior in 1845.[7]

Quarrying was an important industry in the West Riding in the nineteenth century. Henry Crossland rented his quarry from the Ramsden family who were lords of the manor of Huddersfield and owned most of the land in and around that town.[8] By the time of the 1851 census,

7. West Yorkshire Archive Service Kirklees, DD/RE/C/10/32, Ramsden Estate correspondence.
8. The Ramsdens were the most prominent family in Huddersfield and shaped the town as it is today. William Ramsden purchased the Manor of Huddersfield from Queen Elizabeth I in 1599. Over the following three centuries, his descendants increased the amount of the town owned by the family and acquired the nearby estate of Almondbury. In 1920, the Ramsdens sold the town (by then 4,300 acres) to Huddersfield Corporation, earning the town the description of the town that bought itself. Over their 300 years of ownership of large parts of the town as Lords of the Manor, the Ramsdens had a profound influence on the community's development, and the family name and the Ramsden arms are still to be found across the town. Their country seat was Byram Hall near Knottingley in the West Riding. From around 1840, they developed the 'new town' of Huddersfield, bringing a through railway to what had been a small community and building many fine

1.2 Huddersfield College by J.P. Pritchett of York.
This exciting building with Tudor styling, corner turrets and battlements
would have been intended to inspire the college's pupils.

Henry Crossland was a successful businessman employing twenty men
and described as a quarry owner. His success was underlined by the fact
that the census described his sixteen-year-old son, William Henry, as a
scholar. At this time, continuation in education into the teens was unusual
for someone with a working-class background and indicated a sufficiently
comfortable financial standing to allow school fees to be afforded.

## School

William Henry's parents realised that they had a talented son and had the
means to pay for him to have the best education that was available locally.
He became a pupil at Huddersfield College, a school of non-conformist
foundation for boys, taking day pupils from the immediate locality and
boarding pupils from throughout England and from Ireland. The school
was founded in 1838, opening in 1839 in temporary accommodation. The
foundation stone for its substantial purpose-built home was laid in March
1839 in New North Road, Huddersfield. Crossland will have joined the
school at the age of thirteen in 1848, or possibly at age eleven. Either way,
he joined a fairly new but nonetheless prestigious institution in a building

new buildings. (See *The Ramsden Heritage Trail*, published by Huddersfield Local
History Society, www.huddersfieldhistory.org.uk.)

that was meant to impress, designed by J.P. Pritchett of York. The school building was also intended to inspire its pupils, and the architecture would have been exciting to a boy of Crossland's interests, skills and knowledge.

Crossland amply justified his parents' confidence in him. He achieved success at school, winning two prizes in June 1851, at the age of sixteen. This was a considerable achievement for a local boy, as it was the boarders who tended to take most of the prizes since they had the opportunity for more tuition ('instruction') in the evening. The account of the Annual Examination and distribution of prizes in the local newspaper reported that the event took place in the College Hall on 18 June 1851.[9] The work of the pupils was laid out for inspection. Among this work were displayed examples of Crossland's writing and mechanical drawing and it was noted that 'specimens . . . of writing by Master W.H. Crossland and of mechanical drawing . . . were of a high order of merit'.

He was awarded a prize, in the form of a medal[10], in the Mathematical Department for 'Book-keeping and Writing' and another medal prize for an 'extra subject'. This was Drawing, indicating that his artistic skills were well developed by his mid-teens. He also received a special prize: the Vice President's Silver Pen for Penmanship, a prize for the pupil judged best at writing. As well as these prizes, Crossland was awarded a Certificate of General Merit (one of twelve that were awarded). His name was mentioned no fewer than six times in the newspaper account of the prize-giving.

In around 1852, after a successful school career, during which William Henry had demonstrated his ability in English and draughtsmanship, arrangements were made for him to be articled to George Gilbert Scott in London. This was true recognition of the potential of the boy, as Scott had an established and widely recognised reputation. The mid-1850s saw his practice working on 'more commissions for new churches and restorations than the average architect would see in a lifetime'.[11] He ran the largest and best organised architectural practice in England and rose to pre-eminence among architects. He could afford to be selective in the pupils he took into his practice, and it is likely that Crossland's particular talent in drawing won him his place in Scott's office. Scott charged a premium, or fee, that would have placed his practice beyond the aspirations of many would-be architects. At as much as 300 guineas[12], the premium represented a

9. *The Huddersfield Chronicle and West Yorkshire Advertiser*, 21 June 1851, Issue 64, p. 6.
10. http://homepage.eircom.net/~lawedd/MEDALS%20HUDDERSFIELD%20 COLLEGE.htm (accessed 25 November 2014).
11. Law, Part 1.
12. Stamp, Gavin, *Gothic for the Steam Age* (London, 2015), p. 74.

considerable investment on the part of William's father. Additional parental support was also necessary for the not inconsiderable living expenses for the young Crossland in London. The fact that he was able to afford this payment demonstrates clearly the financial strength of Henry Crossland's quarrying business.

How the young Crossland was introduced to Scott is not known. It is possible that Scott visited Henry Crossland's quarry to inform himself of local building materials, as was his practice, in finding local stone for the building of All Souls' Church, Haley Hill, Halifax, for which the foundation stone was laid in 1856. It is possible also that an introduction was through the Reverend Josiah Bateman, who was the vicar of Huddersfield between 1840 and 1855 and who knew Scott.[13] Bateman probably knew Henry Crossland through the latter's role as churchwarden at St John's, a church not far from Bateman's own. George Gilbert Scott's father had been Bateman's tutor, and Bateman had formed a friendship with Scott at that time.

The Reverend Bateman was instrumental in the building of a new church at Longroyd Bridge, near Huddersfield, funded by a local family. Taking advantage of his friendship with Scott, he had commissioned plans, which Scott duly provided.[14] The new church was built between 1857 and 1859, dedicated to St Thomas. Whether or not Bateman was instrumental in introducing William Henry to George Gilbert Scott, the latter is likely to have visited the Crossland quarry, well before construction began, in his search for suitable local building materials for the new church.

## Architectural training

The exact dates of Crossland's pupillage in Scott's office are not recorded. His maximum period of training could have been six years, but it was probably nearer to four years, which was then the normal length of time of articles for architectural pupils.[15] He served his articles between 1852 (when he was eighteen) and finished, at the latest, in 1858 when he established his own practice. He learned his craft alongside several other trainees who were also to go on to become successful and influential architects in their own right, with whom he became well acquainted and formed friendships. Among others, he probably worked with Scott's own sons, George Gilbert Scott Junior and John Oldrid Scott, but they were both younger than Crossland and, as the master's sons, less likely to form close friendships with older

13. Law, Part 1.
14. Law, Part 1.
15. Law, Part 1.

trainees. He may well have become acquainted with fellow Yorkshireman George Frederick Bodley (from Kingston-upon-Hull) even though he was about eight years older than Crossland. Thomas Graham Jackson was the same age as Crossland, but joined the practice at around the time that Crossland left to set up on his own. He also overlapped a year or two with Charles Buckeridge and Thomas Garner.

It would have been surprising if Crossland had not taken full advantage of the entertainments and opportunities offered by the capital. Details are not known, but at some time during his training in London, he became acquainted with a young Londoner named Lavinia Pigot, who was later to become his wife.

All of Scott's trainees absorbed and practised Scott's strong views on architectural style. Scott believed that Gothic was the only truly national style and that it was applicable to all types of buildings. He was, though, primarily a church architect with a mission to bring to the prevailing frenzy of church-building the ideas of A.W.N. Pugin, who had so inspired him. So prolific was Scott himself and so thoroughly and convincingly did he imbue his many pupils with the spirit of Pugin that Gothic became the most used style for churches and chapels in their works, reflecting its wider predominance at the time.

A picture of life in Scott's practice was given by his pupil T.G. Jackson:

Scott's office was a very large one. Counting pupils, salaried assistants, and clerks, I think we were twenty-seven in all. I was put to work in the first-floor room at the back with six others; there were about a dozen more in two rooms on the second floor; the ground-floor front room, which served also as the waiting room, was the sanctum of Mr Burlison, the head man, who made the estimates and surveys. Scott's own room was the ground-floor back, and farther back still were the writing-clerk and the office-boys. The front room first-floor was let to a Mr Moriarty, a barrister, a mysterious person whom we never saw. Of Scott we saw but little. He was up to the eyes in engagements and it was hard to get him to look at our work. I have seen three or four men with drawings awaiting correction or approval grouped outside his door. The door flew open and out he came: 'No time to-day': the cab was at the door and he was whirled away to some cathedral where he would spend a couple of hours and then fly off again to some other great work at the other end of the kingdom. Now and then the only chance of getting instructions was to go with him in the cab to the station. I see I wrote at the time, 'What a fine thing it is to be so busy'; but looking back from my present standpoint I find nothing in such a career to envy, and much to wonder at. It need hardly be said that it is an impossibility really to direct so large a staff as Scott's; but the work had of course to be done somehow. The heads of different rooms were capable men with a good knowledge of construction; Scott had a wonderful power of making rapid expressive sketches and from these his men were able to produce work which, curiously enough, did fall into something of a consistent style that passed for Gilbert Scott's and which one can always recognize wherever one meets with it as coming from that office. There are many amusing tales which show the slight acquaintance he had with what came out of his office: how he admired a new church from the railway carriage window and was told it was one of his own; how he went into a church in process of building, sent for the clerk of works, and began finding fault with this and with that till the man said, 'You know, Mr Scott, this is not your church; this is Mr Street's, your church is farther down the road.'[16]

Jackson paints a picture of an exceptionally busy office, and Crossland will have received his share of delegated work and responsibility, developing not only his skills of draughtsmanship, but also planning, scheduling and financial skills.

The first time the public saw evidence of Crossland's artistic talent was his exhibition at the Royal Academy in 1855 of a view from the Erasmus Chapel, Westminster Abbey.[17] At this time his address was given as 7 Albert Street, Camden Town, close to the area where he was eventually to live when practising in the capital.[18]

## Crossland's first building

Crossland's architectural talent first came to the notice of the public in his home town on 25 March 1856, when his name (spelled wrongly) appeared in the local Huddersfield press for the first time, announcing the opening of the Netheroyd Hill and Cowcliffe School, a building he had designed.[19]

---

16. Quoted in Scott, George Gilbert, ed. Stamp, Gavin, *Personal and Professional Recollections*, 1879 (Stamford, 1995), page k, referencing Jackson, Basil H., *Recollections of Thomas Graham Jackson* (London, 1950).

17. Law, Part 1.

18. This part of Albert Street has been demolished and modern housing is now on the site.

19. *The Huddersfield Chronicle and West Yorkshire Advertiser*, 29 March 1856, Issue 315, p. 6.

He was only twenty and still a pupil in Scott's architectural practice in London. He took no fee for the design, probably feeling (or persuaded by his parents) that, as he was not yet qualified, it was not acceptable to do so. He was not present at the opening of the school so he missed the warm reception given to his first building. It was a small structure, costing around £500,[20] but his parents doubtless glowed with pride. This talented young local architect was as yet unknown so the *Huddersfield Chronicle* was at pains to explain not only his generosity, but also who he was and where he was from: 'The plan was gratuitously furnished by Mr W.H. Crosland, son of Mr Henry Crosland of Longwood House and pupil of G.G. Scott Esq., London.'[21]

The school was in a commanding position on the brow of Cowcliffe Hill. The land for it had been given some four years earlier by Sir John Ramsden, with the purpose of enabling the building of the first school in the area. It was to be a Church of England Sunday School, a school that would teach the poor (adults as well as children) to read the Bible, but not to do writing or arithmetic[22] – very possibly the only education some of the pupils would have. A grant towards the construction had been received from the Council on Education[23] and the remainder of the funds needed was raised through subscriptions.

Netheroyd Hill was where Crossland had grown up, and he began working on the design of the school in 1855, doubtless at his father's insistence and as something of a payback for the family's investment in his education. The local newspaper described the building as having 'a very handsome appearance' and being 'a most appropriate ornament to the locality . . . in the style of architecture which prevailed in England in the early fourteenth century, known as geometrical decorated'.[24] Crossland had followed the principles laid down by the Council on Education and was already demonstrating that he had absorbed the Gothic principles of Pugin that had so influenced his master Scott.

---

20. £1000 in 1860 was worth approximately £92,260 in 2018; £1000 in 1886 was worth approximately £107,000 in 2018. [Source: https://www.measuringworth. com/calculators/ukcompare/relativevalue.php]
21. *The Huddersfield Chronicle and West Yorkshire Advertiser*, 29 March 1856, Issue 315, p. 6.
22. Gillard, D., *Education in England: A Brief History*, www.educationengland.org.uk/ history, 2011 (accessed 25 January 2016).
23. Gillard. Created in 1839, the Council on Education was the first government department with specific responsibility for education.
24. *The Huddersfield Chronicle and West Yorkshire Advertise*, 29 March 1856, Issue 315, p. 6.

1.3 Netheroyd Hill and Cowcliffe School, latterly St Hilda's Church (1856), was Crossland's first building. The extension to the left of the main building was added in 1919. Photograph taken in 2017.

Crossland's training in Scott's office in London continued for about two more years. George Gilbert Scott recognised Crossland's ability, as it was at his master's behest that Crossland returned to the West Riding at the end of his training, and by November 1858, at the age of twenty-four, he had set up his own business – not in Huddersfield, but in Halifax.

*Chapter 2*

# The Halifax office

Over his lifetime, Crossland was to design many buildings in and around Huddersfield, but he never ran a practice in his home town. He probably worked briefly from his parents' home when he first returned to the West Riding, but by 1858 he had opened an office in Harrison Road, Halifax, close to the town centre. This was a prestigious area of the town, with professional offices in fine buildings as well as private residences. Crossland was surely pleased to have found office space in this commercially established part of the town.

He had already been commissioned to design a church for Bradley, close to his family home. This commission likely came through his parents or a family contact and was probably initiated during 1858 as he was planning his move back to the West Riding from London. In September 1859, he placed the first of what would be many similar advertisements over the coming years among the classified advertisements in *The Huddersfield Chronicle and West Yorkshire Advertiser*:

> THE PROPOSED NEW CHURCH AT BRADLEY NEAR HUDDERSFIELD.
> TENDERS REQUIRED for the ERECTION of this CHURCH, each branch of the work to be estimated for separately, and all estimates to be delivered, under seal, on or before Saturday, 9th October, at the Woodman Inn, Bradley.
>
> Plans and specifications can be seen at the Woodman Inn, from Nine o'clock in the Morning until Six o'clock in the Evening each day from the 3rd until the 9th October.
>
> The committee do not bind themselves to adopt the lowest estimates.
> W.H. CROSSLAND, Architect, Halifax.[1]

---

1. *The Huddersfield Chronicle and West Yorkshire Advertiser*, 24 September 1859, Issue 497 and 1 October 1859, Issue 498.

There were delays in the building of the church, due to a strike of masons and, apparently, because the building committee wished to employ only local contractors. They secured a Bradley firm of stonemasons to be the main contractors with subsidiary works being provided by tradesmen from Huddersfield and Halifax. Crossland's youth and inexperience cannot have helped in managing this local dispute, but it seems to have been a useful lesson for him, as in subsequent projects he used local contractors whenever possible. The difficulties with the contractors meant that the building of the Bradley church was to take until 1863. (See pages 38 and 49-50.)

## Marriage

By 1859 Crossland was sufficiently financially secure to marry Lavinia Cardwell Pigot, the Londoner he had met a few years earlier while a pupil in Scott's architectural practice. Their marriage took place on 1 October at the Parish Church of Saint Pancras in London. He was twenty-four and she was twenty-two. In the marriage register, Crossland gave his residence as St John's, Huddersfield, suggesting that, although he was working in Halifax, he was living near his parents' home.

Crossland married well. Lavinia's mother, also Lavinia, was the daughter of John Cumberland, a 'gentleman'. Crossland's mother-in-law enjoyed some prosperity in her own right as the owner of several properties in the London parishes of St Pancras and Islington. Lavinia Cardwell's father had been dead for several years at the time of her marriage to Crossland. Her mother had re-married some nine years earlier in 1850, with her daughter as one of the witnesses. Her mother's second husband, Robert Monach, was a surgeon and one of the witnesses at the Crossland marriage. He and William Henry seem to have gone on to enjoy an amicable relationship.

After their marriage, William and Lavinia set up home at 6 Trinity Place, Halifax, just a short walk from Crossland's office. Built some fifteen years earlier[2], Trinity Place was an elegant, symmetrically designed parade of fifteen houses. The Crosslands' neighbours were mostly people of independent means, but included several tradesmen, a solicitor and two clerics: number 15 was the parsonage for Holy Trinity Church.[3] Crossland will have been anxious to ensure Lavinia had the kind of domestic support that she was used to, so they employed two servants. Fortunately, labour was cheap and even a newly married middle-class couple would expect to

2. Pevsner, Nikolaus, revised Radcliffe, Enid, *The Buildings of England: Yorkshire, West Riding*, (Harmondsworth, 1959), second edition 1967, reprinted 1979, p. 233.
3. Law, Edward, *William Henry Crossland, Architect, 1835-1908*, 1992, Part 4.

2.1 Trinity Place, Halifax: the Crosslands' first home after their marriage in 1859. This was an elegant, modern home for the newly married couple and contributed perfectly to the image of himself that Crossland wished to convey.
Picture taken in January 2017.

employ a minimum staff of two in their household.[4] Their servants were both Huddersfield born: Hannah Beaumont was thirty years old and Mary Wilkinson, who may have been related to Crossland on his mother's side, was twelve.[5] Other than this, little is known about the Crosslands' home life.

## Akroydon

During Crossland's apprenticeship with Scott, his master had been commissioned by the Halifax industrialist Edward Akroyd to build a new church and vicarage at Haley Hill in Halifax, opposite the mills of the textile business (James Akroyd and Son, the largest worsted-spinning concern in the country) that Akroyd had inherited from his father in 1847. Akroyd also commissioned a new village community alongside. Edward Akroyd's commission was important to Scott, his patron's seemingly limitless funds being a huge attraction. Akroyd was not only a leading local industrialist, but also held numerous prominent public positions. He had a considerable personal interest in and knowledge of architecture[6], and Scott and Akroyd

4.  Law, Part 4.
5.  Law, Edward, *William Henry Crossland, Architect, 1835-1908*, 1992, Part 2.
6.  From 1865, Akroyd was MP for Halifax, at which time he became a member of George

cemented their acquaintance through this project. As gratefully noted by Scott in his *Recollections*, Akroyd was one of a small group 'who stuck nobly by me'[7] during the 'battle of the styles' over the Foreign Office building in Whitehall. In 1862, Akroyd published his ideas on housing for poorer people in *On Improved Dwellings for the Working Classes with a Plan for Building Them in Connection with Benefit Building Societies.*

George Gilbert Scott needed an assistant with local knowledge for his important commission for Akroyd. Crossland's credentials amply filled this need, so his move back to the West Riding from his training in London was almost certainly prompted by Scott. Crossland's architectural training in London was possibly not complete when he began assisting Scott in Halifax, but it suited Scott very well to have this capable young local man as his assistant for what turned out to be a large and valuable project. It is possible that Scott brought Crossland into the project as a practical element of his training. Crossland was the perfect assistant for Scott – not only familiar with the locality, but a man whose father operated a nearby quarry, and, since Scott had trained him himself, a man who shared all Scott's Gothic architectural ideas. Certainly, Crossland's assistance in managing a complex project would have been invaluable to his busy master, as well as excellent experience for the young architect. It is likely that Scott encouraged Crossland to set up his first practice in Halifax in order to be near the Akroyd project.

Akroyd was one of the great philanthropists of Halifax and held sincere views regarding the duty of the more successful to help the disadvantaged of society. However, he also sought public recognition, as did the Crossley family, the other important philanthropists of Halifax. Each sought to outshine the other in their philanthropic gestures, including the churches that they both provided for Halifax.

Akroyd's church, which was named All Souls', was later described by Scott as 'probably my best church'.[8] Begun in 1856, when Scott was at the height of his fame, it was almost certainly his most lavish church, prominently located on high ground and visible from much of Halifax. Akroyd poured money into the project, at least partly in an attempt to be seen and remembered as Halifax's first citizen. Rivalry with the ambitious Crossley family led to Akroyd requiring enhancements to his church, resulting in it becoming much more richly appointed than originally

---

Gilbert Scott's 'Spring Gardens Sketching Club' in London (see D. Cole, *The Work of Sir Gilbert Scott*, 1980, p. 141). In 1866, Akroyd become an honorary member of the Royal Institute of British Architects (see *The Builder*, 5 May 1866, p. 329).

7. Scott, George Gilbert, ed. Stamp, Gavin, *Personal and Professional Recollections 1879* (Stamford, 1995), p. 184.

8. Scott, ed. Stamp, p. 176.

intended and acquiring an ever higher spire. In the end, Akroyd enjoyed the satisfaction of knowing that the spire of his All Souls' Church was twelve inches higher than the spire of the Crossleys' Square Church.

Akroyd had been prepared to pay for the very best quality, and Scott 'created one of the crowning jewels of Victorian Gothic, superb in outline and massing, a seamless blend of French and Italian influences with English Decorated architecture, and laden with intense decoration from the best artists of the day'.[9] All Souls' contains decorative work of the highest standard: glorious stained glass by Hardman and Clayton and Bell; delicate ironwork by Skidmore; Minton encaustic floor tiles; naturalistic stone and wood carving; and a magnificent pulpit displaying many colours of marble, effectively announcing that Akroyd was a 'modern man' who embraced the scientific discoveries of the new discipline of Geology. All Souls' Church, including endowments, was estimated to have cost around £100,000 – a truly phenomenal cost. It was consecrated in 1859, and Crossland's support in this massive project, a long way from Scott's busy London base, had been crucial.

Akroyd saw his church, as well as the burial ground and family mausoleum that had been built earlier on a site opposite the church, as the beginning of a new community. Scott's commission had included the drawing up of plans for the houses in the new village. Akroyd held firm views on the duty of those (like himself) with the means to remedy the social evils caused and perpetuated by the rapid industrialisation of society. He believed that a return to a pre-industrial structure of society would contribute significantly to social reform. His utopian dream was to recreate a medieval village with all classes of society represented and with himself at the centre as squire. He believed a return to an earlier hierarchical village society was fundamental to creating a harmonious community. In Akroyd's idealised concept of a medieval community, his intention from the outset was to have a mixture of housing. For this nineteenth-century medieval village, the Gothic style for which Scott was renowned was the only style acceptable to Akroyd.

Akroyd's plan was based on an earlier scheme involving the newly formed Halifax Union Building Society, which, though financially successful, Akroyd nonetheless considered deficient. In particular, the houses were 'devoid of architectural proportion and beauty'.[10] His village therefore had

9. Whelan, A., 'The Victoria Cross in Akroydon', *Transactions of the Halifax Antiquarian Society*, new series, 2004, p. 110.

10. Akroyd, Edward, *On Improved Dwellings for the Working Class: A Plan for Building Them in Connection with Benefit Building Societies* (London, 1862), p. 7. http://www.calderdale.gov.uk/wtw/search/controlservlet?PageId=Detail&DocId=100923

to look attractive in its recreation of a medieval community. Akroyd had already built one model community at Copley on the outskirts of Halifax, and he drew on his experience there in the building of the model village he called Akroydon.

George Gilbert Scott prepared the first designs of the village in what was his first venture into town planning, with Crossland as the 'local architect'. Akroyd and Scott were annoyed when the initial Gothic designs for the village were rejected at an early stage by the Akroydon Building Association (the committee of potential homeowners that was part of Akroyd's planned democratisation of the community). They thought the houses resembled almshouses and 'were antiquated, inconvenient, wanting in light, and not adapted to modern requirements'.[11] They demanded changes to the designs. It seems that, at this stage, the many other demands on Scott caused him to lose interest in the housing development, a project that must have seemed unglamorous alongside All Souls' Church, his cathedral restorations and the possible prize of the Foreign Office project that was then under consideration. Whatever his reasons, he handed Crossland the Akroydon housing project on Haley Hill. Crossland's first commission was therefore effectively a gift from Scott. Crossland can scarcely have believed his good fortune. He revised the plans, and when they were put before proposed shareholders in 1860, they were accepted. The designs were approved in the same year and work began on the houses of Akroyd's idealised society in 1861, about a mile from Halifax town centre along Boothtown Road.

## Architectural competitions and family

Early in 1860, Crossland had somehow also found time to enter the competition for the Manchester Assize Courts. His architectural designs were exhibited at The Architectural Exhibition at premises in Conduit Street, London, in April 1860. Of the five architects mentioned in an article in *The Morning Post*, Crossland was mentioned first and particularly favourably: 'Among the most attractive features of the collection may be mentioned the various designs for the Manchester assize courts, particularly those by Mr W.H. Crossland'.[12] Despite this acclaim, Crossland will have been disappointed not to have been placed among the winning entries.

---

(accessed 1 February 2010 on *From Weaver to Web, Online Visual Archive of Calderdale History*).

11. Akroyd, p. 7.
12. *The Morning Post*, 20 April 1860, Issue 26939, p. 7.

The Crosslands' first (and only) child, Maud Helen, was born on 10 July 1860. She was baptised on 16 October 1860 at All Souls' Church, Haley Hill.[13] Crossland must have been a proud man indeed at the baptismal service in Akroyd's glorious church, the building on which, under supervision, he had tested his new architectural skills.

Work on the Akroydon project continued, and, at the same time, Crossland entered another architectural competition. This was for the Leeds Mechanics' Institute and School of Art, advertised as an open (rather than a local) competition. The time scale was short, particularly after the brief was changed, but Crossland surely burned midnight oil and ensured he met the design brief. *The Builder* commented favourably on Crossland's entry[14] and on that of another entrant, Henry Garling. Yet, when the result was announced, the first three places all went to local Leeds practices, with Cuthbert Brodrick placed first. Extraordinarily, Brodrick had failed to meet all the criteria of the design brief, and there was a strong suspicion that his recent success in the Leeds Corn Exchange building had swayed the adjudicators.

Crossland was understandably furious and with nothing to lose, vented his anger in a letter to *The Builder*, as did Henry Garling. It had been stated at the outset that George Gilbert Scott was to be consulted during the adjudication, so Crossland first checked with his master whether this had happened. Receiving a negative answer, Crossland then wrote to *The Builder* again, publicly asking (while privately knowing the answer) if Scott had been involved. If so, he confidently continued, he would no longer feel an injured competitor. In the knowledge that he and others had been humiliated in the competition, he added that he felt justified in protesting at the underhand behaviour of the committee throughout the competition period. It seems that the judging committee (which sent an abusive response to *The Builder*) not only failed to consult Scott, despite assurances, but sought no other professional advice. Crossland and Garling were left feeling justifiably bitter at their treatment and at the time they had wasted in a competition where the commissioning committee had been shamefully dishonest. Crossland's willingness to complain publically, though, reveals the confidence that he already had in his own ability – not only in his drawing skills, but in his ability to work closely to a brief and to work within a tight timescale.

---

13. https://www.ancestryinstitution.com.
14. *The Builder*, 19 January 1861, p. 43.

## Akroyd and his village

Back in Halifax, the Akroydon project was a curiosity and brought visitors wanting to see what was going on. Crossland plainly worked well with his patron Edward Akroyd and won his confidence. Fanciful though Akroyd's ideas seemed, he sincerely believed his scheme would be the answer to the indisputable evils of industrialising societies and believed that when others saw how well it worked, they would follow suit. His publication, *On Improved Dwellings for the Working Classes,* was intended to explain his

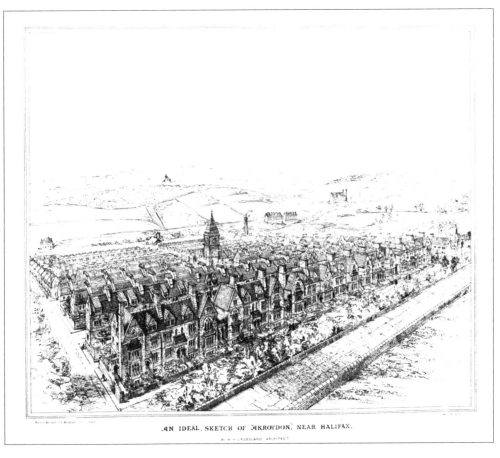

.AN IDEAL, SKETCH OF AKROYDON NEAR HALIFAX.

2.2 Crossland's vision of Akroydon which appeared in Akroyd's publication
'On Improved Dwellings for the Working Classes: A Plan for Building them in
Connection with Benefit Building Societies', published in 1862.
The drawing shows Crossland's considerable artistic skill and
it is one of his few surviving pieces of creative artwork.

ARROYDON.   HOUSES  SHEWING  DETAIL.

2.3 Akroydon: Salisbury Place, design for houses with door details which appeared in Akroyd's publication 'On Improved Dwellings for the Working Classes: A Plan for Building them in Connection with Benefit Building Societies', published in 1862.

ideas, and it included Crossland's plans and elevations for Akroydon. The booklet also featured a detailed picture by Crossland showing Akroyd's 'ideal' vision of the medieval-revival community and clearly demonstrated Crossland's considerable skills as an artist.

The first two blocks of eighteen houses on Salisbury Place were completed in Gothic style by August 1862. The houses were built of stone and roofed in slate. All carried attractive decoration. Akroyd felt vindicated regarding the Gothic revival design, stating that the proposed shareholders' 'prejudices against the pointed style are now finally uprooted'.[15] Crossland personalised some properties with the proud first owner's 'monogram or device, on a stone shield, placed above the door, with the intent to give individuality and a mark of distinction to each dwelling'.[16]

Alongside other work, the project occupied Crossland for several years. He understood Akroyd's requirements and managed to translate Akroyd's romantic vision into reality in the various house designs and overall layout.

15. Akroyd, p. 12.
16. Akroyd, p. 12.

2.4 Akroydon: Ripon Terrace. Photograph taken in April 2010.

2.5 Akroydon: Beverley Terrace. Photograph taken in April 2010.

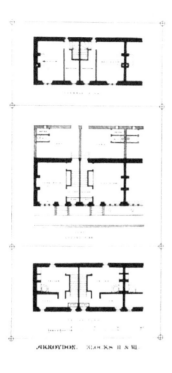

2.6 One of Crossland's plans for terraced houses in Akroydon, which appeared in Akroyd's publication 'On Improved Dwellings for the Working Classes: A Plan for Building them in Connection with Benefit Building Societies', published in 1862.

Houses built to his plans included 2-64 Salisbury Place, 1-9 Beverley Terrace, 8-24 Chester Road and 1-22 York Terrace, although in order to complete the large project, Crossland subcontracted some work to James Mallinson of another local architectural firm, Mallinson & Healey.

The typical plan of the terraced houses consisted of one living room, with two bedrooms above (one small and one large) and a scullery or wash kitchen underneath. At the back were small yards with individual ash pits and lavatories. Larger houses were provided for wealthier tenants, but all had proper drains, water and gas supplies, and were built in partnership with the Halifax Permanent Benefit Building Society.[17]

Also essential to Akroyd's scheme for an ideal English village were communal facilities, including allotments and a co-operative shop. Included in Crossland's designs, therefore, was a co-operative store on the corner of Salisbury Place and Beverley Terrace. Around a first-floor

17. West Yorkshire Archive Service Calderdale, WYHER/10258. *The Akroydon Workers Village*. The Halifax Permanent Benefit Building Society is now 'The Halifax'.

2.7 Akroydon, the junction of Salisbury Place and Beverley Terrace, including the village shop, as depicted in *The Builder*, 14 February 1863; and detail showing the decorated window on Akroydon's village store, as built (photograph taken in April 2010). A stag's head, Akroyd's personal motif, is above the village name with the date of construction underneath.

window he included a substantial stone carving proclaiming the name of the community, surmounted by Akroyd's stag's head motif and the date of its construction (1861), as well as a monogram, probably of the first shopkeeper.

In all the buildings of his village, through Crossland's skill, Akroyd sought to indulge his taste for the decorative detail that he found so lacking in the earlier Halifax Union Building Society scheme. A little further up

2.8 Akroydon: castellated stables, a striking and more costly building
for the patron than those for the new homeowners in the village.
Photograph taken in April 2010.

Beverley Terrace and opposite Akroyd's mansion, Bankfield, Crossland
designed stables for Akroyd. They were decorated more expensively than
the other buildings in the village, with castellation and Akroyd's signature
stag's head over the archway leading into the yard. (See page 39.)

## Schools and almshouses

The work at Akroydon carried a considerable responsibility for an architect so
early in his career, but, despite this, Crossland was careful not to concentrate
all his energy on one project. Akroydon proved to be a perfect shop window
for his work, and he was soon taking on work for other clients. He quickly
became busy, and it seems there was no shortage of commissions. On 12
January 1861, he placed two consecutive advertisements in the classified
section of the *Huddersfield Chronicle and West Yorkshire Advertiser*, looking
for contractors for two different projects in Huddersfield. The sealed tenders
for both were to be submitted to his office in Harrison Road, Halifax, by 30
January 1861. Both these projects were exciting for Crossland, presenting
opportunities to design building types new to him.

The first project was for new schools[18] at Hillhouse, Huddersfield, for St John's Church, Bay Hall, Huddersfield, and he arranged for the plans and specifications to be seen between 23 and 26 January in the school hall in the original ancient house known as Bay Hall. The new schools were to be St John's National Schools, provided by the National Society for Promoting Religious Education. Such schools were developed before the Education Act of 1870 and were intended to provide an elementary education for poor children, in accordance with the teaching of the Church of England.[19] Since Crossland's father was churchwarden at St Johns Church[20], it is likely that this commission resulted through his father's influence. The building included a master's house and was to serve an area of new housing. The site, valued at £350, had been given by a Mrs Clarke Thornhill. When the schools were opened on Shrove Tuesday the following year, with a tea party and sale of work, the buildings were considered by the local newspaper to be 'a great ornament to the new streets formed on Mrs Clarke Thornhill's property'.[21]

The second project was for almshouses in Almondbury, an ancient community about two miles from Huddersfield, and Crossland made arrangements for the plans to be viewed at the offices of a surveyor, Thomas Brook, in New Street, Huddersfield.[22]

This project, known as Nettleton's Almshouses, was paid for by Nettleton's Charity, Almondbury, an organisation established by a Robert Nettleton of Almondbury in 1613 to provide relief for the poor and to fund other charitable acts. Crossland's row of six single-storey cottages was to be built on the north side of the churchyard, replacing six earlier dwellings. They were intended for 'the perpetual relief of the poor of Almondbury'.[23] Doubtless reflecting the budget available for its construction, Crossland's design for the building had no decoration, being simply a practical stone structure with a slate roof and three pairs of front doors. (See page 33-34.)

## Houses and shops

At the same time, Crossland also began taking on smaller projects for private individuals. In 1861, as the construction of Akroydon was beginning, a Mr Richard Flather commissioned two houses to be built at the top of

18. Crossland's school at Hillhouse has been demolished.
19. Such schools were the precursors of the voluntary aided or voluntary controlled primary schools that remain part of the primary education system.
20. Law, Part 1.
21. *The Huddersfield Chronicle and West Yorkshire Advertiser*, 15 February 1862, Issue 622, p. 8.
22. *The Huddersfield Chronicle and West Yorkshire Advertiser*, 12 January 1861, Issue 565.
23. West Yorkshire Archive Service, http://archiveswiki.wyjs.org.uk/index.php? title= Nettleton%27s_Charity,_Almondbury.

Westgate, Elland. Crossland produced plans and elevations for a pair of houses that bore a marked similarity to the Akroydon houses[24], including the lavatory and ash pit at the end of a back yard. The houses were for an irregular corner site on a hill, which Crossland managed by providing the two houses with unequal-sized back yards and a lower basement ceiling for the property higher up the sloping ground. (See page 27, 2.9.)

At more or less the same time, a Mr Jeremiah Peel commissioned Crossland to design a terrace comprising a shop with a house and two further houses in Northgate, Elland.[25] This was a particularly challenging quadrant site on a slope. Crossland's solution to the problem of the site was an asymmetrical frontage, balancing a second-floor gable on the lowest house with a quatrefoil decoration in the large gable over the shop accommodation. A spiral staircase to the bedrooms in the lowest house optimised the limited space and presented an opportunity for a decorative turret. (See page 27, 2.10.)

## Copley Church

Also in 1861, while Crossland was heavily engaged on the Akroydon development for Edward Akroyd, as well as several other local projects, he was commissioned to build a church at Copley, a village built by Akroyd on the outskirts of Halifax. A subscription fund had been launched with Akroyd himself contributing £500. The Copley curate-in-charge, the Reverend James Hope, commissioned the church from Crossland and was an active fundraiser for the project. It seems, though, that hoped-for funds were difficult to raise, and when *The Ecclesiologist* reviewed the building plans in June (devoting a whole page to this proposed church for a small village), it lamented that 'Mr Crossland is unfortunately rather straitened for funds.'[26] This was plainly much regretted since it felt that 'the design has great merits and shows much promise'.[27] This was genuine praise for a young architect who was then only twenty-five years of age. *The Ecclesiologist* also approved of the ritual arrangements, particularly the raised chancel and sanctuary, confirming that Crossland was already seeking to incorporate the principles of the Society into his own designs.

The village of Copley, on the outskirts of Halifax, had been built by Akroyd some fifteen years earlier to house mill workers. As with the Haley Hill mill,

---

24. West Yorkshire Archive Service Calderdale, CMT4/MU:21/23, plans and elevations of two houses at the top of Westgate, Elland (demolished).
25. West Yorkshire Archive Service Calderdale, CMT4/MU:21/24, plans and elevations of three houses, one with a shop, at Northgate, Elland (demolished).
26. *The Ecclesiologist*, Volume XXII, June 1861, CXLIV, new series CVIII, p. 197.
27. *The Ecclesiologist*, Volume XXII, June 1861, CXLIV, new series CVIII, p. 197.

Akroyd had inherited the Copley mill from his father. It was in an isolated location, and most of the workers had to travel some distance to their place of work since, prior to Akroyd's new village, the only housing nearby was a row of seven cottages dating from the beginning of the nineteenth century. When Edward Akroyd erected a second mill in 1847, he also commissioned the housing so that workers could live near their place of work. The village of Copley was built close to the mills and consisted of three terraces of back-to-back housing with Gothic or 'old English' features, as well as four shops. There were also allotments and gardens, schools by 1849 and a library by 1850 – and the hedges were trimmed at Akroyd's expense. The community – housing specifically provided for mill workers – was a novel idea with 'no precedent in weavers' hamlets'[28] and pre-dating the better-known Saltaire on the outskirts of Bradford. However, when built, Copley had no church and worship took place in the village schoolroom.

Since 1845, Copley had been in the new parish of All Saints, Salterhebble. The proposed site for the Copley church, on Wakefield Road, was near All Saints' Church, and the incumbent, the Reverend Warneford, objected to a new church being built so close to his own. It was thanks to the parish of Greetland, on the opposite bank of the River Calder, that Copley was able to have its own church on land provided by Richard Kennett-Dawson. It was an odd arrangement, though, with the planned village church in a different parish and on the opposite bank of the river from the community it was to serve. Regardless, *The Ecclesiologist* was enthusiastic about the location, saying, 'there is an unusually good opportunity for a picturesque treatment, for the church will stand terraced up on the very edge of the stream or torrent, approached by a bridge (which might be worked into the composition), and under the steep slope of a lofty hill, which is thickly wooded'.[29] However, the land agreed for the church, at the foot of a steep bank beside the River Calder, was less than ideal. It was so close to the riverbank that, before any building on the church could begin, substantial work had to be carried out to strengthen the riverbank in preparation for the church foundations. Crossland advertised in late July 1861 for tenders from excavators and masons to build the foundations for the new church, to be submitted by 10 August.[30] The preparatory work began in late 1861.

Strengthening the riverbank in preparation for the church foundations was by no means the project's only problem. It seems Crossland had to remind the Reverend Hope to honour the terms of their contract when it came to payment. In a letter from his Harrison Road office on 25 November 1861,

28. Linstrum, Derek, *West Yorkshire: Architects and Architecture* (London, 1978), p. 135.
29. *The Ecclesiologist*, Volume XXII, June 1861, CXLIV, new series CVIII, p. 197.
30. *The Huddersfield Chronicle and West Yorkshire Advertiser*, 27 July 1861, Issue 593.

Crossland wrote to the Reverend Hope: 'I shall be obliged if you can let me have £50 on account of the Plans for the New Church Copley. Half my commission – $2^{1/2}$ per cent is due to me when the first contract is signed.'[31]

The Reverend Hope responded by paying Crossland just £25 on 7 December. It was plainly a difficult time for Hope, as he was on the point of leaving Copley and his new church project for a new incumbency. Crossland was genuinely sorry that the instigator of the project was leaving when it was barely begun and doubtless had concerns regarding the completion and the payment of his own fee. He replied to the Reverend Hope on 12 December:

> I enclose a receipt for £25 and beg to thank you for your kind letter.
>
> It has always been my desire to do everything possible to meet your wishes, in reference to the new Church; and I very deeply regret that your supervision of the works has ceased. You will, however I hope, cherish the scheme you have so nobly set on foot & watch over the new church with loving care.[32]

Crossland seems to have been anxious not to commit to paper any difference of opinion regarding his payment, as he concluded his letter by saying, 'As yet my mind is unchanged as regards my claim. The reason for my apparent obstinacy I will give up when next I see you.'[33]

His obstinacy may have related to the need to allow the river wall and the foundations to settle before further work could be carried out, leading to a delay in the project. (See pages 33-34 and 57-59.)

## Another shop with houses and a manor house

Meanwhile, in Elland, the houses for Mr Flather in Westgate and for Mr Peel on Northgate had been good advertisements for Crossland. In 1862, he accepted two more commissions: the first to design another terrace of three houses in Westgate, one with a shop, for a Mr Joseph Bayley and the second for a substantial single dwelling, also on Westgate. Both were on straightforward sites.[34]

---

31. West Yorkshire Archive Service Wakefield, WDP59/21, Letters from W.H. Crossland of Halifax, architect, about the Copley commission, 1861.
32. West Yorkshire Archive Service Wakefield, WDP59/21, Letters from W.H. Crossland of Halifax, architect, about the Copley commission, 1861.
33. West Yorkshire Archive Service Wakefield, WDP59/21, Letters from W.H. Crossland of Halifax, architect, about the Copley commission, 1861.
34. West Yorkshire Archive Service Calderdale, CMT4/MU:21/29, terrace of three houses in Westgate, Elland, one with a shop (demolished) and CMT4/MU:21/31, a house in Westgate (demolished).

2.9 (top, left) Elland: elevation of a pair of houses on Westgate, 1861 – a small and simple structure, now demolished, that Crossland accommodated to an irregular corner site. They bore a marked similarity to the houses at Akroydon.

2.10 (bottom, left) Elland: three houses, one with a shop (marked by the large gable with a quatrefoil decoration), now demolished, on a challenging quadrant sloping site at Northgate: front elevation and ground plan, 1861.

2.11 (top, right) Elland: terrace of three houses, one with a shop (identified by pointed arches over the door and windows), now demolished, for Westgate. Front elevation, 1862.

2.12 (bottom, right) Elland: front elevation of a manor house, now demolished, 1862. With greater funding, Crossland was able to be more ambitious in his design for this house.

The development of three small properties for Joseph Bayley was on a rectangular site. Crossland unified the design with symmetrical chimneys and three matching gables for the upper windows. He achieved symmetry on the ground floor in the two houses by placing the square-headed windows and doors in mirror image to each other. The shop was distinguished by pointed arches over both the door and the two-light window with stone-work decoration in the arches. (See page 27, 2.11.)

The second property may have been a speculative development since it was built for the 'Hamerton executors' – the executors of a will. It was a substantial single dwelling, attached to another property on one side and with a side gate on the other. The ground floor contained a kitchen, separate scullery, drawing room and dining room opening off a central hallway. Upstairs, the main bedroom, with a gable window, had both a bathroom and a dressing room opening from it, and there were four further bedrooms on the other side of the landing. The basement was designed to include a wine store and a beer store, as well as the more usual larder and coal store. There was also an attic, which would have served as servant accommodation. This appears to have been Crossland's most ambitious domestic design up to this point in his early career. The design was more complex and called for more imagination than the other three Elland designs and gave Crossland the opportunity to incorporate numerous Gothic decorative features, including a built-out chimney, stonework decoration within a decorated pointed arch, massive door hinges and decorative gutters with further stone carving. (See page 27, 2.12.)

## Ossett Church

Another new church was commissioned in 1862 – and this was a real prize for a young architect. This church was for the community of Ossett, between Dewsbury and Wakefield. Although not far from Crossland's parents' home in Huddersfield, it was far enough for it to be unlikely that the commission was gained through parental influence or contacts, suggesting that his reputation was spreading. It was the highest value commission he had yet received and was to become an important project for him. When the building contracts were signed, Crossland was already being described as an 'established architect'. *The Ecclesiologist* reviewed Crossland's design generally favourably in February 1862, noting, 'The style is the Early-Pointed, in which this gentleman generally designs.'[35]

The Ossett church was an ambitious project for an ambitious town. Ossett had had a church since at least 1409, and Crossland's commission was to replace the then town church in the market place, which had been built in

35. *The Ecclesiologist*, February 1862, Vol XXIII, CXLVIII, new series CXII, p. 65.

1806. Formerly in the ancient parish of Dewsbury, Ossett had been declared a separate parochial district in 1858. By this time the town was a rapidly industrialising community, and the expanding population had become too large for the church. In any case, there was a feeling that a community of increasing prosperity should have a church that made a confident statement about its success. There was no space for expansion on the existing site, so a new location was needed. The site chosen for the new church was on Field Lane, situated on a plateau at the edge of town, some 300 feet above sea level alongside the new Anglican graveyard laid out in 1861. This was a prominent position providing the perfect opportunity to proclaim the status of the town.

Some of the money for the new church was donated by Benjamin Ingham, a member of an Ossett family that had made a fortune in importing wine from Sicily. He subscribed £1,000 towards the construction and was also to fund the stained-glass east window. A further £800 was given by Benjamin Wilson, a wealthy Ossett mill owner and textile manufacturer who was also the organist at the old Church in the market place. The west window was to be funded by the Whitaker family, successful maltsters in Ossett who were related to the Inghams.[36] The foundation stone was laid by the vicar, the Reverend Thomas Lee, on 30 June 1862, when the estimated cost of the church was £8,000. It was to be the new parish church and therefore the most important church in the town. It was, though, only one of at least ten new churches that were built in Ossett between 1857 and 1867 in a demonstration of extraordinary religious fervour and dedication – and this in an area where wages were low and money was concentrated in relatively few hands.

The new parish church was to be Crossland's first large church with a massive cruciform design including a tower and an octagonal stone spire over the crossing. The interior was to be 'elaborate, with constructional colour, low squat marble shafts, archivolts of coloured bricks [and] carved capitals'.[37] In case those funding the project did not like the tower and spire rising from the centre of the church, Crossland prepared an alternative design with the tower and spire positioned at the north-west angle of the church.[38] (See pages 47 and 50-51.)

## Another church and a parsonage

Despite problems with the Copley project, and despite beginning the substantial project at Ossett, by April 1862 Crossland had designed another church, this time for Moldgreen, near Huddersfield. *The Ecclesiologist* reviewed it in the February 1863 edition, stating that 'Mr W.H. Crossland of Halifax

36. http://www.wdco.org/site/Trinity-Church-Ossett/ (accessed 18 June 2013).
37. *The Ecclesiologist*, February 1862, Vol XXIII, CXLVIII, new series CXII, p. 65.
38. *The Ecclesiologist*, February 1862, Vol XXIII, CXLVIII, new series CXII, p. 65.

has designed a very good church for this place'[39], although it criticised some features. Crossland's design included north and south aisles, an apse-ended chancel and a stone tower and spire, described as 'novel in idea and well worked out in detail'.[40] Crossland will have been disappointed that funding allowed for the nave only to be built at this stage, and in June he advertised for contractors to build the truncated new church.[41] (See pages 39-40.)

At about the same time, Crossland was also commissioned to build a parsonage house at Hopton, near Mirfield, to the north-east of Huddersfield. It too was reviewed by *The Ecclesiologist* in February 1863. The journal stated that it liked 'the planning of the house and the general treatment' and considered that 'the whole design exhibits thought and originality'[42], even though it was critical of the fact that the living rooms faced due east and the back door opened due north. Crossland advertised for contractors in September[43], and the house was built during 1863.

## Meeting of the Yorkshire Architectural Society

On a national scale, there was something of a church-building frenzy during the 1860s. This had resulted from the revelation in the 1851 census that the Established Church in England was in a decidedly moribund state, with small congregations and churches often in advanced states of disrepair, while Non-Conformism was attracting ever more followers. These facts provided a profound shock to those in a position to influence public opinion and led to a nation-wide move to build many new Anglican churches. Indeed, the 1860s was to see the greatest number of new churches ever built in one decade. Crossland understood the opportunities this church-building programme offered a young architect, and it is clear that he grasped opportunities both to inform himself about church-building in Yorkshire and also to make his name known among the kind of people responsible for commissioning church buildings.

One such opportunity presented itself in September 1862 when he attended a meeting of the Yorkshire Architectural Society at Driffield in the East Riding of Yorkshire.[44] He went with William Bakewell (1839-1925), an architect colleague from Halifax, and they found themselves among

---

39. *The Ecclesiologist*, February 1863, Volume XXIV, CLIV, new series CXV11, p. 65.
40. *The Ecclesiologist*, February 1863, Volume XXIV, CLIV, new series CXV11, p. 65.
41. *The Huddersfield Chronicle and West Yorkshire Advertiser,* 7 June 1862, Issue 638.
42. *The Ecclesiologist*, February 1863, Volume XXIV, CLIV, new series CXVIII, p. 66.
43. *The Leeds Mercury*, 25 September 1862, Issue 7630; 26 September 1862 Issue 7631; and 27 September 1862, Issue 7632.
44. *The York Herald*, 20 September 1862, Issue 4690, p. 10.

2.13 Hawnby:
All Saints
Church,
restoration
1863.

clerical and lay men from different parts of Yorkshire, many of whom were the incumbents of churches. He was able to acquaint himself with a diverse range of people, among whom many were likely to be considering commissioning new buildings. After the meeting, they viewed the parish church at Driffield and then stayed at the Blue Bell Inn overnight. The following day the group had a tour of churches, including the remains of Watton Abbey, all of which were sources of interest and ideas to young architects like Crossland and Bakewell.

## Hawnby Church

Crossland's first known church restoration was of the ancient church of All Saints at Hawnby, about seven miles from Helmsley on the North Yorkshire Moors and may well have been an immediate product of the Architectural Society meeting in Driffield. Hawnby was so far from his general area of work in West Yorkshire that the commission is more likely to have resulted from such a meeting than from a local contact. The restoration was well reported in *The Ecclesiologist* in February 1863 (making it the third Crossland project reported in this edition of the journal) as 'an effective restoration by Mr Crossland of an unpretending little First-Pointed church'.[45] The restoration was completed during the same year. His self-promotion at the Driffield meeting of the Yorkshire Architectural Society already seemed to be paying off.

45. *The Ecclesiologist*, February 1863, Vol XXIV, CLIV, new series CXVIII, p. 69.

*Move to Leeds*

Sometime late in 1862, Crossland decided to move his business to Leeds, opening an office there in 1863, but maintaining the Halifax office for some months into that year. Why he moved to Leeds is not clear. The fiasco of the competition for the Leeds Mechanics' Institute and School of Art, in which he seemed to have been overlooked simply because he was not from Leeds, may have suggested to him that the town would provide more career opportunities. Leeds was developing fast, and he probably anticipated that there would be more large and interesting projects there than in Halifax. Since the construction of Cuthbert Brodrick's fine town hall, ahead of similar plans in Wakefield, Leeds had effectively become the most important town in the West Riding, and Crossland probably calculated that he would have more opportunities there than anywhere else in the West Riding. He was ambitious and wanted the opportunity to carve out his place in the architectural vanguard as the pace of industrial and civic development gathered speed.

*Chapter 3*

# The first Leeds office

A large project was not Crossland's reason for moving to Leeds (as it was when he opened his office in Halifax), for he had no commissions in the town when he moved his office in 1863, but he probably believed he would have a better chance of success in any future Leeds architectural competitions if he were resident there. In any case, there was more construction going on in Leeds than in Halifax.[1] He took with him oversight of his ongoing projects at Akroydon, Almondbury, Hopton, Copley, Moldgreen, Hawnby and Ossett when he moved, necessitating correspondence and frequent travel between Leeds, Huddersfield and Halifax, and further afield, to ensure the works were progressing satisfactorily and to deal with any problems. Of these projects, Nettleton's Almshouses in Almondbury (see page 23), the parsonage house at Hopton, Mirfield[2], and the church restoration at Hawnby, were completed the same year.

The premises in Leeds to which Crossland moved were at 17 Albion Street.[3] It is likely that the building was already condemned and that he rented his office on a short lease as development was planned.[4] He therefore probably knew from the outset that his tenure of this office would be short. Nonetheless, it provided him with a town centre location, probably at a low rent, close to the main thoroughfares of The Headrow and Boar Lane, as well as Park Row, where most of the banks were located.

Of the works begun before his move to Leeds, the church at Copley (see pages 24-26 and 57-59) probably caused Crossland the most sleepless nights, as it continued to be beset with problems. Although it had been

1. Douglas, Janet, *William Henry Crossland,* unpublished notes of lecture delivered at Cannon Hall, Cawthorne, South Yorkshire, 21 April 2012.
2. The parsonage house at Hopton was demolished in the 1960s.
3. The building in Albion Street where Crossland had his office has been demolished for a retail development.
4. Wrathmell, Susan, *Leeds: Pevsner Architectural Guide* (New Haven and London, 2005), p. 105.

3.1 Almondbury: Nettleton's Almshouses, 1863. The simplicity of this stone structure with a slate roof, three pairs of front doors and no decoration reflects the low budget available for its construction. Photograph taken in 2015.

commissioned in 1861, it was 5 June 1863 before the foundation stone was laid by Edward Akroyd on its wooded hillside site above the Calder Valley, across the river from the model village that Akroyd had built in 1847 for the employees of his Copley woollen mills.

The first time one of Crossland's advertisements for contractors showed he had moved to Leeds was two months previously, on 18 April 1863, although he also included the Halifax office address in the advertisement. The particular advertisement was for the various trades needed to build the Copley church following the completion of the strengthening of the riverbank. Plans and specifications were made available at his Halifax office.[5]

Crossland seems to have run both a Leeds office and a Halifax office for a few months into 1863; with several projects ongoing and a family to move, he probably judged it the easiest way to manage the transfer. It has to be assumed he employed several assistants and he presumably made good use of them in keeping his two offices open.

## Birstall Church

Crossland began to take on new work within a short while of opening his office in Leeds. In what was to turn out to be one of his most important projects, Crossland was commissioned to restore the medieval church of St Peter at Birstall, near Dewsbury. This restoration was destined to turn into a complete rebuilding of the church, except for the ancient tower, which was retained.

---

5. *The Huddersfield Chronicle and West Yorkshire Advertiser*, 18 April 1863, Issue 684, p. 3; *The Leeds Mercury*, 18 April 1863, Issue 7805; and *The Huddersfield Chronicle and West Yorkshire Advertiser*, 25 April 1863, Issue 685.

The commission was to build what would be the fourth stone church on the site, the first having been built around 1100 and dedicated to St Peter and St Paul. When the third church was built in 1490, St Paul was removed from the dedication, and over the next 375 years this church was extended and altered. By the 1860s it had become too dilapidated to repair.[6] In rebuilding this ancient church, Crossland sought to be sympathetic to the old building, incorporating material and structures where possible. It was a project that was to last about seven years, during which time Crossland's architectural skills, in terms of design, planning and decoration, were to develop with great sensitivity and increasing confidence. Development of the plans to the point that the church congregation was happy to go ahead would take nearly two years, before any thought of laying new stones was contemplated.

His plan for enlarging the Birstall church was unusual. There were already north and south aisles, and these he planned to extend by adding a further aisle to both north and south. The result would be a particularly wide building. The church thus gained sufficient internal space without having to be heightened or lengthened by the use of double aisles, a rare feature in English parish churches and quite a surprising innovation by Crossland at such an early stage in his career.[7]

This plan meant that he could retain the low profile of the church he was replacing. (See pages 48, 50 and 96-98.)

## *Family*

Crossland's personal life and how it related to his business life remains shadowy, but there are occasional glimpses. A letter dated 22 April 1863, sent from his home in Halifax to the Birstall church, explained that an illness affecting his daughter had interfered with his work: 'My little girl has been dangerously ill at Southport and I have been obliged to be a good deal with her – consequently have been unable to get through my work. I am engaged on a Report to accompany the Plans. I hope I send off the plans tomorrow night.'[8]

It is not known why Maud was in the resort of Southport, but Crossland and his wife possibly considered the sea air would help recovery from whatever condition affected her. The use of notepaper printed with his

6.  West Yorkshire Archive Service Wakefield, WDP5, Birstall St Peter, parish records.
7.  Whitaker, L.J., *W.H. Crossland* (master's degree thesis), University of Manchester, 1984, p. 52.
8.  West Yorkshire Archive Service Wakefield, WDP9/244, letters concerning plans for St Peter, Birstall.

3.2 Huddersfield, Lockwood Gatehouse, Meltham Road, 1863. Crossland gave this house much architectural interest. The three gables at the front of the house are of different depths and have different decorative detailing. He placed a small circular tower with a spire at the back. Also noteworthy are the different window styles, variation in roof design, patterning in the tiles and decorative carving around the front door. The house was restored in 2017. Photographs taken in 2019.

home address implies that he had relinquished his office premises in Halifax by this time, having probably maintained them for about five months after opening his Albion Street office in Leeds.

## Lockwood Gatehouse

At the beginning of May 1863, and little more than a couple of weeks after advertising for contractors for the Copley church, Crossland took on a project for a gatehouse to Woodfield House at Lockwood, near Huddersfield. He advertised in the Huddersfield, Halifax and Leeds newspapers for contractors for this project. Signing himself as an architect of Halifax and Leeds, but giving the address of the Leeds office only, suggested that new work was being taken on through the Leeds office.[9]

The project was a villa (sometimes referred to as Woodfield Villa) for Bentley Shaw, a wealthy local brewer, and it was completed later in 1863. It was described as a gatehouse, as it stood at one of the entrances to the Woodfield House estate. It is a pleasing building with a great deal of architectural interest, including gables, of which the three to the road frontage each have a different depth. There is also a small circular tower and spire at the back, decorated chimneys, several different window styles, patterning in the roof tiles and much decorative carving, particularly around the front door. Edward Law considered that Crossland was given substantial independence on the design of the property, and it seems he took the opportunity to experiment with a variety of architectural ideas. This resulted, in the opinion of Law, in the building being the most interesting of any of Crossland's domestic works, even when compared to larger later projects.[10]

## A house in Leeds

Also in 1863, Crossland began a house in Cookridge Street, Leeds, for a Dr Craig, known only from an advertisement to tender in May 1863.[11] Cookridge Street turns off The Headrow, the principal west-east thoroughfare through the town. It is where Cuthbert Brodrick's Mechanics' Institute is located and is close to Brodrick's town hall and other municipal buildings. The road itself had been extended northwards in 1861 to

---

9. *The Huddersfield Chronicle and West Yorkshire Advertiser,* 2 May 1863, Issue 685 and 9 May 1863, Issue 686.
10. Law, Edward, *William Henry Crossland, Architect, 1835-1908,* 1992, Part 4.
11. Law, Part 4.

Woodhouse Lane[12], giving rise to much new building. Crossland will have been pleased to have had an opportunity to make his mark on this developing central area of the town.

## Bradley Church

The church at Bradley, commissioned about 1858 (see pages 10-11), was completed in 1863 with 'eccentric details: the rounded pier growing from the SW corner of the W gable, the twin turrets flanking the E gable of the nave and the wild ironwork of the W doors'.[13] Built on sloping ground in coursed dressed sandstone, it has a steeply pitched slate roof. Crossland's design included a five-light east window and a fine rose window over the west door. There are also smaller quatrefoil windows. Such details contribute to an original appearance indicating that Crossland was trying to put his own stamp of individuality on his work. It displays considerable confidence in an architect at the beginning of his career and was an early demonstration of the 'vigorous and quirky detail characteristic of the architect'.[14] The church was consecrated in August and dedicated to St Thomas. (See pages 49-50.)

## More houses and more cottages in Leeds

In September 1863, Crossland placed two advertisements for contractors. They were for two commissions in Leeds itself. The first was placed on both 12 and 19 September for a small development of a block of houses in Belle Vue Road[15], in the Little Woodhouse suburb to the north of the town. The road itself had been constructed in 1860, and several terraces of housing were soon added by various architects, displaying both classical and Gothic detailing.[16] Crossland would have sought to make his mark with his characteristic Gothic styling.

The second was for a project to design eighteen 'model cottages' at Armley Hall for the Leeds Model Cottages Society.[17] This non-profit group had begun

---

12. Wrathmell, p. 146.
13. Harman, Ruth and Nikolaus Pevsner, *The Buildings of England, Yorkshire West Riding, Sheffield and the South,* 2017, p. 351.
14. Heritage England listing (accessed 10 November 2015). This church has been redundant since 1975. The north aisle was added in 1879, the porch and vestry in 1891.
15. *The Leeds Mercury*, 12 September 1863, Issue 7931 and 19 September 1863, Issue 7937.
16. Wrathmell, p. 193.
17. Douglas, Janet, List of works by W.H. Crossland, 2012.

Perspective View

3.3 Crossland's drawings of model cottages at Armley Hall for the Leeds Model Cottages Society. This image is the only one that has been found of this 1863 project and appears in *W.H. Crossland* by L.J. Whitaker (picture 9 between pages 43 and 44).

in the previous decade, with objectives similar to those of Edward Akroyd in Akroydon. The group aimed to enable skilled workers to build their own homes by acting as their guarantor for loans. At the same time, they sought to ensure good quality and good design by providing plans for dwellings.[18] With his experience of the model community at Akroydon, Crossland was well placed to provide the kind of designs that were required.

While working on this and other new projects, and perhaps surprisingly, Crossland seems to have gradually withdrawn from the development of Akroydon. By 1863, the first houses had been offered for sale, and, in the same year, Crossland began handing over to local architect William Swinden Barber, who continued with the project into the 1870s. Dormers on the houses were avoided in the light of the early criticisms that they made the properties look like almshouses. The properties were built with two stories and a basement, except for those in Chester Road, which had three stories. By 1873, Barber had overseen the completion of almost 100 houses of the 350 planned at Akroydon, many of which were to Crossland's designs.[19]

## Moldgreen Church

The church at Moldgreen, Huddersfield, having been begun the previous year (see pages 29-30), was consecrated in October 1863 and named Christ Church. It was much smaller than Crossland's original design, the final building being very simple because of limited funds. At £2400, it was one of Crossland's cheaper churches, but he still managed to provide an attractive church for the local community, with a bell-cote on the south side instead of the planned tower and spire. From the start, though, it was planned to replace the bell-cote and also to add a chancel, but a further

18. http://www.utopia-britannica.org.uk/pages/YORKS.htm (accessed 21 June 2016).
19. The Victorian Society, *Leeds and Saltaire*, Notes for AGM, 25-27 July 2005. By 1866, thirty-eight houses had been built, and by 1872 almost 100 houses (of 350 planned) had been completed. The last houses of Akroyd's model community were built around 1900.

3.4 Huddersfield, Moldgreen: Christ Church, 1863. The church was smaller
than Crossland's original design, with no chancel and a bell-cote instead of a
tower and spire. Date of photograph unknown, but before 1904 when G.F.
Bodley extended the church forward with the addition of a chancel.

£2000 remained to be raised for this.[20] Worshippers had to wait some forty
years for a chancel to be added by another architect[21], and a tower and spire
were never built.

## Architectural competition for Rochdale's Town Hall

In January 1864, Crossland entered another competition. This was to design
a town hall for Rochdale, an ancient community to the north of Manchester
that had grown dramatically with increasing industrialisation. It was around
thirty-five miles from Crossland's practice in Leeds and eighteen miles from
his home town of Huddersfield, over the Pennines in Lancashire.

The gestation of the initial idea for Rochdale's town hall had been a
protracted affair. Rochdale had been incorporated as a borough in 1856
and within two years the possibility of building a town hall was being

20. Law, Part 4.
21. The chancel, organ chamber and vestries were added in 1904 by G.F. Bodley, https://
    huddersfield.exposed/wiki/Christ_Church,_Moldgreen (accessed 19 June 2019).

discussed. Even when the idea was agreed in principle, there was wrangling over sites and the amount of money to be allocated. In 1858-59, there had been strong opposition to the proposed site and to spending the estimated £15,000-£20,000. Nonetheless, at a Council meeting in 1859, the decision to build was taken by a majority of one. The main protagonist was George Leach Ashworth, one of the town's councillors, who had opposed a scheme for a town hall for several years. Even with the decision taken, there was a later proposal to defer the decision until councillors could move closer to unanimity and the idea was put in abeyance until 1863. Vested interests, including those of Ashworth, continued the wrangling.

The General Purposes Committee of Rochdale Council commissioned a report, which made recommendations costed at £20,000 for the shell of the town hall. The motion for the adoption of the report was made and seconded, but an amendment was moved by Ashworth, limiting the cost of the building to £15,000 (the amount of the loan permitted by the 1853 Improvement Act to erect certain civic buildings). After discussion, the amendment was withdrawn and the original motion for £20,000 was unanimously carried. A competition was announced in January 1864 for the design of the new town hall, with the offer of prizes for winning designs: the first prize to be £100, second £60 and third £40.[22] The site recommended had been recently purchased by the Council beside the River Roch with a steep wooded slope behind. In addition to the usual public offices, it was intended to include a large hall for public meetings.

With both enthusiasm and economy in mind, Ashworth headed the subcommittee delegated to visit other town halls to learn how other communities had approached the problem of constructing such a building. They visited Blackburn (by James Paterson) and Preston (G.G. Scott) in Lancashire as well as Halifax (Charles and E.M. Barry) and Leeds (Cuthbert Brodrick) in Yorkshire, and it is likely that actually seeing the size and quality of these civic palaces convinced Ashworth that the £20,000 earmarked for Rochdale was insufficient for the sort of civic statement Rochdale wanted to make. (See pages 44-46, 56, 70-71, 92, 109-119.)

## A hotel, shops and a fine house

Once Crossland had submitted his entry in the competition for a design for Rochdale Town Hall, he continued looking for other, more certain, work, and he seems to have secured a commission to build a hotel at Elland, to which he added two shops and two dwellings the following year. Details of this project are scant, but Edward Law noted:

---

22. *The Leeds Mercury*, 8 January 1864, Issue 8031.

In March 1864 an advertisement to tender for the erection of a new hotel at Elland appeared in the *Halifax Guardian*, in association with an invitation to tender for the quarrying of stone on a site adjacent to the Crown and Anchor Inn. It is thought from this that the new hotel was the present Royal which stands at the southern end of Elland Bridge, and backs on to a quarry face. The neighbouring building to the west is two shops believed to be those which Crossland designed in 1865. . . . The letting of the building of two shops and two dwellings at Elland was advertised in April 1865. In October a further advert invited tenders for the slating and plastering of the buildings which were stated to be at Bank Bottom. The shops which lie to the west of The Royal (qv) are perhaps the least attractive of Crossland's designs; the doorways in particular are poorly proportioned, appearing very elongated.[23]

By April 1864, Crossland had been commissioned by James Priestley, proprietor of a woollen mill, to build a substantial house at Taylor Hill, near Huddersfield. He advertised for contractors, as usual, in the *Huddersfield Chronicle and West Yorkshire Advertiser*. With his office now in Leeds, he thought better of requiring potential contactors, who were likely to be in business in Huddersfield, to make the journey to Leeds to see the plans and specifications. They were therefore made available to view for just one day on 13 April at Priestley's own offices: B. Vickerman and Sons, 52 New Street, Huddersfield. Tenders were to be delivered to the same office by 20 April. Crossland signed himself as W.H. Crossland, Architect of Leeds and Halifax, but did not bother with an office address, which further suggests he had probably closed the Halifax office by this time, but had not moved his home.

When completed, the Taylor Hill house was known as Bankfield House.[24] It was a fine two-storey property with a three-storey tower, topped by a four-faced conical roof. Interest was added by several gables and a variety of window styles, including a bay window at ground-floor and first-floor levels with a decorative parapet above the upper floor, square-headed windows with quatrefoil lights above each, as well as several pointed arch windows. A pointed arch also drew attention to the front door, and there was much decorative stone carving.[25]

Within a few months of the Taylor Hill commission and only a year after moving to Leeds, Crossland had left the office in Albion Street and set up his practice a short distance away in the prestigious new Corn Exchange building.

---

23. Law, Part 5.
24. *The Huddersfield Chronicle and West Yorkshire Advertiser*, 2 April 1864, Issue 733.
25. The building was demolished in 2007 for a housing development. Photographs of Bankfield House can be found in the Flickr collection.

## Chapter 4

# The second Leeds office

By the summer of 1864, Crossland had moved his office to 23 Corn Exchange Gallery, one of the business premises in Cuthbert Brodrick's much-acclaimed new Corn Exchange building. By any yardstick, his year or so in the Albion Street office was a remarkably short tenancy, but the development of Albion Street[1] was probably the reason for his move. At the same time, Crossland was ambitious and would have wanted to be seen as among the vanguard of the new generation of architects. Brodrick's oval building with a partly glazed dome would have been seen as different, stylish and fashionable. Its two stories provided fifty-nine offices around the perimeter of the building, with those on the second floor, where Crossland's office was located, accessible from a balcony. It would have suited Crossland well to be part of such an environment at that particular time. Furthermore, Brodrick was well known as a result of the Town Hall building, the Mechanics' Institute (the competition for which had caused Crossland such anguish), as well as other buildings in the town and now the extraordinary Corn Exchange building. Crossland may have anticipated that, with an office there, a little of Brodrick's stardust would rub off on him. He took with him to the Corn Exchange office several projects, including the slowly progressing church project at Copley.

By this time, Crossland had almost certainly moved his family to East House in Roundhay, a northern Leeds suburb. During the 1820s a few grand houses had been built in Roundhay[2] and East House, which Crossland rented, may well have been one of these.

---

1. Wrathmell, Susan, *Leeds: Pevsner Architectural Guide* (New Haven and London, 2005), p. 105.
2. Wrathmell, p. 227. No remaining evidence has been found of Crossland's Roundhay home.

4.1 Leeds Corn Exchange. Crossland's office was number 23
at the top left-hand side of the picture. Photograph taken in 2016.

## Rochdale Town Hall

In what was to become by far his most significant and important
commission to date, July saw him secure the sort of reward for which he
had worked so hard. His Rochdale Town Hall competition entry won first
prize. He had submitted his design in January, along with twenty-seven
other hopeful architects[3], as he had submitted designs for other prestigious
public buildings. He must have been surprised, but utterly delighted to
win. The outcome of the competition was announced in the press on 8
July 1864:

> Town Hall for Rochdale – At the monthly meeting of the
> Rochdale Town Council, held yesterday, presided over by the Mayor,
> on the recommendation of the General Purposes Committee, the
> prize of £100 for the best design for a Town-hall for the borough

---

3. Grime, William, 'An Architect with Genius Leaves behind a Mystery', *Rochdale
   Observer*, 21 August 1971, p. 10.

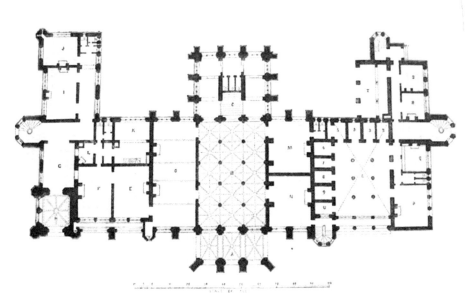

ROCHDALE NEW TOWN HALL — Plan

4.2 Rochdale: Crossland's design and plan for the Town Hall
from *The Builder*, 24 November 1866, p. 869

(costing £20,000), was awarded to Mr W.H. Crossland, architect, New Corn Exchange, Leeds; a gentleman, who we believe gained the second or third prize by his design for the Manchester assize courts. . . . The Council, by a majority of sixteen to six, then decided that the proposed Town-hall should be erected from the design of Mr Crossland, with such alterations in the details as the committee might think necessary.[4]

He was a virtually unknown Yorkshire architect, aged only thirty. His design stood out from the others as a report of the Council meeting that chose the winning entry made clear: 'He was the only competitor who spoke with distinctness and confidence.'[5] This recognition of his ability and the superlative building that was handed over to Rochdale a few years later was to assure Crossland a national reputation. Having surprised himself by winning the competition, this was, by a considerable margin, to be his largest building so far. His design and plan for the Town Hall were published in *The Builder* on 24 November 1866. (See pages 40-41, 56, 70-71, 92, 109-119.)

## St Chad's, Far Headingley

In 1864, Crossland began what must have been one of his most difficult commissions, working for a client who chose not to recognise Crossland's work publicly. This was the church that would become St Chad's at Far Headingley, just north of Leeds. His clients were the Beckett banking family. The church was to be built at the joint expense of Mr Edmund Denison of Doncaster and his son Mr E.B. Denison QC[6] (later Lord Grimthorpe), and endowed by the former with £200 a year. The land was given by Sir Thomas Beckett, the elder brother of Mr Edmund Denison.

The Becketts were responsible for several good works in the area. They purchased the Baptist chapel that had to be demolished for George Gilbert Scott's new infirmary building in Leeds and rebuilt it where a new church was needed in another part of the town. Later, they contributed to the restoration of the Parish Church[7] and also paid for two more new churches to be erected in the Leeds area. The family also built new schools on their property nearby.[8]

4.  *The Leeds Mercury*, 8 July 1864, Issue 8187.
5.  Law, Edward, *William Henry Crossland, Architect, 1835-1908*, 1992, Part 2.
6.  *The Bradford Observer*, 8 September 1864, Issue 1595, p. 4.
7.  *The Leeds Mercury*, 18 January 1868, Issue 9287.
8.  *The Bradford Observer*, 8 September 1864, Issue 1595, p. 4.

Mr E.B. Denison QC, had talents that were quite separate from his knowledge of the law, including a particular interest in clocks and bells and a considerable skill in their operation. In 1851, he had designed the mechanism for the clock at the Palace of Westminster responsible for the chimes of Big Ben, and he was elected to the presidency of the British Horological Institute in 1868. He believed that he had architectural skills also. According to Denison's biographer, Peter Ferriday, 'Interfering with architects had brought him much pleasure and some renown'.[9] Following work on St George's Church, Doncaster (where he was reported as having tormented the architect, Crossland's master, George Gilbert Scott), he turned his attention to the Far Headingley church, contributing to its design.[10]

The church was to be built on land provided from the Kirkstall Grange estate, where the mansion of the Beckett family was located. This new church was, according to *The Bradford Observer*, 'intended to be the church of a new district in the old parish of Leeds'.[11] The Beckett family wanted a grand church on their land, and the newspaper went on to describe the ambitious plans for the church:

> The foundations cover 140 feet in length and 63 feet wide, exclusive of the porch, and comprise a nave and aisles of six bays, with a five-sided apse and periapse, the aisles being carried round the chancel, and a tower 30 feet square at the base, which is shown in the plans with a spire 180 feet high.

Crossland almost certainly received this commission through a recommendation from George Gilbert Scott who, in addition to the new hospital for Leeds, had also designed the building for Beckett's Bank on Park Row in Leeds. After his experience with Edmund Beckett Denison in Doncaster, Scott himself had probably had enough to do with the Beckett family. It is also possible that Crossland first became acquainted with E.B. Denison when building Holy Trinity Church, Ossett, for which Denison designed the bells.[12]

Denison gave Crossland no credit for the design of St Chad's. The local papers, using information given to them, reported similarly. *The Bradford*

---

9. Ferriday, Peter, *Lord Grimthorpe, 1816-1905* (London, 1957), p. 68.

10. In the 1880s and 1890s, Lord Grimthorpe was to rebuild parts of the cathedral at St Albans, work generally considered unsympathetic to the character of the ancient building.

11. *The Bradford Observer*, 8 September 1864, Issue 1595, p. 4.

12. Whitaker, L.J., *W.H. Crossland* (master's degree thesis), University of Manchester, 1984, p. 89.

*Observer* report in September, for instance, credited Denison with the designs for the church, though recognised Crossland's involvement by adding 'with the assistance of Mr W.H. Crossland, of Leeds, Architect'.[13] (See pages 92-96).

## Personal life

A newspaper report of February 1865 gave a rare glimpse into Crossland's private and social life. He and his wife, Lavinia, attended the annual Masonic Ball at the Masonic Hall, South Parade, Huddersfield, being described on the guest list as a Leeds architect.[14] Despite now having his office in Leeds and previously having lived more than five years in Halifax, Crossland was still part of society in the town of his birth. He was not a Freemason, so he and Lavinia were invited guests. The ball was apparently one of 'the most successful and pleasant gatherings' that the brethren and their friends had ever enjoyed in Huddersfield, taking place in a beautifully decorated room with excellent music and 'a numerous, fashionable and cheerful company'. Crossland would have seen an occasion like this as a valuable opportunity to make and reinforce contacts in the professions likely to provide him with commissions. It was reported that the dancing at the Masonic Ball continued until half past three in the morning 'with unabated pleasure and vigour'.[15] One might wonder whether Crossland allowed himself and Mrs Crossland to dance the night away with so many building projects demanding his time and attention the next day.

## Work on churches

In April 1865, Crossland was ready to advertise for contractors for the rebuilding of the ancient church of St Peter's, Birstall, commissioned two years earlier. (See pages 34-35.) The development of the scheme for the replacement of this medieval building had taken him much time. The original plans were dated 1863. Alterations were made to plans for the chancel in 1864 and plans for the pulpit were added in the same year. In both the planning of the much-enlarged church and in its decoration, Crossland demonstrated skill and imagination in satisfying the demands of his client. The unusual plan of a double-aisled church fulfilled the requirement to increase the size of the church while accommodating to a limited footprint.

---

13. *The Bradford Observer*, 8 September 1864, Issue 1595, p. 4.
14. *The Huddersfield Chronicle and West Yorkshire Advertiser*, 4 February 1865, Issue 776, p. 5.
15. *The Huddersfield Chronicle and West Yorkshire Advertiser*, 4 February 1865, Issue 776, p. 5.

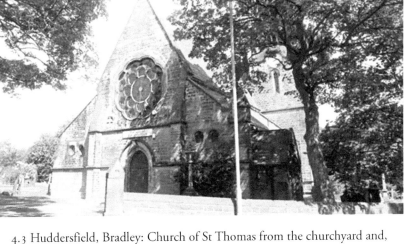

4.3 Huddersfield, Bradley: Church of St Thomas from the churchyard and, below, the west end. The church was completed in 1863 with many interesting details including a fine rose window and twin turrets marking the east gable of the nave. Crossland added further interest in 1865 with the asymmetrically placed broach-spired bell tower. The building is now used as a gymnasium. Photographs taken in 2019.

He invited tenders for the 'restoration and additions to Parish Church, Birstal [*sic*]', with plans and specifications available at his New Corn Exchange office from 19 April and tenders to be delivered to his office by 4 o'clock on 27 April.[16] St Peter's was to turn out to be a lengthy project that was to stretch his creativity and supervisory skills over the next five years. (See pages 96-98.)

At around the same time, in 1865, Crossland was recalled to the church of St Thomas at Bradley on the outskirts of Huddersfield. (See pages 10-11 and 38.) To the church he completed two years earlier, he added a bell tower with a broach spire, costing around £400.[17] He placed the tower asymmetrically on the south side of the church, making the outline of the building particularly striking.

Work on the huge church at Ossett (see pages 28-29) continued into 1865. When the vicar, the Reverend Thomas Lee, placed the final stone on top of the steeple in May 1865, it was clear that Crossland had truly delivered what the people of the town wanted in producing a Gothic Revival design for a building that would dominate the area and of which the ambitious citizens of Ossett could be proud. It immediately became 'the principal building in Ossett'[18] and drew comment: 'The new church is a beautiful structure, quite a surprise to anyone seeing it for the first time.'[19] Though initially estimated at £8,000, alterations and additions to the original plans took the final cost of construction to at least £16,000, but probably well over £20,000.

Designed in Crossland's usual Decorated style, its plan is a Latin cross, with a chancel, vestry and south porch, as well as space for an organ. The high nave is separated from the chancel by a tall arch and is provided with a clerestory above small, low side aisles and polished granite columns with foliated capitals on tall stone bases. Window tracery is geometrical and of a high standard.

Both the east and west windows are of stained glass by O'Connor of London. The east window carries an inscription underneath honouring the Inghams, one of the families whose funding had made the construction of the church possible. The west window has a dedication to the Whitakers, another family who provided substantial funds for the building of the church. Crossland provided seats for a congregation of 1,000.

The roof is steeply pitched, and the main entrance at the west end has archivolts of coloured bricks and huge wooden doors with magnificent large decorative hinges. The high quality interior ornamentation is restrained

---

16. *The Huddersfield Chronicle and West Yorkshire Advertiser*, 22 April 1865, Issue 786.
17. Law, Part 4.
18. Banks, W.S., *Walks in Yorkshire: Wakefield and its Neighbourhood*, (London and Wakefield, 1871), p. 486.
19. Banks, p. 487.

and quantity may have been sacrificed to pay for the desired size of the church. Exterior decoration is limited too, except for banding around the tower and its crocketed pinnacles.

The church's glory is its soaring spire, rising from the tower at the intersection of the nave and transepts. The spire is over 200 feet high, ensuring it can be seen on its hilltop position for miles around. The ringing chamber is reached by a spiral staircase, and the unusually large and heavy ring of eight bells was intended to ensure nobody in the locality missed the call to services. With its pinnacles, tracery and magnificent spire, this remains one of Crossland's finest churches.

The consecration of the church at Ossett, the new parish church, was announced for 14 July 1865 at 11.00 a.m., followed by a public luncheon, costing three shillings a head, in the Church School Room. Dedicated to the Holy Trinity (now called Trinity Church), the church was consecrated by the Bishop of Ripon. The church was of such an enormous size that, during the dedication service, the bishop described the church as 'this miniature cathedral'. The opening of the church was reported in *The Builder* on 22 July 1865.

In 1865, Crossland took on two more church restorations. The first was for St Chad's Church, at Middlesmoor, near Masham and around eight miles north of Pateley Bridge, on the border of the North Riding of Yorkshire. How Crossland obtained the commission is unknown, but it may well have been another outcome of the meeting of the Yorkshire Architectural Society at Driffield in September 1862. The location is outstandingly beautiful, enjoying spectacular views down the Nidd valley, but its remote hilltop location at the end of a minor road, at the head of Nidderdale, made access a challenge for Crossland.

As with the Birstall church, it was to turn out to be effectively a rebuilding and was described by *The Ecclesiologist* as a new church.[20] There had probably been a church at Middlesmoor since the fourteenth century, but it gained its own separate ecclesiastical parish only in 1863. Becoming a parish is likely to have been the impetus for rebuilding, at the instigation of the incumbent, a tribute to whom was placed in one of the stained glass windows in the chancel. Crossland's advertisement for tenders appeared in May 1865[21] and was for demolition and rebuilding.

In his rebuilding, Crossland incorporated into the new structure many elements from the old church that would have been of importance to local people. These included the font, which was probably Anglo-Saxon, and three windows from the south side that were reinserted in the north side. He also brought into the back of the church an old preaching cross dating from

20. *The Ecclesiologist*, Vol XXVI, February 1865, CLXVI, new series CXXX, p. 49.
21. Law, Part 5.

4.4 (below, top, right) Ossett: Trinity Church, 1865: a distant view.
The church's hilltop position still ensures that it can be seen for miles around.
Photograph taken in 2013.

4.5 (below, middle, right) Ossett: Trinity Church: viewed from churchyard.
Photograph taken in 2015.

4.6 (below, left) Ossett: Trinity Church: the huge west doors with large decorated
hinges and archivolts of coloured bricks. Photograph taken in 2013.

4.7 (below, bottom, right) Ossett: Trinity Church: Crossland's grand interior
of the church included polished granite columns.
The pews have now been replaced by chairs..

the tenth or eleventh century, which, according to legend, belonged to St Chad.[22] The high-backed pews and pulpit (both dating from 1775) were also retained.[23] Local marble was used in the rebuilding, which included a lean-to north aisle, as well as arches and columns with foliated capitals separating the north aisle from the nave. A new east window and new south wall windows were installed. The tower was entirely rebuilt and hung with six bells.

*The Ecclesiologist* suggested that the original design included 'a thin octagonal spire banded and with spire lights on the cardinal sides'[24], but this was never built. Overall, the journal wrote favourably on the design, which Crossland based on that of the fourteenth-century church he replaced, treating it 'with much dignity'.[25] The church was reopened on 26 September 1866, having cost £2,000 and intended to seat 400 worshippers.[26]

4.8 Middlesmoor: St Chad's Church, rebuilding 1866. Photograph taken in 2016.

July saw Crossland beginning the second restoration. This was at the twelfth-century parish church of St Mary the Virgin in Elland. This commission would have had special significance for him since his own baptism had taken place in the church. The work was to be extensive, including the removal of galleries, the removal of the ceiling in the nave in order to restore the original open roof, and the removal of the large south window. In addition, it required refurnishing the sanctuary, choir and nave, as well as laying new tiles on the nave and aisle floors. The restoration plan amounted to a restructuring of much of the church, causing resentment among some parishioners, one reputedly even defending his family pew with a drawn sword.

Nonetheless, Crossland continued with the work. He sought tenders from the various necessary trades by 14 July, having provided the plans and specifications at his own office in the Leeds Corn Exchange and in the schoolroom in Elland from 3 July.[27] With considerable care, Crossland completed the

22. https://historicengland.org.uk/listing/the-list/list-entry/1174129 (accessed 15 June 2016).

23. The present low-back oak pews were installed in 1939, according to information inside the church.

24. *The Ecclesiologist*, February 1865, Vol XXVI, CLXVI, new series CXXX, p. 49.

25. *The Ecclesiologist*, February 1865, Vol XXVI, CLXVI, new series CXXX, p. 49.

26. *The Ecclesiologist*, October 1867, Vol XXVIII, CLXXXII, new series CLVI, p. 287.

27. *The Huddersfield Chronicle and West Yorkshire Advertiser*, 8 July 1865, Issue 796.

4.9 Elland: the Parish Church of St Mary
the Virgin, restoration 1866. Photograph
taken in 2017.

restoration the following year, at a cost of £1,500, all of which was raised through fundraising. The church reopened on 16 July 1866, providing seating for an extra sixty worshippers. *The Ecclesiologist* praised and vindicated Crossland's restoration, saying, 'It is a good specimen of what a church may have been if built towards the end of the eleventh century.'[28]

In 1865, Crossland carried out a restoration of St Mary's, Lockington, near Beverley in the East Riding. This was so well outside his usual area of operations that it seems likely to have been another commission resulting from the meeting of the Yorkshire Architectural Society he attended nearby in Driffield in 1862. This church is of an unusual design and was reviewed at considerable length in *The Ecclesiologist*, which saw it as an 'interesting' church, commenting on the Romanesque elements and giving close attention to the 'large and picturesque western tower and spire of unusual design and proportions'. It argued that 'the conception does the architect great credit'.[29]

## Holiday

Another rare glimpse into Crossland's private life was provided by newspapers in the summer of 1865, hinting that his hectic business had an unfavourable impact on his family life. He seems to have been managing too many projects to be able to take time to have a holiday with his family in August. His wife and daughter (Maud was then five), together with Crossland's mother, went to Llandudno to enjoy three weeks of the summer in the resort. Their arrival was announced, as was then usual practice, in the *Original Llandudno Directory and List of Visitors*, which was published every Saturday morning in conjunction with the local Bangor newspaper, the *North Wales Chronicle*. It stated, 'Mrs W.H. Crossland and family from Roundhay, Leeds and Mrs Crossland of Huddersfield to 10 Neville Crescent, Llandudno.'[30]

---

28. *The Ecclesiologist*, October 1867, Vol XXVIII, CLXXXII, new series CLVI, p. 285.
29. *The Ecclesiologist*, December 1865, CLXXI, new series CXXXV, pp. 373-74.
30. *North Wales Chronicle*, 5 August 1865, Issue 1972 and *North Wales Chronicle*, 26 August 1865, Issue 1975 (Advertisements & Notices).

4.10 Lockington:
St Mary's Church,
restoration 1865.
Although the church
has lost its spire,
its design remains
'interesting' as
described by *The
Ecclesiologist*.

Crossland was plainly not with them. It is possible that he managed to join them for a few days, although his next classified advertisements seeking contractors were placed in the middle of the family holiday period. This time he was looking for craftsmen to build a new rectory or parsonage house, commissioned at Methley, near Leeds. It was to be a large and grand property, appropriate to the social status of the rector at the time, who was the Hon Philip Yorke Savile, son of the 3rd Earl of Mexborough.[31] *The Ecclesiologist* liked the design: 'A good design by Mr Crossland, embodying several suggestions which we have made for such houses. For instance, the dining room, study and drawing room are *en suite* . . . the architectural detail is good, though plain and simple in character.'[32]

Advertising for contractors in both the Huddersfield and Leeds local newspapers, Crossland made plans and specifications available at his Corn Exchange office between 28 August and 6 September, by which date tenders had to have been submitted to his office.[33] It is possible that he left a clerk to deal with potential contractors, but there is little evidence of Crossland delegating work. There is also no hint in any of his surviving records that he took on any pupils or that he delegated entire projects to assistants. It may be that having experienced at first-hand the continual frenzy of Scott's office, he determined to organise his professional life differently. He undoubtedly used assistants with the measuring up and drafting needed for projects, but it seems unlikely that they assumed further responsibility

31. http://www.methleyarchive.org/mppt011.html (accessed 9 February 2017).
32. *The Ecclesiologist*, December 1865, CLXXI, new series CXXXV, p. 371.
33. *The Huddersfield Chronicle and West Yorkshire Advertiser,* 19 August 1865, Issue 802; *The Leeds Mercury*, 19 August 1865, Issue 8538 and 23 August 1865, Issue 8541.

for buildings, at least at this time. The implication is that Crossland was always immersed in building projects, personally juggling several at any one time and leaving little time for holidays. The rectory at Methley seems to have been a straightforward commission and was completed the following year.[34]

## Rochdale Town Hall

Crossland's main preoccupation, however, while his family were on holiday, was the large project in Rochdale. (See pages 40-41, 44-46, 70-71, 92, 109-119.) More than a quarter of the £20,000 originally agreed for the project was 'swallowed up in the estimate for preparing the ground and constructing the cellars, even before the laying of the foundation stone'.[35] This ceremony took place on 31 March 1866 by John Bright, then Liberal Member of Parliament for Birmingham, but a native of Rochdale. Costs continued to spiral, but Crossland found himself generally supported by Councillor George Leach Ashworth in ever more ambitious ideas for the building. In his position as chairman of the town hall committee, Ashworth was 'concerned to see the whole palace completed'[36] and fought for all the extras that were eventually to bring the final cost of the project to many times over the original budget.

Working from his winning competition entry, Crossland began preparatory work on Rochdale's Town Hall. The size and grandeur of the project excused him from the tedious requirement to personally seek tenders for the work. The task of doing this was taken on by the town clerk, Mr Zach. Mellor, and the drawings and specifications were made available for viewing both at the town clerk's office and at Crossland's own office between 20 September and 2 October 1865. Specified quantities were obtainable from Messrs Bulmer and Holtom, surveyors of Dewsbury, or from the town clerk himself. Tenders were required by 2 October, although the deadline was extended to 9 October by an advertisement that was reissued several times.[37]

---

34. West Yorkshire Archives Leeds, WYL555/36: plans, elevations, specifications and related papers for a parsonage house, Methley, 1865-66.
35. Sharples, Joseph, *Rochdale Town Hall*, Rochdale Metropolitan Borough Council, undated, p. 1.
36. Cunningham, Colin, *Victorian and Edwardian Town Halls* (London, Boston and Henley, 1981), p. 71.
37. *The Leeds Mercury*, 25 September 1865, Issue 8566; 26 September 1865, Issue 8567; 29 September 1865, Issue 8570; 3 October 1865, Issue 8572; and 5 October 1865, Issue 8574

## St Stephen's Church, Copley

While working on the huge Rochdale project, Crossland was also wrestling with problems at the site of his church at Copley. (See pages 24-26 and 33-34) Ever since the commissioning of the church in 1861, the project had presented Crossland with challenges. In particular, it is likely that, from the outset, the building suffered from settlement and water seeping in from the riverbank on which it was built. The laying of the foundation stone was delayed until June 1863, and there were further delays due to mistakes on the part of the contractors, resulting in considerable annoyance on the part of the building committee. Nonetheless, by the summer of 1865, the church was nearing completion and the consecration was arranged.

A lych gate leads to the church. Constructed of sandstone with a slate roof and an apsidal chancel, the church was built high and narrow, to accommodate 450 adults and 220 children. Heavy buttresses support the building to the west front and between the nave and the chancel. There is much rich stone carving, and high on the outside west wall, Crossland placed a three-dimensional roundel in white stone of a figure with his hands in the gesture of a blessing. In the opinion of *The Ecclesiologist*, it was intended to be St Stephen, but it is more likely that it represents Christ. A bell-cote with two bells rises over the east nave gable. If a bell-cote was considered to be a sign of a poorer church, the glorious interior was an unexpected surprise.

Crossland provided a nave with a high waggon roof, a chancel with a polygonal apse, a south porch, low aisles and a transept chapel. The lavish decorative scheme, by Clayton and Bell, included paintings of saints on the south wall of the chancel and stencilling on the roofing timbers of the nave and aisles, as well as a small frieze around the chancel below window level, most of which no longer remains. Other fittings include a wrought iron chancel rail and gates, 'idiosyncratic' benches designed by Crossland[38], and a reredos and pulpit, both richly decorated with mosaic panels by Heaton, Butler and Bayne.[39] There is also high-quality stained glass by Hardman[40], depicting scenes from the life of the patron saint. The font was given by the Reverend James Hope, who had been, at the time of commissioning, the curate-in-charge at Copley. *The Ecclesiologist* was generally complimentary ('All is polychromatised very effectively'[41]), although the journal felt the reredos, altar and screen insufficient when compared to the richness of the rest of the church.

---

38. Howell, Peter, *St Stephen's Church, Copley, West Yorkshire,* undated, p. 6.
39. Harman, Ruth and Nikolaus Pevsner, *The Buildings of England, Yorkshire West Riding, Sheffield and the South,* 2017, p. 184.
40. Harman and Pevsner, p. 184.
41. *The Ecclesiologist*, Vol XXIII, 1865, p. 368.

4.11 Copley: exterior of
St Stephen's Church, 1865.
Photograph taken in 2010.

4.12 (opposite) Copley:
St Stephen the Martyr.
Lithograph of the rich interior of
the church by J. Drayton Wyatt
in *The Ecclesiologist*, December
1865, facing p. 368.

The original estimate for the church had been £3,600, and Edward Akroyd, Crossland's satisfied patron at Akroydon, had agreed to pay for the chancel, vestry and decoration in the church. The rest was to be financed by public collections, originally organised by the Reverend James Hope. Akroyd had also agreed, though, to make up any shortfall. The final cost of the building was around £9,000, including some £3,000 for the rich interior decoration. Akroyd was generous in helping to provide this particularly fine place of worship for his Copley millworkers, finally paying around two-thirds of the cost of the church and contributing to the vicar's stipend.[42] As the major contributor to the funding of the development, and with an informed personal interest in architecture, Akroyd had had a strong influence on the design. In recognition of his generosity, the other subscribers were willing to accept Akroyd's choice of vicar, the Reverend John Benson Sidgwick.

The church was eventually consecrated on 30 October 1865 by the Bishop of Ripon and dedicated to St Stephen the Martyr. Despite the difficulties experienced during the construction of the church, the lavishness of the building's interior must have given Crossland much pleasure and satisfaction. The architectural richness was another demonstration of Akroyd's own commitment to architecture. Indeed, the following May, his contributions to architecture were acknowledged when he was admitted to the Royal Institute of British Architects as an honorary member.[43]

As a member of The Ecclesiological Society, Crossland sought opportunities to publicise his work through the Society. The accounts of his new churches and restorations that appeared in *The Ecclesiologist* were almost

---

42. West Yorkshire Archive Service Wakefield, WDP/59, Copley, St Stephen's Church parish records.
43. *The Builder*, 5 May 1866, p. 329.

S. STEPHEN'S CHURCH, COPLEY, NEAR HALIFAX.

VIEW OF THE INTERIOR, LOOKING EAST.

certainly submitted by himself, several at a time. This would account for
some editions carrying details of as many as three of his works while others
had none. On 7 November 1865, he shared much of his ongoing work
(as well as initial plans for two new churches) with the committee of the
Society. He included 'photographs of the recently consecrated church of St
Stephen, Copley, . . . detailed drawings of his new Town Hall for Rochdale,
and his designs for new churches at Staincliffe and Marsden, Yorkshire, and
for the restoration of Lockington church in the same county.'[44]

## New church projects

While overseeing the complex and costly project in Rochdale (where
building probably began early in 1866), as well as projects in Elland,
Birstall, Far Headingley and Methley, Crossland continued looking for new
commissions to maintain a continuum of work and income, and he took
on several new projects, including both restorations and commissions to
build new churches.

   One of his new-build commissions, the plans of which he had shared
with the committee of the Ecclesiological Society the previous year, was for
a church for Staincliffe, a small community that was expanding with the
growth of the woollen industry. The new parish was the first of several in the
area to be carved out of the ancient parish of All Saints, Batley, to provide
for the increasing population and to counter the growing influence of Non-
Conformism. Crossland's invitation to tender for this new church appeared
in local newspapers in December 1865. The laying of the foundation stone
took place in April 1866, on land given by a Mr J.B. Greenwood, who
also provided £1,500 for the building fund. A further £100 was provided
by the Church Building Society, on condition that 500 free sittings were
provided.[45]

   *The Builder* published a detailed description of the plan of the building.[46]
It included two porches and a three-stage tower with angled turrets, an
embattled parapet and an octagonal stone spire. *The Ecclesiologist* also
reviewed Crossland's designs, noting the 'good ritual arrangements' in the
raised chancel and sanctuary and 'proper chancel seats and subsellae . . .
credence and sedilia'. Crossland was clearly trying hard to design according
to the Society's precepts. The journal thought the clerestory windows
were too small, but praised the rich design of the large windows: 'The
west window is a good composition . . . the east window is a still richer

44. *The Ecclesiologist*, December 1865, CLXXI, new series CXXXV, p. 367.
45. Banks, p. 469.
46. *The Builder*, 28 April 1866, p. 312.

Geometrical design. We commend in this design the dignified effect, externally, of the larger and more ornate windows in the chancel.'[47] (See page 74.)

Undaunted by the demands of working on ancient buildings with clients who had clear ideas of what they wanted of their architect (as at Birstall and Elland), Crossland took on two further restorations in 1866: St Mary's Church, Masham and All Saints Church, Broughton in Craven.

The Church of St Mary the Virgin in Masham was a building going back to the twelfth century, and the advertisement for tenders in March 1866 related specifically to a new roof.[48] Masham, north-west of Ripon, was quite remote, necessitating a horse cab for the ten miles from Ripon station.[49] As his clients had come to expect, Crossland provided the ancient church with a magnificent new roof. Other works were carried out in the later nineteenth century, including a remodelling of the chancel, the restoration of the octagonal lantern and spire following a lightning strike in 1855, alterations to the windows and the removal of box pews[50] – it is likely Crossland was responsible for these too.

4.13 Masham: St Mary's Church, restoration, 1866. Photograph taken 2016.

All Saints, Broughton in Craven, is another remote church not far from the market town of Skipton, between the villages of Broughton and Elslack. It is on land owned by the Tempest family, who have owned nearby Broughton Hall for many generations. The Tempest family became patrons of the church on their arrival in the early fifteenth century, and there are several memorials to them in the church. How Crossland gained the commission is not known, but it was very likely through the personal acquaintance of one landowning family with another.

The church has rubble walls and a stone slate roof, and probably dates from the fifteenth century on twelfth-century foundations, although there was probably some sort of religious building as early as the tenth

47. *The Ecclesiologist*, December 1865, CLXXI, new series CXXXV, p. 370.

48. Law, Part 5.

49. Masham did not have its own station until 1875. It was on a branch line from Ripon (http://www.disused-stations.org.uk/m/masham/).

50. Cleeves, Rev David, *St Mary's Church, Masham*, undated.

century.[51] Crossland's commission was to restore the chancel.[52] His plan for the work[53], signed and dated 1866, was for a large chancel, turning the Tempest Chapel into the Sacristy. The Tempest family may have objected to this, as the restoration was not carried out.

In 1872, the matter was addressed again, and the restoration was completed in 1873 to an unsigned and undated alteration to Crossland's plan[54], which included resiting the pulpit to the opposite side of the church, reducing the size of the chancel and no alteration to the Tempest Chapel. In the balance sheet for the restoration, dated October 1873[55], there is no fee to Crossland or any other architect: this suggests (in addition to the unsigned alteration plan) that Crossland was not responsible for the work that was carried out. According to the church guide, the work on the chancel has never been popular with parishioners: 'The chancel has suffered most heavily from the Victorian alterations. The heavy woodwork, most especially the pulpit, shows little sympathy for the proportions of the rest of the church, or the remnants of earlier and more subtle woodwork.'[56] So, although the restoration work in this church is attributed to Crossland, it seems certain that the heavy-handed work carried out – which was quite uncharacteristic of Crossland's sensitivity – was not his responsibility.

---

51. Historic England, https://historicengland.org.uk/listing/the-list/list-entry/1132291 (accessed 16 June 2016).
52. North Yorkshire County Record Office, PR/BGT 6/1, All Saints, Broughton in Craven, parish records: restoration of the chancel; elevation and plans for restoration of the chancel, 1866.
53. North Yorkshire County Record Office, PR/BGT 6/1, All Saints, Broughton in Craven, parish records: restoration of the chancel; elevation and plans for restoration of the chancel, 1866.
54. North Yorkshire County Record Office, PR/BGT 6/2, All Saints, Broughton in Craven, parish records, ground plan of part of the church, undated. This unsigned and undated plan is for the chancel and to the same scale as Crossland's plan. It could easily have been traced from Crossland's plan and then adapted by an unqualified person. The work carried out is heavy and does not respect the proportions of the ancient church.
55. North Yorkshire County Record Office, PR/BGT 6/5, All Saints, Broughton in Craven, parish records: balance sheet and subscription list for the restoration of the church, 1873.
56. The parish church of All Saints, Broughton-with-Elslack, visitors' guide, http://www.bmtparish.co.uk/welcome/?page_id=23 (accessed 28 July 2019).

*Chapter 5*

# The third Leeds office

According to his classified advertisements seeking contractors, by August 1866 Crossland had moved his office in Leeds once again. Edward Law suggests he moved earlier in the year, probably by March. Speculating on the reason for his move, it seems likely that the Corn Exchange office proved an insufficient 'shop window'. The nature of the building was such that the only passers-by were those who had already decided to enter the building and walk around its gallery and other interior spaces. Crossland probably realised that many potential clients walked past the building without ever entering. He may also have thought better of any association with the much-acclaimed Cuthbert Brodrick and his buildings while he was striving to make his own way. Crossland was finding Brodrick's stardust elusive, and, as an ambitious architect, he would have been anxious to avoid any suggestion that he was in another architect's shadow.

He moved to 25 Park Square, a prestigious professional area of Leeds. He may have had his eye on this sought-after part of the town for some time, patiently waiting until a suitable office became available. Park Square had been built between 1788 and 1810 on the site of the medieval park of the Manor of Leeds and was originally intended as a high-class residential estate. By the mid-nineteenth century, these high-quality homes had become the offices of various professions. Potential clients of an appropriate calibre frequented the area, and Crossland would have seen this as helpful in furthering his professional ambitions. He was to remain at 25 Park Square until 1870, sharing premises with two other professional men.[1] One of these men was probably the architect William Bakewell[2], whom he may have employed for a while. He had known Bakewell since at

---

1. Quoted from Kelly, E.R., 'The Post Office Directory of the West Riding of Yorkshire' (London, 1867), Part 2, p. 581 in Whitaker, L.J., *W.H. Crossland* (master's degree thesis), University of Manchester, 1984, p. 3.
2. Correspondence with Janet Douglas, 2 August 2017.

5.1 Leeds, 25 Park Square.
Crossland's third office in Leeds was
in a prestigious area of the town where
various professionals had their offices.
Photograph taken in 2016.

least the time of the meeting of the
Yorkshire Architectural Society, at
Driffield in 1862, which Crossland
had attended with Bakewell.

Despite coming to national
notice through the Rochdale
competition, it probably seemed
to Crossland that the project was
a flash in the pan, a one-off or a
chance success. He was to win no
more large projects for the rest of the
decade, despite several attempts, for
which he drew mixed comments.
For example, his entry for the
Manchester Exchange building
competition won some praise from
*The Builder* in November 1866:
'The best gothic interior exhibited,
broad in treatment and delicate in
detail. The architect has succeeded
in making a purely Gothic design,
suitable to an exchange.' Clearly,
though, the journal felt Crossland's skills needed further honing as far as
exterior design was concerned, as it was criticised as being 'not quite equal
to the interior'. Although *The Builder* found the design of the principal
front 'well carried out and would look imposing', it criticised the main
entrance, which it considered 'stunted and not important enough'.[3] Such
caustic comments neutralised the praise for the interior, and, coming from a
well-respected and much-read publication, they will have been profoundly
disheartening for Crossland. However, they also served to motivate him.
It is clear that the ambitious Crossland was anxious to take a larger and
more important part on the architectural stage. It was important to him,
therefore, to continue to find time to prepare designs for carefully chosen
competitions and to look for possible entries to the architectural scene of
Manchester, the largest city in the north of England.

However, having been unsuccessful with the Exchange competition
in gaining the entrée he so craved to Manchester, Crossland continued
to restore ancient churches and to design new churches, as well as a few
domestic buildings almost exclusively in the West Riding of Yorkshire in
the same way as he had done before winning the Rochdale project.

3.  *The Builder,* 3 November 1866, p. 807.

## Flockton Church

In the summer of 1866, at around the same time that he moved his office to Park Square, he was commissioned to build a new church for Flockton, south-east of Huddersfield, near Wakefield. It was to be the third Anglican church in Flockton, replacing buildings of 1697 and 1762 on adjacent land that was bequeathed by the Reverend Torre, rector of nearby Thornhill. Funds were limited and Crossland designed the church 'with the utmost regard to economy'.[4] In fact, the church was built largely due to the efforts and at the personal expense of the incumbent at the time, the Reverend Robert Jackson French. In August 1866, Crossland advertised for contractors for the new church, making the drawings, specifications and bills of quantities available for inspection for the week 22-29 August at his office in Leeds. Tenders were required by 30 August.[5] The foundations were begun the same year and were above floor level by the time the cornerstone was laid on 9 May 1867. The church was consecrated on 9 September 1869, dedicated to St James the Great.[6]

It was built as economically as possible. The limited funds meant Crossland put little detailing on the outside, and a small bell-cote rather than a tower had to suffice. The account of the church in *The Builder*[7] spoke of the severity of the interior, implying the economy of design was necessitated by the tight funding. The original plan included no chancel because of the low budget. As a member of the Ecclesiological Society, this expedient would have disappointed Crossland. He and others of the High Anglican movement will have been relieved, therefore, when funds for a chancel were forthcoming from a member of the local aristocracy. As a result, Crossland was able to provide a church that conformed to the criteria laid down by the Ecclesiologists with the final plan including a chancel, nave, north aisle and a porch on the south side.

Crossland appears to have been asked particularly to maximise the use of interior space within the limited budget for the Flockton Church and designed a wide chancel arch, allowing a clear view to the altar. By including no transepts, he managed to fit in 400 sittings. The church was built of roughly cut local stone with pressed red brick facings on the internal walls

---

4. Brookes, Laurie, *(Revised) Brief Notes on the Church of St James the Great, Flockton,* 2009, p. 1.
5. *The Huddersfield Chronicle and West Yorkshire Advertiser,* 11 August 1866, Issue 852; 18 August 1866, Issue 853; and *The Leeds Mercury,* 11 August 1866, Issue 8839.
6. Brookes, p. 1.
7. *The Builder,* 29 September 1869. p. 773.

and stone columns. The incorporation of brick was becoming acceptable in architectural circles by this time and, as a cheaper building material, allowed Crossland to squeeze more out of the low budget. The re-use of some fittings from the previous church (including the font and bell) and several gifts also helped to stretch the available funds.[8]

Despite working to a tight budget, Crossland achieved a spacious interior with a warm intimate atmosphere[9], helped by the use of red brick. There were some uncarved stops, suggesting that the low budget did not allow some of his planned items of decoration. Nonetheless, he managed certain decorative elements, including a pulpit with painted panels by John Roddam Spencer Stanhope, son of a local landowner, an associate of the Pre-Raphaelite circle of artists and almost certainly a personal acquaintance of Crossland.[10] He also included oak and vine carving for the capitals and a fine window for the east end, with stained glass by George Baguley of Newcastle upon Tyne.[11] The vicar, the Reverend Jackson French, sought Crossland's advice in connection with this window. Crossland's reply to the vicar (in syntax suggesting it was written in great haste) is preserved among the church papers:

> 17 Apl 1869
> My Dear Sir,
> I have looked carefully over the designs for your east window and if drawing is worth anything Bagully design is out and out the best.
>    I hope you will allow the central front to go as he shows it the noble figure of our Lord never can be made to look well in glass and the other arrangement is more medieval.
>    Yours faithfully,
>    W.H. Crossland[12]

At £3,075, although exceeding the original quote of £2,600 (and probably accounted for by the late addition of the chancel), St James was still a low-cost church, earning Crossland just £231-1s. Despite it being one of his smaller churches, the time Crossland spent on St James was well used as he went on to apply a variation of the style to a later commission.

---

8. Brookes, pp. 5-7.
9. Whitaker, p. 95.
10. Douglas, Janet, unpublished lecture notes from study weekend *Stanhope Country*, Cannon Hall, Cawthorne, South Yorkshire, 21 April 2012.
11. The window was moved to become the West Window in 1937.
12. Law, Part 5.

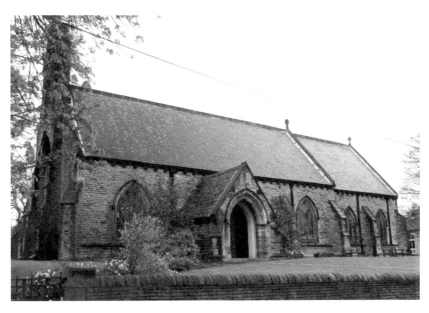

5.2 (above) Flockton: St James the Great Church, 1867. The bell-cote and simple exterior announce that the church was built to a tight budget. Photograph taken in 2012.

5.3 (left) Flockton: St James the Great: the East window, set in red brick. Despite an austere exterior, Crossland achieved some high-quality decoration inside the church, including this window by George Baguley of Newcastle upon Tyne. The red brick created a feeling of warmth. Photograph taken in 2012.

## Marsden Church

Despite funding issues, the Flockton church proved to be a reasonably straightforward project, which was more than could be said for another new project, the plans for which Crossland had shared with the committee of the Ecclesiological Society the previous year. This was to replace the parish church, dedicated to St Bartholomew at Marsden, near Huddersfield, in hilly country at the head of the Colne Valley. This was an ancient church, dating from sometime between 1433 and 1455, when it was built as a chapel of ease because of the difficulty local people had in travelling to Huddersfield to worship. A new church had been built on the same site in the middle of the eighteenth century, increasing capacity to over 600. By the second half of the nineteenth century, the church was serving a population of about 2,700 with most of the inhabitants working in mills or as weavers at home. Furthermore, all the 600 or so seats were considered personal property with pew rents paid for them, implying that the church was only for the use of worshippers of some personal means. The earth floor of the church allowed burials inside the church, but by 1865 it was so crowded that the decision was taken to build a completely new church on a site on the other side of Church Lane.

When applications for funding were made to replace the existing church, it was described as old, dilapidated and insufficient. According to the local press in 1867, a grant of £50 had been received and a further grant application had been made to the Ripon Diocesan Society. Assistance with funding was also sought from other organisations, including the relatively new Society for Rural Extension within the Deanery of Huddersfield. The new church, the application stated, was to be built near the old one, with a new burial ground alongside, on glebe land that was to be purchased from the incumbent. The proposed cost of the church, including a tower with a spire, was £7,235, of which only £2,700 had already been raised.[13]

Crossland drew up plans for the new church to seat a congregation of about 800.[14] By the time of the grant applications, Crossland had already signed a contract with the church to build the nave and aisles, and work had begun. In October 1866, just two months after beginning the Flockton church, Crossland advertised for excavators and masons to carry out the preparatory work of constructing the foundations and basement of the new

---

13. *The Huddersfield Chronicle and West Yorkshire Advertiser*, 4 May 1867, Issue 889, p. 6.
14. http://www.achurchnearyou.com/marsden-st-bartholomew/ (accessed 15 September 2015).

church at Marsden. Plans and specifications were available for inspection both at his Leeds office and at the vicarage in Marsden. Crossland required tenders for this part-project by 29 October 1866.[15]

However, the project seems to have been beset by problems from the outset, one of which was undoubtedly funding. At their meeting in May 1867, the Society for Rural Extension within the Deanery of Huddersfield, which had a total of only £500 to award in grants, voted a grant of £100 towards the rebuilding.[16] Given the limited funds available, this was generous, but left a great deal still to be raised. Nonetheless, Crossland must have been confident of the balance being made up, since, by the beginning of July 1867, he advertised for contractors for 'all or any' works in building the new church at Marsden. Plans and other documentation for potential contractors to examine were made available at his office from 29 July with tenders required by 12 August. (See pages 70 and 230.)

## *Fellow of the Royal Institute of British Architects*

By this time, Crossland had achieved an enormously important milestone in his professional life by becoming a Fellow of the Royal Institute of British Architects. He had begun signing his advertisements as 'W.H. Crossland, F.R.I.B.A., Architect, Leeds,'[17] and must have added these letters after his name with great pride. A basic condition for election to the rank of Fellow was the completion of seven years in practice. Proposed by his master, George Gilbert Scott, as well as by E.R. Robson and J.P. Seddon, he was elected a Fellow of the R.I.B.A. on 28 January 1867. This was a mark of recognition of a practitioner at the top of his profession, and although there were various architectural associations and societies at the time, the Royal Institute of British Architects was almost certainly the best recognised and respected, albeit mainly in London.[18] Probably encouraged by Scott, the ambitious Crossland already had his eye on London and the opportunities it offered and counted on his R.I.B.A. Fellowship to open new doors. He was elected a Fellow without having held a lower level of R.I.B.A. membership such as an Associate of the R.I.B.A..[19] His parents were undoubtedly very

15. *The Huddersfield Chronicle and West Yorkshire Advertiser*, 20 October 1866, Issue 862 and 27 October 1866, Issue 863.
16. *The Huddersfield Chronicle and West Yorkshire Advertiser*, 4 May 1867, Issue 889, p. 6.
17. *The Huddersfield Chronicle and West Yorkshire Advertiser*, 6 July 1867, Issue 898; 13 July 1867, Issue 899; 20 July 1867, Issue 900; 3 August 1867, Issue 902; and *Manchester Times*, 13 July 1867, Issue 501.
18. Correspondence between author and R.I.B.A., 3 June 2016.
19. R.I.B.A., W.H. Crossland biographical file, letters to and from Peter Crossland, 4 August 1983.

proud of their son. His mother died in April of the same year at the age of only fifty-five, and Crossland must have found some consolation in his bereavement that she had lived long enough to celebrate this accolade.

His advertisements for contractors for the Marsden project appeared, as usual, in local newspapers, but he also advertised in the *Manchester Times*. It is possible he did this routinely when looking for contractors, but more likely, perhaps, Crossland wanted to use such an advertisement to promote himself to the city of many potential clients now that he had become a Fellow of the foremost architects' professional body.

The foundations of the new St Bartholomew's were constructed, but the new church was not to be. There was a dispute between the contractor and the building committee, and the foundations were covered over. Remarkably, the congregation then abandoned their plans for a new church and instead repaired and renovated the old chapel, continuing to worship there for around another thirty years.[20] (See page 230.)

## Rochdale Town Hall

The project that most preoccupied Crossland throughout his entire period of practice in Leeds was Rochdale Town Hall. (See pages 40-41, 44-46, 56, 92, 109-119.) The protracted time taken for the project to be agreed after the incorporation of the borough in 1856 had caused local comment. Once the project began, the steadily increasing costs, for which Crossland was blamed, generated even more local comment and caused Crossland much anguish. At times during the construction, Crossland feared it was going to destroy him professionally. A letter, written from his Park Square office to Mr James Kitchin, the clerk of works, on 12 September 1867, gives a flavour of his concerns and shows that he felt the problems associated with the project threatened his personal reputation.

> 25, Park Square Leeds
> 12 Sep 1867
>
> Dear Sir,
> The more I reflect upon what I heard at the meeting yesterday, the more anxious I become to impress upon you the necessity of spreading a report about Rochdale contradicting the present received opinion of my character and intentions.

20. http://www.achurchnearyou.com/marsden-st-bartholomew/ (accessed 15 September 2015) and www.marsdenparishchurch.org.uk/history.htm (accessed 15 September 2015).

I look to you to do this and I feel that you will not disappoint me. Your opinion in the future if asked for must be

1st    That the works are progressing perfectly satisfactorily now.

2nd   That we had some trouble at first to get Messrs Warburton to do the right thing.

3rd   That we have every confidence in a satisfactory finish.

You must on no account whatever express an opinion unasked for, unless to the Chairman, beyond the above & always go to the Chairman or come to me when any difficulty arises.

I have been told that you are in the habit of telling people that the work you got at the Baths is far superior to that you are getting at the Town Hall. *I do not believe it.*

I should be very much annoyed if I thought you made any such remark or compared the 2 buildings in any way.

I know you have my interest at heart & beg to assure you that the report now going through Lancashire is simply ruinous to me & it must be stopped.

When the Town Hall is finished I shall, I do not fear, be reinstated in public favour. In the meantime I trust implicitly in your acceding to my wishes.

See if the entrance gates cannot be kept locked & if necessary get Mr Ashworth to allow a Porter to be placed there.

I am

Dear Sir

Yours faithfully

W.H. Crossland

To Mr James Kitchen[21]

Also evident in this letter is Crossland's self-confidence and his complete belief in his own capabilities to achieve an entirely satisfactory outcome with the complex Town Hall project.

Alongside Rochdale Town Hall, Crossland continued to take on an exhausting number of new commissions and restorations. Although they were almost all in the West Riding, and although each project had a clerk of works, travel from project to project to supervise the ongoing work in this large county took considerable planning and a great deal of time. The railway network was good by the mid-1860s, but journeying from the final station to a project would have been a slow and uncomfortable journey by horse-drawn carriage.

---

21. Law, Part 2.

## Womersley Church

The restoration at the church of St Martin at Womersley near Selby was one such restoration.[22] While still in the West Riding, this church was well outside the area with which Crossland was familiar, and with no station in the immediate vicinity, it added considerably to the logistics of managing his various projects between 1866 and 1870. A church in Womersley was recorded in the Domesday Book, and over the centuries many improvements had been carried out, funded by prosperous patrons with features from as early as the thirteenth century remaining

5.4 Womersley, near Selby: St Martin's Church, restoration, 1867. The ancient church was closed for a year for Crossland's restoration.

in the church.[23] Around 1867, Crossland was commissioned to restore the fabric of the building and to remove fittings that compromised the medieval character of the church.

The church was closed for about twelve months for Crossland's restoration. His work involved lowering the whole church floor by around twelve inches to return it to something like its original level. In so doing, he uncovered the bases of the nave pillars, which had been buried as the floor level had risen over the centuries. He also removed a wooden gallery and the high-backed pews, replacing them with open pine pews that were rearranged to increase the number of worshippers that could be accommodated. A new stained-glass window by Hardman, funded by a local benefactor, was installed in the chancel, and some other windows were replaced in the south aisle and transept, allowing more light into the church. He supervised the stripping of old plaster from the interior and repointing, as well as the cleaning and recarving where necessary of the

22. Further restoration work was carried out by G.F. Bodley towards the end of the nineteenth century, leading to Crossland's contribution to the restoration of the church now being generally overlooked.
23. https://www.achurchnearyou.com/womersley-st-martin/ (accessed 19 December 2016).

capitals of the columns. The harmonium was replaced by an organ, paid for by the parishioners, with decorated front pipes and a screen case designed to harmonise with the structure of the church. In removing some of the accretion of several centuries, Crossland restored coherence to the interior. Such was the sensitivity of the work that on completion in the summer of 1868, the impression was of a well maintained medieval church rather than a church in the contemporary idiom.[24]

## Kellington Church

It seems that the Womersley project led directly to further work in the vicinity as, at much the same time in 1867, Crossland also took on the restoration of the church in Kellington, a small village in a lonely location between Pontefract and Selby, about two miles from the nearest dwelling. The fact that it was close to Womersley suggests that Crossland was probably recommended for the work in Kellington because of the quality of his work at Womersley. This project was to restore the twelfth-century Church of St Edmund, where the main concern was the dilapidated condition of the north aisle. Crossland was commissioned initially to assess what restoration work was necessary. While still in the West Riding, like Womersley, the location of this church was unfamiliar and scheduling supervisory visits would have been a further complication in his project management.

In the restoration, old plaster and whitewash were removed to reveal the stone wall, which was repointed. Crossland demolished the dilapidated north aisle and rebuilt it with a lean-to roof, using new stone to match the original stone. The south chancel wall was found to be so much out of plumb that it was considered unsafe, so it too was taken down and rebuilt. The whole roof was renewed, restoring the carved bosses at the intersections in the nave and the north chapel, thereby preserving the character of the old roof. Mindful of the Ecclesiologists' principles, Crossland took the opportunity to add a new chancel arch and to enlarge the chancel with a roof of hammer-beam structure, a style that became typical of Crossland's work. The east chancel wall was rebuilt and rebuttressed, and a new five-light east window was installed. A new window was also installed at the west end, for which Crossland drew the style (square headed with cusped lights) from that of the north clerestory. He also provided new oak pews and an open traceried screen to separate the north chapel and the vestry from the chancel. The old seating was replaced with more practical pews. The priest's doorway was removed internally, but left complete outside, preserving the appearance of the building. The porch was also restored.

24. Whitaker, p. 118, and *The Builder*, 22 August 1868, p. 630.

Despite these substantial changes, Crossland handled the project sensitively and left intact many of the earlier fittings, including the font, which dated from 1663. Three Early English windows were preserved and returned to their original position in the new south wall, and, as far as possible, original materials were reused, including the lead from the roof, which was recast.[25]

Crossland's restoration included the rescue of the 'Kellington Serpent Stone'. This stone slab, generally presumed to be the lid of a knight's coffin, was, according to village tradition, the coffin lid of a shepherd who, with his dog, slew a 'noisome snake' as a result of which both man and dog died

of poisoning. The stone was originally in a niche in the north wall of the Chantry Chapel, but had been put in the churchyard in the sixteenth century. Through exposure to weather, the carving deteriorated, and to prevent further damage, and as part of the restoration, it was brought back into the church in 1869 and placed near the font. Crossland's restoration cost about £3,000 and was paid for by a Miss Mary Ann Eadon, whose memorial tablet was placed on the wall near the high altar.[26]

5.5 Kellington: St Edmund's Church, restoration, 1869. Crossland carried out substantial works at this church, handling the work sensitively and preserving many of the early fittings.

## Staincliffe Church

On 12 November 1867, Crossland's church in Staincliffe, near Batley, commissioned in 1865 (see page 61), was consecrated in the name of Christ Church by the Bishop of Ripon, in whose diocese it then belonged. The church, in a mixture of medieval styles, was built on a hill, and its large tower was to become a local landmark. The design of the church had been described in some detail in *The Builder* in April of the previous year[27] and in *The Ecclesiologist* in 1865[28], but Crossland clearly had to contend with a shortage of funds for the work.

25. *The Builder*, 8 January 1870, p. 34 and Whitaker pp. 117-18.
26. http://tyates.com/page2.htm (accessed 29 June 2016).
27. *The Builder*, 28 April 1866, p. 312.
28. *The Ecclesiologist*, February 1865, no. CLXVI (new series no. CXXX), pp. 369-70.

After costings, Crossland's original plan had proved to be too expensive, leading to cost-cutting by the parish council and the consequent loss of the spire and porches[29], as well as much external decoration. The planned school and schoolmaster's house were also abandoned. Crossland will have been disappointed by the compromises to the external appearance that had to be made to cut costs (including his own fee). In particular, blocks of stone that Crossland had intended to become decorative carvings were left unworked on the four pinnacles of the tower as well as elsewhere on the exterior of the building, having the effect of making the outside appearance particularly austere. Overall, the exterior of the building was never completed as Crossland intended.[30] It seems that funds for decoration were diverted to the interior, although all the windows were probably of clear glass at the time of consecration and the tracery on the east and west windows was more modest than originally designed.

Huddersfield stone was used for the tracery and dressings and the floor was of Westmorland slate. The building was broad and spacious 'and consequently rather bare'[31] with clerestory windows and a roof of Crossland's familiar hammer-beam construction to the nave. The piers between the nave and the aisles, each comprising four clustered columns, had foliated capitals of oak and vines, of a high quality, each one different. The large chancel (about half the length of the nave) was provided with a wide arch, which was also finely carved on both sides. Cast iron grilles were installed in the floor as part of an underfloor heating system. The nave and both the north and south aisles were filled with pews. Along the length of the south aisle were square stops. As with the blocks outside, it seems certain that these blocks were intended for carvings and they provide further evidence of cost-cutting. The high standard in Crossland's other churches would have precluded them from being intentionally squared.[32] The final cost was £4,620.[33]

A vicarage was also commissioned from Crossland, and it was built next to the church a couple of years later in 1869, at the cost of £1,183.[34]

---

29. Although the porches in Crossland's design for the north and south sides were not included in the original building, they were added just a few years later.

30. Whitaker, p. 46.

31. Banks, W.S., *Walks in Yorkshire: Wakefield and its Neighbourhood*, 1871, p. 469.

32. Whitaker, p. 88.

33. http://staincliffe.weebly.com/ (accessed 22 October 2015). The account of the church is largely taken from this website.

34. Whitaker, p. 88.

5.6 (top) Staincliffe, Dewsbury: Christ Church, 1867. The exterior of the building was never completed as Crossland intended. Photograph taken in 2015.

5.7 (middle) Staincliffe: Christ Church: Blocks of stone were left unworked where there should have been carvings. Photograph taken in 2015.

5.8 (bottom) Hoylandswaine: St John the Evangelist Church, 1868. A small but substantial church, built to a high-quality of local stone for a small working class village. Photograph taken 2012.

## Hoylandswaine Church

Among Crossland's new churches in 1867 was a commission for a church and vicarage at Hoylandswaine, a small working-class village near Penistone, to the south-east of Huddersfield. An application had been made to Ripon Diocesan Church Building Society in 1861 to build a church for this community, but the laying of the foundation stone by the Bishop of Ripon was delayed until November 1867. It was on a site provided by Francis T.V. Wentworth of Wentworth Castle, and the parsonage, funded by the local Stanhope family of Cannon Hall, was largely already complete by then.[35] Crossland's church for the village, in the Decorated style, was small and simple, but substantial, built of local stone and of a high quality. It was rectangular in shape with a high and spacious chancel, a massive low square tower at the west end, with battlements and pinnacles, a north porch, an organ chamber and a south aisle running into a small vestry. It cost around £3,000.

The cost of the church was largely borne by the Stanhope family, in memory of Louisa Stanhope, who had died in 1867.[36] There were a few smaller subscribers, including F.W.T.V. Wentworth who contributed £700. Eighty pounds was provided towards the building by The Incorporated Society for Building Churches, on condition (according to a plaque at the back of the church) 'that all the sittings be free and unappropriated'. Accordingly, when the church was consecrated on 30 July 1869, dedicated to St John the Evangelist, it provided 322 free sittings[37] for the local farmers and farmworkers, weavers, coal miners and nail-makers.

Decoration in the church is limited except for a spectacular east end. This includes a fine window by Morris & Co. to a design by Edward Burne-Jones, depicting the crucifixion. The church's most remarkable feature is a magnificent large wall painting above the east window, with the title *The Ascendancy of Christ*. This is by John Roddam Spencer Stanhope and depicts Christ with saints and angels.[38] Roddy, as Stanhope was affectionately known, was the son of the principal benefactor, acquainted with the Pre-Raphaelite artists and almost certainly also with Crossland.

The parish was created shortly after the consecration. A small school was built at the same time as the church and was almost certainly also designed by Crossland.

---

35. *The Sheffield & Rotherham Independent*, 14 November 1867, Issue 4076, p. 3.
36. Poë, Simon, 'Stanhope Country', unpublished notes from lecture delivered at Cannon Hall, Cawthorne, South Yorkshire, 21 April 2012.
37. *The Sheffield & Rotherham Independent*, 31 July 1869, Issue 5008, p. 8.
38. Stanhope's wall painting was painted over in 1961 and restored in 2014.

## *Church project, Armley, Leeds*

In the same year that he began the Hoylandswaine commission, Crossland secured a commission to build a new church in Leeds. He must have been pleased to have secured, at last, another commission in the town where he ran his business, but the Armley project was to cause him many time-consuming problems.

A public meeting had been held in August 1866 to consider forming a new parish and building a parish church, and a building committee was formed. The principal contributors to the proposed church, apart from the Leeds Church Extension Society which gave £3,000, were local industrialists John and William Ewart Gott who gave respectively £2,000 and £1,000. In November, Crossland was asked to provide a plan that satisfied the requirements of the building committee, seated 700 and was within a budget of £5,000. According to Edward Law[39], the following month Crossland submitted two plans, but reported that 'a very plain church without either tower or spire to accommodate the number required could not be built for less than £5,000 to be substantially built'.

A meeting in December resolved to advertise for plans for a church of 650 adult sittings with a transept and a tower for eight bells at a cost of about £5,000, and they added that a thoroughly good and substantial building was required. Several plans were received and considered by the building committee. Meantime, a sub-committee was formed to examine the church Crossland was building for the Beckett family at Far Headingley, and it reported back that the workmanship on the stone at the Beckett church was very good.

At a meeting in February 1867, there was a motion that alternative Leeds architects, Messrs Adams and Kelly, be appointed architects of the Armley church, but the motion lacked a seconder. The outcome was that Crossland was appointed architect of the project, and later in the same month, he submitted his plans and specifications. The estimate for the building was £6,255, or £6,055 if the interior was not to be plastered. However, Crossland was away in London, delaying further progress until late March, at which time he was instructed to obtain tenders without any unnecessary further delay.

Matters stalled again until July when Crossland was again asked to seek tenders, which he apparently did immediately. When the tenders were

39. This account of the commissioning of the Armley church is derived entirely from Edward Law, *William Henry Crossland, Architect, 1835-1908*, 1992, Part 5.

examined, they were all well beyond the estimate, and Crossland was asked for an explanation. Matters came to a head on 28 September 1867 at a meeting of the building committee when it was minuted:

> Mr Crossland having furnished no data to enable the Committee to understand the discrepancy between his estimate and the tenders sent in the Committee feel under the necessity of stating that unless Mr Crossland will guarantee that the cost shall not exceed £6,255 complete, they will consider themselves at liberty.

On 8 October, the Committee issued a statement following a meeting saying that they had met 'purposely to consider the explanation offered them by Mr Crossland, and having carefully gone into the same, [did] not feel that they [were] justified in proceeding, and therefore they decide[d] to return the plan to Mr Crossland together with a copy of this resolution'.

The architects subsequently appointed were the alternative Leeds architects, Messrs Adams and Kelly, and the new plans were drawn up after visits to other churches, including (surprisingly, given the circumstances) Crossland's church project at Staincliffe. Problems continued as the new Armley church took shape: there were resignations from the building committee, some contractors refused to take instructions from the architects and the clerk of works was dismissed. In the light of all the subsequent issues, Crossland must have been relieved that he had been able to cut his losses at a relatively early stage.

## Ripon Churches

The following year, 1868, saw Crossland taking on several more new projects, including two in Ripon, which was well outside the area of the West Riding he knew well. These were a restoration (amounting to a rebuilding) of the ancient church of St John in Bondgate and a replacement for the ancient church of St Mary Magdalen. These two churches were associated with medieval hospitals, of which there were several associated with Ripon Cathedral. The Charity Commissioners had reported in 1820 on the estates of both churches and in 1864, these estates were reorganised, enabling the premises to be rebuilt.[40] How Crossland came to be awarded these rebuilding commissions is unknown, but it is likely that it was through George Gilbert Scott, who was working on the restoration of Ripon Cathedral at the time.

---

40. *Historic England,* http://www.britishlistedbuildings.co.uk/en-330124-chapel-of-the-hospital-of-st-mary-magdal#.VtR4oZyLRn4 (accessed 29 February 2016).

The hospital of St John Bondgate was founded in 1109 by the Archbishop of York to provide hospitality for poor travellers. The original hospital chapel fell into disuse in 1722, and from 1812 to 1854 it was used to house the National School. Crossland's commission was to build a new church. He designed a small chapel, which was built of sandstone, on the site of its medieval predecessor with an apsidal chancel and a large stone bell-cote with a finial cross, plain white walls and wooden pews. It cost just £1,300.[41]

The chapel of St Mary Magdalen was founded in about 1115, also by the Archbishop of York. It served the Hospital of St Mary Magdalen, which cared for lepers, blind priests and poor travellers. By 1868, the congregation had outgrown the small chapel, and Crossland was commissioned to build a new church on the opposite side of the road from its medieval predecessor. The medieval church was not demolished, but used for a while as a farm building.[42]

## Secular commissions

Back in Huddersfield, 1868 saw Crossland design what was described as a pair of semi-detached houses. These are in Edgerton, an affluent area of the town, and were built for a local solicitor, Henry Barker, who was on the building committee of a new church in Leeds Road, Fartown, Huddersfield, which Crossland was commissioned to design the following year. Barker probably became acquainted with Crossland during the discussions that led to the building of the church and negotiated the designing of the villas at the same time. He planned to live in one himself, and the other was to be for his mother.[43]

The term 'semi-detached' poorly describes this particularly clever development, which Crossland designed to look like one large property, very likely to offer the option of converting it to one large home at some future time. The substantial building was constructed on a bank and cut into a steep hill, making it considerably higher than the level of the road and giving both houses a steep back garden. The houses are approached on separate entrance drives, each with striking gateposts bearing the name of the house. Their front doors are at right angles to each other. For his client's own home, which was named West Mount, Crossland designed the more imposing front entrance, positioning it

---

41. http://riponcathedral.info/the-chapels/ (accessed 29 February 2016) and http://www.shipoffools.com/mystery/2010/1960.html (accessed 29 February 2016).
42. Jones, Revd Gareth T., *A History of the Chapel of the Hospital of St Mary Magdalen, Ripon*, revised 2016.
43. Law, Part 5.

5.9 (top, left) Ripon: the chapel of St John, Bondgate, rebuilding, 1868.
A small and low-cost chapel with an apsidal chancel. Photograph taken in 2016.

5.10 (top, right) Ripon: Crossland's new church of St Mary Magdalen, 1868,
which was used for worship while the original medieval church became a farm
building. Now converted to a private residence, the medieval church has been
restored to its original purpose. Photograph taken in 2016.

5.11 (bottom, left) Huddersfield, Edgerton: West Mount, 1868. The fine porch
suggests the entrance to a grand property, rather than to a 'semi-detached' house.
Photograph taken in 2017.

5.12 (bottom, right) Huddersfield, Edgerton: Marshfield, 1868.
This is half of the same building as West Mount, the two houses being described
as 'semi-detached'. Both houses have gateposts bearing the name of the house but
the approach to Marshfield is less grand than that to West Mount.
Photograph taken in 2017.

to one side of the development, in a deep and steeply gabled porch. The front door of Marshfield, the house for his client's mother, is halfway along the façade that fronted the road. The whole building is attractively gabled and incorporates a variety of Gothic motifs. It still presents an air of opulence in this well-to-do area, but cost the original client considerably less than two separate houses.

In the same year, Crossland also designed a larger and grander domestic building, near to Ripponden, to the west of Huddersfield. This was Rishworth Lodge, a shooting lodge in domestic Gothic style for Henry Savile, a member of an important local family. Crossland gave the building interest through a variety of roof levels, several elaborate chimneys, and the Savile monogram and coat of arms (an owl) carved into the walls.[44] The staircase was provided with stepped pointed arch windows, a motif Crossland employed on several of his buildings, including Rochdale Town Hall.

1868 seems to have been a particularly busy year for Crossland. He took on some new work in Rochdale, associated with his increasingly grand Town Hall project. project. This was essentially landscaping work and entailed building a wall to control the River Roch with the addition of some parapets. The work was advertised for tender in February 1868, calling specifically for the ashlar and stone to be from the Summit and Todmorden quarries.[45]

## Two new churches and an unsung restoration

In the same year, Crossland also began two new churches, both well outside his usual area of work. The first was a church at Broomhill, Sheffield. Plans and other details were made available at his Park Square office from 30 June with tenders required by 11 July, and the foundation stone was laid in October. It was to be a large church, with 950 sittings and took until 1871 to complete, at a cost of £12,000. It was consecrated on 31 May 1871, dedicated to St Mark and was described as one of the finest churches in the city.[46] This may have been an example of journalistic hyperbole, as a few years later it was described as 'one of the plainest . . . churches in the town' with an 'almost total absence of colour' with the only decoration in the carved reredos.[47] The architect of the vicarage of

---

44. www.britishlistedbuildings.co.uk/101277090-rishworth-lodge-ripponden. The building has now been divided into flats.
45. Law, Part 5.
46. Law, Part 5.
47. *The Sheffield & Rotherham Independent*, 30 September 1878, Issue 7497, p. 3.

5.13 Rishworth: Rishworth Lodge, 1868, a shooting lodge built for a member of the locally important Savile family. Its location is still isolated and the building has been divided into several homes. With road access at the back, the principal elevation looks out across a valley. The side view shows Crossland's lively variation in roof style and stepped pointed arch windows marking the staircase. Photographs taken in 2019.

5.14 Sheffield, Broomhill: St Mark's Parish Church, 1871. The tower, spire and porch are the only parts of the original church that remain.

St Mark's is not recorded, but the building is attributed to Crossland.[48] It was probably built over a decade later (being known to have been first occupied in 1885), using French motifs that were characteristic of Crossland's work at that time.[49] Except for the tower with spire and the porch, the church was destroyed by a German bomb during the Second World War.

The second new church was at Sutton-in-Craven in the large parish of Kildwick in the Aire valley, between Keighley and Skipton. A number of daughter churches had been planned as early as the 1850s, including a church in Sutton. These plans came to fruition in 1868, at the instigation of the vicar of Kildwick, when the opportunity of funding presented itself. In his will, a wealthy local man, Thomas Bairstow, who had already paid for the Sutton National School, provided a bequest for the building of the church, and his widow had the church built in his memory.

At his office in Park Square, Crossland made available plans, specifications and bills of quantity for the various relevant trades, with tenders required by 30 July.[50] The foundation stone was laid in November, and the new church was consecrated on St Thomas's Day the following year, 21 December 1869, dedicated to St Thomas. It is a small church, built on

48. Harman, Ruth and Nikolaus Pevsner, *The Buildings of England, Yorkshire West Riding, Sheffield and the South*, 2017, p. 584.
49. In 1885, Crossland was completing Royal Holloway College for Thomas Holloway in Surrey, for which he visited France several times, recording motifs from châteaux to be incorporated into the vast building. It would have been entirely natural for Crossland to apply such details to other buildings on which he was working at the same time, including the vicarage of St Mark's Church, Broomhill.
50. *The Leeds Mercury*, 20 June 1868, Issue 9419; *The Bradford Observer*, 2 July 1868, Issue 1793 and 23 July 1868, Issue 1796.

rising ground providing seating
for 350 at a total cost of £4,000,
including an endowment. The
sturdy tower at the west end,
with crocketed pinnacles at each
corner and an external staircase
turret with arrow-slit light
openings, was built to carry a
spire that was never added.

The interior is relatively
plain, although the foliage
carving on the column capitals,
to Crossland's designs and each
one different, is of a high quality.
The plainness of the interior is
easily overlooked by the size of
the pulpit, which overwhelms

5.15 Sutton-in-Craven:
St Thomas' Church, 1869, a daughter
church for St Andrew, Kildwick.
Photograph taken in 2015.

the inside space. Made of local Monkton Moor stone (as is the font), it is
decorated with a large carving of an angel and banner, as well as carvings
representing Matthew, Mark, Luke and John.

Thomas Bairstow's widow ensured that she and her husband were
remembered by placing a memorial plaque under the five-light east window.
The window depicts the Ascension with the eleven disciples at the feet of
Christ. The other windows in the new church were of clear glass, many to
be replaced by stained glass in later years as memorials to various people,
including other members of the Bairstow family.

At around the same time (1868-69), Crossland is also known to have
designed two fittings for Kildwick parish church itself. Other restoration
work was carried out simultaneously on this ancient church, some of
which had a direct bearing on Crossland's recorded work. Useful details
of the restoration are included in a history of Kildwick Church, written
between 1901 and 1908 by the vicar of the church at the time[51], but much
of the work carried out in 1868-69 is unattributed. However, because this
restoration work and Crossland's known contributions were all part of the
same reordering, and because Crossland is not known to have worked with
other architects, it seems likely that Crossland was responsible for the design
and supervision of the whole restoration project. Seemingly, he became
a victim of architects' invisibility. Such 'invisibility' could be the fate of
those who carried out sensitive and high-quality restoration work that was

---

51. Brereton, Revd E.W., *History of the Ancient and Historic Church of St Andrew, Kildwick-
in-Craven*, Crosshills, Yorkshire, 1909 (details taken from pp. 17-20, 66-67).

5.16 Sutton-in-Craven: St Thomas' Church. The fine foliage carvings on the column capitals are all different. Photograph taken in 2015.

5.17 Sutton-in-Craven: St Thomas' Church. The heavy decoration on the large pulpit overwhelms the church. Photograph taken in 2015.

5.18 Kildwick-in-Craven: St Andrew's Church, restoration 1869. Crossland's large and beautiful font cover, designed to be like the one destroyed in 1825. Photograph taken in 2016.

5.19 Kildwick-in-Craven: St Andrew's Church. With ten bays, the church is exceptionally long and probably dates from the tenth century. Crossland's restoration of 1868-69 seems to have been completely forgotten in the twentieth century. Photograph taken in 2016.

so appropriate to the style and character of the original that, on completion, it was difficult to see what had been carried out. Such work is also often poorly documented, particularly if followed a few years later by more major work that effectively overshadows the earlier work. This is probably the case at Kildwick, where Paley and Austin of Lancaster carried out substantial work on the church less than forty years later.

Assuming that it was indeed Crossland who restored the church of St Andrew Kildwick between 1868 and 1869, he left the ancient building looking as it might have done for centuries in the absence of the earlier interventions that he erased. The work included the removal of the gallery, installed in 1825, and of the ringing chamber at the west end, thereby opening out this part of the church. A new base was provided for the ancient font, to suit its octagonal form, and the two south doorways were raised to the level of the church. The two or three steps inside the church from each door were taken to the outside and into the porch respectively. Additionally, a door in the middle of the south side was walled up, the roof restored and the oak ceiling was stripped of the plaster that had covered it.[52] The old vestry, at the west end of the north aisle, was removed and a new one at the east end of the south aisle was flagged and panelled in oak; new seats were put in and a new heating system was installed; the roof and woodwork were oiled; the interior walls re-coloured; and the pillars and side walls painted. A stained-glass window, by Clayton & Bell, was installed in the tower and stonework renewed. Another new window by Heaton & Bayne was placed in the east end of the south aisle.[53] The organ was also installed at this time, replacing a harmonium.[54]

These were substantial alterations. The only work actually documented as by Crossland were an oak screen across the bottom of the tower arch at the west end (no longer in place) and an elaborate 'very beautiful canopy

52. Brereton, pp. 20-21.
53. Brereton, p. 67.
54. Brereton, p. 19.

or font cover, the gift of Mrs. Tennant, of Kildwick Hall'.[55] This new font cover is fourteen feet in height and weighs over four hundredweight[56] so a new beam had to be installed from which it could be suspended, the old one not being sufficiently sound.[57] This beam could not have been installed without the removal of the gallery at the back of the church. It seems clear, therefore, that Crossland's documented works were integral to the whole restoration scheme.

The 'very beautiful canopy or font cover' replaced the original canopy that had been removed in 1825 to create space for a gallery at the back of the church and, extraordinarily, 'cast aside and afterwards made into chairs, and sold by public auction.'[58] Forty-three years later, Crossland created the replacement 'after the pattern of the old one destroyed in 1825'[59], implying a sketch of the original had been retained. This beautiful piece of craftsmanship, by an unknown woodcarver, remains a superlative example of Crossland's outstanding design skills.

Whether the Kildwick commission or the Sutton commission was first is unclear, but it seems certain that one came as a result of the other. Crossland's work at these two churches, just a couple of miles apart, demonstrates starkly the extremes of his style. The restoration work at the ancient church at Kildwick, in particular the exquisite reproduction of a medieval font cover, demonstrated true sensitivity to the environment within which he was working. On the other hand, he showed at the Sutton church that 'he could "brutalise" Gothic forms' (presumably to satisfy the client), selecting, according to Whitaker, 'only the most essential shapes and placing them in a nineteenth century context'.[60]

## New relationship with the Ramsden Estate in Huddersfield

Most satisfyingly for Crossland in 1868, he was, at last, to enjoy the beginning of a new relationship with the Ramsden estate in his home town of Huddersfield. This was one of the largest estates in the region, and the new relationship was of the utmost importance in enhancing Crossland's reputation.

As a town, Huddersfield was in the unusual position of having virtually only one ground landlord: the Ramsden family owned, with two small exceptions, all the land on which the town of Huddersfield stood. When the railway

---

55. Brereton, p. 17.
56. Four hundredweight is equivalent to about 203 kilograms.
57. Brereton, p. 67.
58. Brereton, p. 17.
59. Brereton, p. 67.
60. Whitaker, pp. 245-46.

arrived in Huddersfield in the 1840s, the Ramsdens opened up new areas of the town for development. They granted leases that reserved them the right to exercise building control, with particular reference to design. The Ramsden development was laid out in grid form, and all proposed designs were submitted to their representative for approval. The vetting was not simply a formality, as anything that did not harmonise with the scheme was rejected.[61]

Though by now established as a church architect in the West Riding, Crossland must have yearned for the prestige of a commission from the Ramsdens in his home town. Up to this point, though, Sir John William Ramsden had doggedly retained the services of William Tite (who planned the overall scheme for the new centre of Huddersfield) and later Edward Blore, both London architects. Ramsden must have been well aware of the young local architect called W.H. Crossland, going back to 1856 when the Ramsdens made a gift of land for the Cowcliffe and Netheroyd Hill School that Crossland designed while still a pupil of George Gilbert Scott. Furthermore, Crossland's father had leased quarries on Ramsden land for at least two decades and would have been regularly in contact with the builders and architects in the town, and with the Ramsden estate's local agent and surveyors.

Sir John Ramsden was clearly not willing to trust building work on the estate to a young architect who, in his view, had not amply proved himself. By 1868, though, with Rochdale Town Hall approaching completion and Crossland's reputation increasing through the high quality of his growing list of completed buildings, and not least through his election as a Fellow of the Royal Institute of British Architects, Ramsden was ready to entrust a large, strategically placed and transformative building to Crossland.

The Ramsden Estate Office was, at that time, located at Longley Hall, the old Ramsden family home, which the family used for occasional visits and which was conveniently situated midway between their main estates of Almondbury and Huddersfield. By the 1860s, however, the railway in Huddersfield had led to the rapid development of the town while Almondbury remained rural and undeveloped. It made sense, therefore, for the Ramsden estates to be managed from the growing town. The expansion of the Ramsdens' commercial interests in Huddersfield included new trading arrangements and the letting of new leases, which necessitated inspecting new work and liaison with the town council.

Huddersfield was incorporated as a borough in 1868. This formalised planning control, but as almost the only landlord in Huddersfield, the Ramsden family remained able to develop the town according to their own ideas. Critically, they realised that appearance and efficiency were of prime

61. Law, Part 4.

importance in attracting business to the town. Wide, straight streets of attractive buildings with efficient drainage and sewerage systems, as well as good service access, all increased the appeal of the town.

Commercial buildings were still a relatively new building type, but the growth of industry had led to an increasing demand for large purpose-built industrial and commercial buildings that swept away the small premises of the eighteenth century, which had often differed little from domestic buildings. Fine premises made a confident statement about a business and its owner. The abolition in 1851 of a tax on windows quickly led to larger windows in new building designs, which were particularly appealing to tenants looking for new shop premises. Architectural decoration was also important in making premises more attractive to potential tenants.

Sir John Ramsden had ambitious plans for Huddersfield. In the same year as incorporation, together with his local agent, R.H. Graham, and his cashier, Isaac Hordern, he began redeveloping the north side of Westgate as far as the parish church. The existing small buildings, typical of a country market town, were to be demolished and replaced by grand buildings to provide an impressive foretaste of the streets of the new town. Crossland's trademark Gothic style was becoming more popular for large public buildings and Crossland's new status as Fellow of the Royal Institute of British Architects reassured Sir John that Crossland was the architect to turn his ideas into reality. On 22 May 1868, Crossland was commissioned to design a town-centre office for the Ramsden Estate, and the commission was announced in *Building News*.[62]

Until the Ramsden Estate Offices, new buildings in Huddersfield had been classical derivations. However, Sir John Ramsden was now pleased to embrace the Gothic style with which Crossland had established his reputation. Crossland's commission was to design a prominent block of buildings opposite the station in the centre of Huddersfield. The site was chosen not only because it would be seen from the station, but also because the buildings that would have to be demolished were poor and unattractive and, it was realised, an unfitting welcome for visitors to the expanding and ambitious town.

The site for the Ramsden Estate Building fronted two main thoroughfares: Railway Street and Westgate. The Railway Street frontage was to be the more ornate, housing the Ramsden Estate Offices in the central portion. All the offices necessary for the running of a large estate were to be here, including a large hall where estate tenants would come to pay their rents. The decorative detailing of this side of the building was to include a series of sculpted armorials depicting the Ramsden family's marriage alliances.

62. *Building News*, 22 May 1868, p. 351.

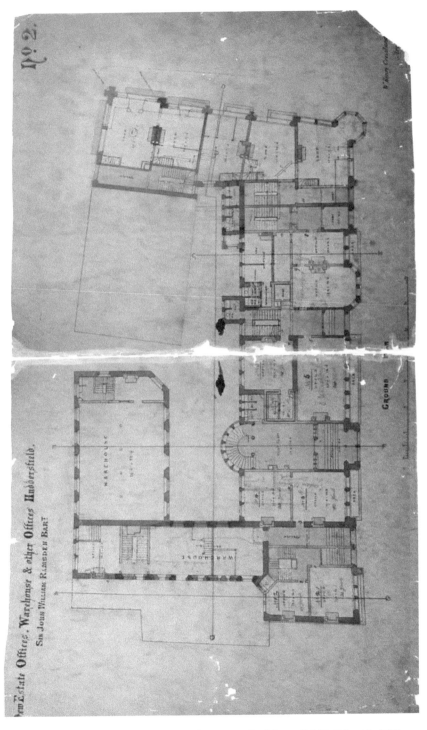

5.20 Huddersfield: plan of the Ramsden Estate Buildings (1868-74), titled 'New Estate Offices, Warehouses & other Offices, Huddersfield'. Crossland sought to separate unobtrusively the public and private parts of the building.

The Ramsden arms, their crest and the date of construction were to appear on the eastern elevation. The cost of the whole project was estimated at about £35,000.

Crossland designed a fine building for the Ramsdens, strikingly different from other buildings in the town. In it he sought to manage issues similar to those with which he had already wrestled in the design of Rochdale Town Hall. In particular, he had to resolve the problem that some parts of the building were to be private space and function independently of other areas, while other parts were to be open to the public with limited circulation.[63] He advertised in May, inviting tenders 'for erection of Estate Offices, Warehouses and other offices at Huddersfield for Sir John William Ramsden, Bart'.[64] Plans and specifications would be made available at his Park Square office in Leeds, and he required estimates by 20 June. Construction began the same year, and advertisements for the letting of the building appeared as early as May 1868. (See pages 103-106.)

In 1869, there was some correspondence between Crossland and the Ramsden estate about building a new market for Huddersfield. A letter of 6 May 1869 from Crossland to the estate's agent R.H. Graham set out 'probable costs' of 'the proposed New Market at Huddersfield'. The site lay at the bottom of the town on land surrounded by Kirkgate, Cross Church Street, King Street and Old Kirkgate, and it was proposed to develop it in four phases as various tenancies became available. The likely cost was over £33,000.[65] However, the project did not come to fruition. Law suggests it may have been simply the floating of an idea or that it was shelved.[66]

## Completing earlier church commissions

Meanwhile, other projects continued to demand Crossland's time. Alongside the large Rochdale Town Hall project (see pages 40-41, 56, 70-71, 109-119), the cost of which continued to escalate, and the Ramsden Estate Building, on which his reputation in his home town depended, he had the various new churches and restorations taken on after the office move to Park Square and several ongoing projects from previous years.

The new church for the Beckett family in Far Headingly, commissioned in 1864 (see pages 46-48), took until 1868 to complete. At the planning stage, Crossland had been given no credit for the design of St Chad's, all

---

63. Whitaker, pp. 159-60.
64. *The Huddersfield Chronicle and West Yorkshire Advertiser*, 16 May 1868, Issue 944.
65. Law, Part 4.
66. A new market building for Huddersfield was finally opened in 1880, designed by local architect Edward Hughes.

responsibility for the project being claimed by Edmund Beckett Denison. In practical terms, the amateur architect Denison probably put his ideas for the church on paper and went on to supervise the execution of the building.[67] Managing the whims of the demanding Denison over the construction of the church presented Crossland with many difficulties that had resulted in the protracted build-time between commission and completion.

Pevsner described the church as 'a proud and prosperous church, lying on its own, away from the bustle of the road'.[68] Though intended to be the church for a new district within the parish of Leeds, it was effectively an estate church, built in the grounds of New Grange, then the home of the Beckett banking family. In Early English style with Decorated detailing, it was almost as large as Crossland's vast church in Ossett. The Beckett family wanted their new church seen, and it was therefore, unusually, orientated almost north-south rather than the usual west-east, to provide a more pleasing vista from Otley Road, the main road through Headingley. It was situated on a ridge on a gently rising slope, and its unusual orientation ensured it fitted its location well. Crossland used a fine stone on the reredos, pulpit and font, as well as for the foliated capitals[69], but otherwise the church was built of 'Rough Rock' gritstone – a much-used coarse local sandstone, which included pebbles of quartz and feldspar. The building was constructed from regularly shaped and sized blocks, quarried specially for the purpose[70], probably from the local Harehills quarry or the small quarries in nearby Meanwood.

Crossland provided the church with a nave of six bays and a five-sided apse with the unusual feature of a periapse (aisle carried round the apse). The windows were of plain glass and the reredos was decorated with mosaic. Philip Webb designed an east window for the church[71], but it was never executed. This was possibly because of the unusual orientation of the building, but also because the periapse, in the finished form, precluded any large window behind the high altar.

The church was one of the few Crossland designed that was completed with a spire. It was 186 feet high, octagonal in design, slender and well-proportioned with diaper patterning. The bell tower originally had just three bells, designed by Denison himself, and cast in 1867 by Taylors'

---

67. Wrathmell, Susan, *Leeds: Pevsner Architectural Guide* (New Haven and London, 2005), p. 260.
68. Pevsner, Nikolaus, revised Radcliffe, Enid, *The Buildings of England: Yorkshire, West Riding* (Harmondsworth, 1959), second edition 1967, reprinted 1979, p. 323.
69. *The Builder*, 25 January 1868, p. 66.
70. Church information board outside the church, 25 August 2015.
71. *The Victorian*, July 2015, p. 13.

5.21 Leeds: Far Headingley: St Chad's Church, 1868. This picture is reproduced
from a page in a stewardship leaflet given to the author in 2015. The church was
much altered when a chancel was added in 1909-11 by J. Harold Gibbons
of Manchester, at which time Crossland's east end was demolished.

foundry in Loughborough. The total area of the church was an impressive
5,500 square feet, and the height of the interior lent it an air of opulence,
which was doubtless Denison's intention.

With the exception of gas fittings by Francis Skidmore of Birmingham,
Crossland's tradesmen were all from Huddersfield and Halifax[72], suggesting
that, even around five years after moving to Leeds, he had not established

72. *The Builder*, 25 January 1868, p. 66.

such good working relationships in Leeds as he had made at the beginning of his career. The church was consecrated on 11 January 1868 by the Bishop of Ripon and dedicated to St Chad, an Anglo-Saxon Bishop of Mercia. The Beckett family held the patronage of the church, which had cost them about £15,000 including an endowment of some £7,000.

5.22 Leeds, Far Headingley: St Chad's Church. This image, taken in 2015 from an old photograph inside the church, shows Crossland's periapse.

During the consecration service, the Bishop of Ripon commented that 'St Chad's Church was one of the most beautiful edifices he had ever consecrated, and he was persuaded it might become a model for other churches.'[73] This sentiment was expanded by the report of the consecration in the local press: 'there are few that surpass in elegance of design or general appearance the church of St Chad at Far Headingly.'[74] Denison must have been pleased with himself and took all the praise for the church. Crossland's name was not mentioned at all by Denison in his remarks on the church[75], and he gave Crossland no credit for the design. Instead a commemorative plaque began:

> This Church dedicated to St Chad was consecrated on the 11th of January 1868. Designed by Edmund Beckett Denison Esq QC afterwards the First Lord Grimthorpe who, together with his father Edmund Denison Esq defrayed the costs & endowed the living . . .[76]

Fortunately, *The Leeds Mercury* recorded the true situation for posterity: 'Mr W.H. Crossland of Leeds is the architect and the work has been executed from designs prepared by that gentleman and partly suggested by Mr E.B. Denison'.[77] The following week, *The Builder* gave Crossland his due among its wider professional readership, stating simply, 'Mr Crossland was the architect'.[78]

---

73. *The Leeds Mercury*, 18 January 1868, Issue 9287.
74. *The Leeds Mercury*, 18 January 1868, Issue 9287.
75. Ferriday, Peter, *Lord Grimthorpe, 1816-1905*, 1957, p. 68.
76. To the present day, there remains no reference to Crossland in St Chad's Church.
77. *The Leeds Mercury*, 18 January 1868, Issue 9287.
78. *The Builder*, 25 January 1868.

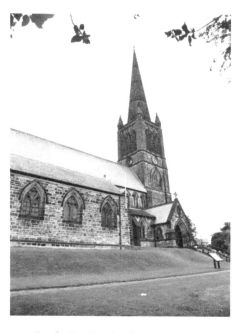

5.23 Leeds, Far Headingley:
St Chad's Church. The tower and spire.
Photograph taken in 2015.

The rebuilding of St Peter's Church, Birstall, originating from Crossland's commission for a restoration in 1863 (see pages 34-35, 48 and 50), was eventually completed in 1870. It was on an ambitious scale, and Crossland worked sympathetically with the church community over the seven years in ensuring that they obtained a new church that fitted their requirements. He handled the project and expectations sensitively, and although, except for the tower, he completely rebuilt the church, he respected the original church and its twelfth-century elements.[79]

His design was in sympathy with the Tudor church he replaced and which had become too small for the congregation. He lengthened the chancel and broadened the church by the unusual expedient of providing double aisles.[80] In Crossland's design were the best features of the church's architecture from the preceding centuries[81], including the conserved Norman tower, with its fifteenth-century bell stage. Memorials from before the rebuilding were incorporated into the walls of the ground floor of the tower, as was a medieval window of St Peter and St Paul. Another medieval window was incorporated into the wall of the vestry. The octagonal font, with a panelled bowl and stem, dating from the fifteenth century, was retained. Medieval choir stalls with blind tracery, poppy heads and armrest carvings of foliage and animals were also retained. Some medieval pew ends were kept, displaying the carvings of family or farm symbols that had originally helped the illiterate find their places in the church. Some medieval grave slabs were also retained, as well as a brass to a Mrs Popeley, who died in 1623. All these retentions demonstrated Crossland's care in keeping as much from the previous church as possible. He also reused stone from the

79. Whitaker, p. 117.
80. Whitaker, p. 245.
81. West Yorkshire Archive Service, Wakefield, WDP5, Birstall St Peter parish records.

5.24 Birstall: St Peter's Church, rebuilding, 1870. The east window and back of the church, showing the church's unusual width. Photograph taken 2015.

5.25 Birstall: St Peter's Church. The interior, showing the church's double aisles and Crossland's fine stone pulpit. Photograph taken 2015.

previous church, much of it already well worn. He built in a mixture of styles in ashlar sandstone with a graded slate roof, keeping the low profile of the previous church and adding west-end porches to the north and south.

The decoration both outside and inside was lavish. He provided exterior battlements and pinnacles, doors with ornate strap hinges, much high-quality wood and stone carving, and traceried windows. He gave the chancel roof his favoured hammer-beam style, finished with flying angels holding their hands together in prayer. The high-quality carving in the chancel was by Samuel Ruddock[82] whose carved bench ends of the choir unusually included pigs and lions. The north chancel-aisle chapel was given a mosaic floor. Crossland designed the large stone pulpit, decorated with figurative carving, stone steps and a wrought-iron balustrade. He installed new west windows to the aisles, taking the style from the openings in the retained medieval tower. Apart from the retained medieval stained glass windows, the windows contained clear glass, the present stained glass having been installed after Crossland's church was complete.

The final cost of the church was around £18,000, making it one of Crossland's most expensive churches. The wide building with its double-aisled nave provided seating for 1,050 worshippers. The chancel rebuilding was completely funded by local benefactor Percival Wormald, who also made a large contribution towards the building of the nave. St Peter's was probably Crossland's most attractive church. It was certainly his most interesting church plan and generous funding allowed more decoration than at his other churches.

## Another new church for Crossland's home town

Despite the large project for the Ramsdens in Huddersfield, the as yet unfinished Rochdale Town Hall and numerous other incomplete projects, in 1869 Crossland accepted an assignment from the committee on which Henry Barker (of West Mount and Marshfield, Edgerton) was a member, to build a new church, dedicated to St Andrew, together with a school and vicarage in Leeds Road, Fartown, Huddersfield. The church was to be built on a site provided by Sir John Ramsden, and Crossland sought tenders in March 1869 from his Park Square office.[83] The foundation stone was laid on 21 July of the same year.

The plan of the church is asymmetrical. It is of a compact design, similar to the church in Sutton-in-Craven, built of stone from the local

---

82. Harman and Pevsner, p. 127.
83. *The Huddersfield Chronicle and West Yorkshire Advertiser*, 13 March 1869, Issue 987 and 3 April 1869, Issue 990.

Crosland Hill quarries with slate roofs and a bell-cote. It has sloping roofs over the side aisles and noteworthy exterior decorative detail. This includes some fine carving, especially a figure of Christ with outstretched hands (now badly weathered) in the gable above the steeply pitched porch, similar to that at the Copley church. There is also a series of heraldic shields under the single transept window. The trefoil

5.26 Huddersfield: St Andrew's Church, Leeds Road, 1870. The disused church has fallen into a sorry state of dereliction. Photograph taken in 2017.

motif design of the chancel window is repeated in the transept window and unusual circular clerestory windows allow light into the nave. As Crossland designed it, the interior was plain but spacious, with a finely carved stone pulpit and a typical Crossland hammer-beam roof. The church was intended to have a tower with a spire, but this was never built. The cost of building was £4,167, and the church was consecrated on 10 August 1870, providing 550 sittings on long open benches.[84]

5.27 Huddersfield: St Andrew's Church, Leeds Road. This exterior detail of carved heraldic shields shows the fine quality of stonework on the church. Photograph taken in 2017.

As it turned out, the vicarage was never built, and there was a delay in realising the school project. By now, though, Crossland was moving into an altogether more exciting stage of his career, and it is possible that without pressure from the church itself, he simply overlooked it until prompted a few years later.[85]

---

84. Whitaker, p. 11.

85. St Andrew's Church was declared redundant in 1975, after which it was used by the local Roman Catholic congregation until about 2001. By 2017, it was boarded up and dilapidated and its future was uncertain.

*Chapter 6*

# London and Huddersfield offices

Crossland had opened an office in London by April 1869, while the tendering for his Leeds Road church in Huddersfield was being completed and before the foundation stone for that church was laid. With so much work in Yorkshire, Crossland's reason for opening an office in London is obscure. Only the previous year, he had won the trust and patronage of Sir John Ramsden, the most important person in Huddersfield, and had the prospect of plenty of work for Sir John in his home town. He may have been tempted to London by George Gilbert Scott, who perhaps considered his talented ex-pupil's skills were under-exploited in Yorkshire and convinced him that his Fellowship of the R.I.B.A. would open fashionable and lucrative new doors. It may be that the income from Rochdale Town Hall and the Ramsden estate commissions in Huddersfield provided the financial confidence he needed to open an office in London. It may be also that his London-born wife, Lavinia, wanted to return. Not least, the availability of offices in the heart of the metropolis (in the building where Scott had begun in practice), must have been attractive. Indeed, Scott may well have told him of their availability.

Having trained in London, Crossland knew the city well. Over the previous decade, he had continued to visit from time to time, almost certainly to maintain contact with George Gilbert Scott, but also to keep in touch with the other architects with whom he had trained and who had set up their practices in London. The creative hub of the profession was undoubtedly London, and it enhanced Crossland's reputation to have strong connections with the capital.

Whatever the reason for his move, he was to continue designing buildings for Huddersfield, even though the supervision of the construction of these buildings must have been difficult from a distance of some 200 miles. Crossland's London office was at 2 Carlton Chambers, 4 Regent Street. This was a prestigious address, in the heart of the fashionable West End.

6.1 London:
Carlton
Chambers, 4-12
Regent Street.
Crossland chose
a prestigious
location for his
first London
office.

It was also near to Scott's office, suggesting that Crossland remained keen to maintain a link with his master. Carlton Chambers had been designed by Decimus Burton who had bought up the leases of a number of plots in Regent Street, including 4-12 Regent Street. Dating from around 1820, it was a fine building, offering sets of chambers arranged around a public staircase, much as at the Inns of Court, for gentlemen and professional men.[1]

As early as 4 May 1869, within a month of opening his office in London, Crossland applied for membership of the Junior Carlton Club, a club with strong leanings towards the Conservative party. This early application to join a London club implied that his new presence in London was intended to be permanent. He gave the Regent Street office address as his London address, suggesting that he opened his office in London before he had a permanent residence in the city. He gave the address of his home in Roundhay, Leeds, as his country residence. It is likely that his proposer for membership was Robert Monach, his step father-in-law. His seconder was J.M. Sagar Musgrave, Lord of the Manors of Roundhay, Seacroft and Shadwell who lived at Red Hall, Shadwell, near Leeds. Crossland was not elected a member until almost three years later, on 5 March 1872, implying that there was a waiting list to join the club.[2]

By 1870, his home was 12 Park Village West, Albany Street, near Regents Park, where the household comprised himself, his wife, Lavinia, and their daughter, Maud (then aged ten), as well as a cook and a maid.[3] This was a very fine home for a man in his mid-thirties. Park Village, separated into East

---

1. https://londonstreetviews.wordpress.com/2015/02/13/carlton-chambers/ (accessed 25 July 2016).
2. Law, Part 3.
3. https://ancestryinstitution.com, *1871 England census*, census RG 10 203 f6 p. 5.

6.2 London:
12 Park Village
West, Regents
Park: Crossland's
remarkably
opulent first
home in London.
Photograph taken
in 2016.

and West, was a development of the 1820s by John Nash, completed by his pupil and successor, James Pennethorne. Park Village West is a particularly picturesque crescent of about twenty individual villas in a variety of styles. Among these exceptionally prestigious homes, number 12 is 'possibly the most impressive villa in the whole development'.[4] In an Italianate design, its pedimented front door faces the road at the base of a three-storey octagonal tower. Previous occupants of the house included Dr James Johnson, physician to King William IV and the enormously successful painter William Powell Frith. This home made a supremely confident statement of success for an architect only recently arrived in London. Indeed, renting this property may well have been an act of supreme overconfidence since, busy though Crossland always was, the rental of office space in Regent Street and a home in an exclusive and fashionable development near Regents Park must have been a considerable financial strain.

## New work for the Ramsden Estate in Huddersfield

From his London office in 1870, Crossland supervised the beginning of his next project in the development of Huddersfield for the Ramsden Estate, even before the Estate Office was complete. It seems the new development was seen by the Estate as a continuation of the Estate Office project. Estate correspondence from earlier the same year endorsed this:

4.  http://hidden-london.com/gazetteer/park-village/ (accessed 23 January 2017).

In February 1870 Captain Graham [the Ramsdens' agent] wrote to Sir John Ramsden 'I shall be glad to receive your sanction to my authorising Mr Crossland to get in tenders for the work.' That letter is endorsed 'proposed new building Westgate and Station Street.' . . . It is clear therefore that it was seen from the start as part of a larger scheme.[5]

Sir John Ramsden was plainly well satisfied with his new architect, as sanction was quickly given. In May, and then a further three times in June, Crossland advertised for tenders 'for the erection of the first portion of a block of buildings comprising shops, warehouses and offices'[6], to be built alongside the Estate Offices on Westgate. This was to become the Byram Buildings (the name deriving from the Ramsden's family country house near Knottingley, West Yorkshire). Crossland included both the Leeds office address and, for the first time, his London office address in his advertisements. Tenders for these commercial buildings in Huddersfield were to be submitted by 30 June, and Crossland stated in his advertisements that the plans and specifications would be available from 20 June at both his London and Leeds offices. (See pages 106 and 134.)

Shortly after this, despite his ongoing projects in Huddersfield and despite the fact that he continued to take on further new commissions in the West Riding, Crossland closed his Leeds office. His local presence seems to have transferred to Huddersfield in the person of his senior assistant, Mr A.J. Taylor, who had occupied this role since about 1867. In Huddersfield, Taylor worked out of an office within the Ramsden Estate Office, surveying for Crossland and dealing with general office business. It meant that Crossland effectively had, at last, but in absentia, an office in his home town of Huddersfield.

The Ramsden Estate Building (see pages 90-92) opened without ceremony on 14 September 1870, although the building was not completed until 1872 and the complex of buildings of which it was part was not fully finished until 1874. From the station exit, a fine view of the building faced people arriving by train. The management of the Huddersfield part of the Ramsden Estate was moved to the new Estate Buildings from Longley Hall in the same year. Crossland provided rooms for the Ramsden's agent and manager, cashier and surveyor, as well as a drawing office, general offices and, effectively, an office for himself – the architect to the Ramsden Estate – in the guise of the office of his chief assistant, A.J. Taylor.

---

5. Law, Part 6.
6. *The Huddersfield Chronicle and West Yorkshire Advertiser*, 28 May 1870, Issue 1050; 4 June 1870, Issue 1051; 18 June 1870, Issue 1053; and 25 June 1870, Issue 1054.

6.3a and 6.3b (top and middle) Huddersfield: the Ramsden Estate Building, *The Builder*, 23 March 1872, p. 227 and today. Photograph taken in 2015. The first Gothic style building in Huddersfield, with a striking corner tower, it was richly decorated with symbols of the Ramsden family.

6.4 (bottom) Huddersfield: the Ramsden Estate Building, roofline detail. Photograph taken in 2015.

In addition to the Ramsden Estate accommodation, the building also contained warehousing, offices, shops and a considerable area for the newly founded and prestigious Huddersfield Club. At the end of 1870, the Ramsdens' Huddersfield agent, Captain Graham, enthused: 'nothing could be more successful than the [Estate Office] undertaking has proved'.[7] Crossland achieved 'grandeur' and 'eloquence'[8] as a result of the privilege of an unrestricted site. A three-sided, four-storeyed construction, enclosing a narrow courtyard, it was built entirely of Yorkshire stone, except for marble shafts on a corner tower and a slate roof. The floors were designed to be fireproof throughout. The original contract costed the building at £27,000, but the final cost was over £40,000.[9]

The Ramsden Estate Building was quite different from anything built previously in the town. In a Gothic style inspired by the new Houses of Parliament in London, the magnificent frontages to Westgate and Railway Street were linked by a striking corner tower topped by a short octagonal spire with a weathervane. The roofline was highly original and the whole building displayed a wealth of decorative designs. It was described in *The Builder* in March 1872 as 'a romantic free gothic' building 'with turrets, round-arched windows, pointed arch windows and square-headed windows with also trefoil-headed windows and wide segmental arches on the shop fronts in the Westgate.[10] The corner tower had elaborate battlements and blind tracery. The Estate Office entrance on Railway Street had fine wrought iron gates, which led to an ornate semi-circular staircase to the Estate Manager's office. There was also much sculptural work, carved on-site, particularly fronting Railway Street, including flowers, foliage and birds. There were even 'the naked bottoms of men illicitly carved by a cheeky mason, proving beyond doubt that intricate sculptural carvings of this sort were carried out on the building rather than being placed in position ready carved'.[11]

The building was designed as three separate areas. The Railway Street frontage housed the Ramsden Estate Offices and had the most ornate exterior. The interior of this wing was also richly decorated, with linenfold panelling, plaster relief work, decorative wrought ironwork and windows decorated with heraldic motifs. The Westgate front housed shops with the central shop converted to the vestibule and entrance hall for the Huddersfield

7.  Law, Part 6.
8.  Whitaker, p. 179.
9.  R.I.B.A., W.H. Crossland biographical file.
10. *The Builder*, 23 March 1872, p. 227.
11. Gibson, Keith and Albert Booth, *The Buildings of Huddersfield* (Stroud, 2005, reprinted 2009), p. 99.

Club, which occupied the whole of the first floor. The entrance hall was
opulently appointed with oak panelling, painted glass windows and a black
and white tiled floor. Crossland apparently also designed the furniture and
fittings for the club, to harmonise with the building itself.[12]

The rest of the building had simpler detailing and provided offices and
warehousing space with shared amenities. There were also three boiler
rooms, a large heating chamber, a strong room, coal stores and a service
lift to all floors.[13] Windows were large, allowing maximum daylight into
the building, and Crossland's design of the building intended maximum
flexibility in use. A suite of rooms in the basement, extending beyond
the building line under Westgate was provided for a resident porter, with
natural light brought in through windows opening on to a light well.
Crossland's visually arresting design for the Estate Building not only
provided plush and attractive centrally located offices for the Ramsdens,
thereby reinforcing the key role the family held in Huddersfield, but also
provided space for letting, providing the Ramsdens with an immediate
return on their investment.

Contracts for the Byram Buildings (see page 103) were accepted in 1871,
and the estimated cost, including Crossland's architect fees, was £7,100.
Law suggests that the reason the two buildings (the Estate Buildings and
the Byram Buildings) were not progressed as one project was that relocation
of the tenants whose premises were to be demolished and the payment of
compensation to them delayed the overall development. Compensation to
the value of £15,369 was paid to enable the construction of the Byram
Buildings on Westgate.[14] (See page 134.)

## St Chad, Rochdale

Despite the substantial works being carried out for the Ramsden Estate
and the fact that his main home was now in London, between 1870
and 1872 Crossland accepted a commission from St Chad's Church
in Rochdale. St Chad's was an ancient church, steeped in folklore and
tradition, as the following extract from a nineteenth-century local history
describes:

> The mother church of the parish is of great antiquity, and stands
> on a commanding eminence, the ascent to which is by a flight of
> 124 steps. The church was erected in the 12th century, and has

12. Law, Part 5.
13. Whitaker, pp. 162-63.
14. Law, Part 5.

undergone various changes, alterations, and renovations. The local legend is that the site of the church was, in point of fact, the place chosen by spirits and fairies for the purpose. On several occasions, as the story relates, the materials brought together for the erection of the church, on an entirely different site, were removed from the place originally selected to the hill or eminence on which St. Chad's stands. That this removal was the work of superhuman agency, was the firm belief of our forefathers in those far-distant days; and we should be sorry to do or say anything which could in the remotest manner interfere with this time-hallowed belief, which has been handed down to us, and which, with vast numbers among us, is received with the greatest deference and respect.

The site ultimately adopted, under such supernatural pressure, led, of course, to the formation of the celebrated church steps; to ascend which is always considered a necessary piece of work to be performed by all visitors to our good old town. To come to Rochdale and not mount the steps is considered a breach of good manners, as well as a serious deprivation of a very agreeable exercise. The steps, in fact, are among our most cherished possessions; and they form a most important thoroughfare, with which it would be very unwise to intermeddle to the great prejudice of the inhabitants.[15]

The 'improvement' of such a cherished place could only have been entrusted to an architect in whom the town's decision-makers had confidence.[16] The restoration had been planned in 1867 using another architect, who considered that the tower should be raised. The vicar disagreed, feeling it would spoil the proportions of the church, and the project was shelved. Three years later, Crossland's substantial reputation in Rochdale had been established, following the success of the soon-to-be-opened Town Hall. The parish decision-makers also knew of Crossland's successful restoration work elsewhere, so he was the obvious architect to invite for their second attempt at restoration. Unfortunately for the incumbent, Crossland was of the same opinion as the earlier architect: raising the tower (parts of which dated from the thirteenth century) was also part of his plan. His intention was to make the appearance of Rochdale's parish church much more commanding.

---

15. Robertson, William, *Rochdale Past & Present, a History and Guide* (Rochdale, 1876). http://freepages.genealogy.rootsweb.ancestry.com/~todmordenandwalsden/St.Chads.htm (accessed 5 January 2016).

16. Further restoration work in the 1880s was carried out by another architect.

6.5 Rochdale: St Chad's Church, 1872.
Crossland's top stage of the tower is clearly evident.

The specification in December 1870 of the works to be carried out called for 'stone from the finest selected beds of the Todmorden quarries'.[17] The work done by Crossland included work on the south aisle and the porch[18], as well as raising the tower. His restoration, largely in his usual Decorated style, provided the building with 'offset angle buttresses surmounted by carved heads and decorative pinnacles, an elaborate bell-stage, gargoyles and crocketed pinnacles', while the south porch had 'diagonal weathered buttresses, grotesque gargoyles, crocketed pinnacles, a statue of St. Chad and an arched opening with a heavily enriched ogee shaped surround'.[19] Crossland added the thirty feet that constituted the top stage of the castellated tower. His bill for the work was £86.[20]

---

17. Law, Part 6.
18. http://historicengland.org.uk/listing/the-list/list-entry/1045812 (accessed 7 January 2015).
19. http://historicengland.org.uk/listing/the-list/list-entry/1045812 (accessed 7 January 2015).
20. Law, Part 6.

6.6 Rochdale: Town Hall, 1871. The tower was noticeably higher than in the planned elevation published in *The Builder* in November 1866 (see page 45). In front of the building, Crossland designed a spacious esplanade behind the wall built to control the River Roch.

## Rochdale Town Hall

When Rochdale's Town Hall was officially opened on 27 September 1871, ablaze with gaslight and likened to the House of Lords by the local newspaper, Crossland was well established in London. Rochdale must have seemed a long way off and belonging to an altogether different part of his life. It was, though, his most important building to date, and he was immensely proud to be present and to see the design completed in all its spectacular glory. Councillor George Leach Ashworth, who, after initial misgivings, had championed the building of a town hall for the town, was then mayor of Rochdale. He too was a proud man, having seen the ambitious project through from idea to opening. Designs had been much elaborated since Crossland had won the competition to design the building, to a budget of £20,000, and costs had therefore spiralled. The final cost on which Crossland's commission of 5% was payable was an extraordinary £154,755[21], meaning that, together with the premium

21. Cunningham, Colin, *Victorian and Edwardian Town Halls* (London, Boston and

for first place in the competition, Crossland earned over £7,000 on the building[22] – a very large sum that had put him into the income bracket of the affluent.

In replying to a toast to the architect at the opening banquet, Crossland modestly said he felt that more credit had been given to him than he deserved, and he attributed much of the success of his work to the fact that he had under him the greatest talent in England. The Town Hall that Crossland provided for Rochdale is the finest of buildings. Indeed, it remains one of the finest town halls in the country[23], with a spacious esplanade fronting the River Roch. In his opening speech, Councillor Ashworth justified the huge expense saying 'we cannot have beauty without paying for it'.[24]

Crossland's decorative scheme for the Town Hall was spectacular, demonstrating his understanding of Gothic architecture at least as well as in his churches. Indeed, his design is an exemplar Gothic Revival building in that he made the different parts of the building evident from the outside, with each section of the building under a distinctly separate roof. Similarly, the location of the spiral staircases is made clear by the sloping sills of the windows that follow the rise of the treads. By following the advice of Scott and turning to continental sources, Crossland produced a building that was both romantic in its associations and practical in its arrangement.[25] As well as mythical and naturalistic motifs, he also drew on themes of local history and industry, which provided immense pride and satisfaction for the people of Rochdale. He achieved an extraordinary richness of decoration, both inside and outside, by combining the work of different artists and craftsmen, including stone and wood carving, and stained glass and mural painting, mostly related to local themes or to the function of a particular room. Some detractors felt the decoration made it too much like a church, but in general, Crossland's building was much admired.

Described as 'one of the dozen most ambitious High Victorian town halls of England'[26], the plan of the building is in the shape of a letter

Henley, 1981), p. 270.

22. Law, Part 2.

23. Rochdale Borough Council no longer has offices in Rochdale Town Hall. Civic administration has moved to modern premises, and the Town Hall has become a popular location for a wide variety of events, including weddings. There are regular tours of the building.

24. Sharples, Joseph, *Rochdale Town Hall: An Illustrated Guide,* Rochdale Metropolitan Borough Council, undated, p. 1.

25. Whitaker, p. 246.

26. Harman, Ruth and Nikolaus Pevsner, *The Buildings of England, Yorkshire West Riding, Sheffield and the South,* (New Haven and London, 2017), p. 594.

'E', combining three buildings in one.[27] The long north side is the main front and three wings project towards the south. A monumental staircase, occupying the middle wing, leads up to the borough court and a large hall for public meetings. Administrative offices for the borough, rooms for the mayor and a public library were in the eastern wing while the western wing originally housed the fire and police services, including a courtroom, cells and a house for the chief constable. Centrally placed spiral staircases in both the eastern and western wings provide access to those parts of the building, as well as access to the upper floors so that the three parts of the building were able to function independently.

Crossland had created a building with almost fairy-tale interest in its picturesque profile and decoration: 'towered, traceried, mullioned, crocketted and spired – in mixed fourteenth century Gothic, part French, part English, part Flemish'.[28] He did not waste funds on the back of the building, leaving it generally plain while providing pleasing decorative detailing to the exterior sides. He lavished the most decoration on the main front with additional textural richness achieved by projections and recesses.

This north façade contains a large centrally placed vaulted porte-cochère with four golden lions keeping watch from the parapet above. This leads to a grand entrance, which in turn opens into an impressive entrance hall. This was originally intended as an exchange hall for the sale of local goods, particularly woollen textiles, but ideas changed during construction, and it was never used as such, providing instead a grand entrance hall to the public rooms in the central section of the building. It has a low ceiling vaulted in bands of pink and grey stone with columns of polished red and grey granite. Crossland employed Thomas Earp to carve the Bath stone capitals, which are of a very high quality displaying naturalistic features, including plants, birds and animals. The spectacular encaustic-tiled floor by Minton is filled with heraldic designs depicting the Royal Arms, alternating with those of the Duchy of Lancaster and the Borough of Rochdale. The designs were by Heaton, Butler and Bayne, who also supervised and contributed to the entire decorative scheme for the Town Hall. The stained glass in the windows of the entrance hall, which continues to be known as The Exchange, celebrates Rochdale's commerce.

---

27. The description of Rochdale Town Hall draws substantially on Joseph Sharples, *Rochdale Town Hall: An Illustrated Guide*, Rochdale Metropolitan Borough Council, undated.

28. Crook, J. Mordaunt, 'Mr Holloway's Architect and Mr Holloway's Château' in *Centenary Lectures 1886-1986*, ed. Moreton Moore, (Egham, 1988), p. 29.

6.7 (left) Rochdale: Town Hall. Crossland drew on themes of local history and industry, which provided pride and satisfaction for the people of Rochdale. This window, on a subsidiary staircase, contains images of the suspended fleece of Rochdale's crest representing the wool industry. Photograph taken in 2011.

Opposite page:
6.8 (middle, left) Rochdale: Town Hall, porte-cochère.
Photograph taken in 2011.

6.9 (middle, right) Rochdale:
Town Hall: two of the four guardian golden lions on the parapet
above the porte-cochère. Photograph taken in 2011.

6.10 (bottom, left) Rochdale: Town Hall: the banded pink and grey vault of the
entrance hall. Photograph taken in 2011.

6.11 (bottom, right) Rochdale: Town Hall: detail from the spectacular encaustic
tiled floor of the entrance hall. Photograph taken in 2011.

From the subdued light of the Exchange, with its low ceiling and few windows, Crossland designed a spectacular approach to the first floor, with the broad main staircase rising through a high and brightly lit vault. Located in the central wing of the building, light streams in through tall windows. The windows are all filled with stained glass, creating a bright mosaic of colour in the stairwell. The designs are largely heraldic, depicting the Royal Arms and the arms of textile-producing towns in Lancashire and Yorkshire, as well as those of countries supplying raw materials and the British ports from which Rochdale's products were shipped. Also depicted are contemporary technological inventions that had made possible the growing prosperity of Rochdale. From a half-landing, the staircase divides in two and leads to a pair of richly carved doorways into the grand and majestic Great Hall, which occupies the whole of the first floor of the central part of the building.

The spacious Hall, with a magnificent 'Crossland trademark' hammer-beam roof, was modelled on medieval halls such as Westminster Hall. It is richly decorated with painting, gilding, carving and stained glass. The hammer beams terminate with an angel (very similar to the design at St Peter's Church, Birstall), from the hands of each of which originally hung a gasolier.

The east end of the hall is filled with a mural by Henry Holiday entitled *The Signing of the Magna Carta* while the rest of the walls are covered with a stencilled floral pattern, with wood panelling and built-in benches at the

6.12 (opposite) Rochdale: Town Hall, the Great Hall.
*The Builder*, 12 February 1876, p. 147.

6.13 (top, left) Rochdale: Town Hall, staircase.
Photograph taken in 2011.

6.14 (top, right) Rochdale: Town Hall. The hammer beams in the Great Hall
each terminate with an angel, which originally held a suspended gasolier.
Photograph taken in 2011.

6.15 (bottom, right) Rochdale: Town Hall, Great Hall, stained glass.
Photograph taken in 2011.

base. Crossland provided the western end of the hall with a triple-arched opening for an organ.[29] The glory of the hall is its stained glass that was 'of a richness probably unequalled among civic buildings'.[30] Crossland designed the hall to occupy the full depth of the building and to rise higher than the adjoining blocks. It therefore has windows on all four sides, allowing an extraordinary play of colour in the huge space, weather permitting, throughout the day. The windows are filled with portraits of British monarchs, mostly taken from known likenesses. The two rose windows in the gables are of Queen Victoria and Prince Albert, the latter surrounded by the symbols of human endeavour that the Prince Consort encouraged. These include a representation of Architecture, above which is a view of the north front of the Town Hall itself.

The original council chamber (later the reception room) is on the ground floor of the central part of the building, on the east side of the Exchange. This too is richly decorated with stencilled patterns on the walls and ceiling, representing both the wool industry, illustrated by the suspended fleece of Rochdale's crest, as well as spindles and shuttles. The cotton industry is also represented, by cotton flowers, cotton bolls and teasels. A frieze around the top of the walls depicts the technological advances of the textile industry in the eighteenth and nineteenth centuries, as well as textile production through history in various parts of the world. Crossland's most striking features in this room are two finely carved stone fireplaces and the four pierced stone arches that span the room, supporting the flat stencilled ceiling and the Great Hall above.

Also in the east wing of the ground floor, are the Small Exchange (intended as a vestibule to the Mayor's Suite), the original Mayor's Reception Room (later a committee room) and the Mayor's Parlour, all of which Crossland ensured were richly decorated. The Small Exchange is painted in rich reds, greens and gold in a complex decorative scheme. Stylised vines cover the walls above the panelling. An elaborate frieze at the top of the walls depicts animals, chosen to illustrate sources of clothing before the invention of spinning and weaving. The panelled ceiling has representations of the arms of Rochdale, the suspended fleece symbol, and the various trades and crafts of the town. The windows have the arms of England, Wales, Scotland and Ireland depicted in the stained glass, as well as each country's plant emblem. The floor of Minton tiles has further heraldic representations. Two pointed arch doorways are filled with opening glazed oak screens, both of which are framed by octagonal oak columns terminating the panelling and supporting carved lions that hold the arms of Rochdale.

29. The organ was not installed until 1913.
30. Sharples, p. 8.

The original Mayor's Reception Room opens off the Small Exchange and the Mayor's Parlour is beyond. The decorative style of both is lighter than the majestic decoration of the large public rooms. The decorative scheme of the Reception Room is broadly on the theme of day and night, with a stencilled floral pattern on the walls in black, red and gold on a muted green, above which is a frieze including native animals and birds. There is much interesting detail here, including an owl hiding from the sun being taunted by smaller birds, while on the next wall, by the light of the moon, the owl is taking its revenge. The panelled pale blue ceiling is also stencilled with naturalistic representations, including swallows and butterflies. The lower part of the walls has rich oak panelling. Under the windows is an integral oak bench with magnificent carved finials in the form of mythical creatures. The windows contain stained glass and take up the theme of day and night with representations of the hours of morning, noon, evening and night. The story of Jack and the Beanstalk is an unexpected decoration of the window surround. Another quirky highlight of this room are the four corbels that support the beams of the ceiling, which are carved as representations of four local dignitaries: Mayor Ashworth, who had seen through the ambitious building scheme from beginning to completion; Alderman Edward Taylor, the Treasurer[31], shaking a fist presumably at the escalating cost of the whole project; Councillor W.A. Scott and the fourth, holding dividers and a building plan, is Crossland himself.

6.16 Rochdale: Town Hall. This corbel in the original Mayor's Reception Room (one of four) represents Crossland. Photograph taken in 2011.

The Mayor's Parlour has a relatively simple naturalistic design of white and gold rosettes painted onto light bluish-green walls. The extravagant ceiling is its highlight with a mythological tree design springing from above a fine Gothic fireplace and spreading into the four corners of the room, with fruit in purple and gold, dragons, birds of paradise and peacocks. The corbels supporting the ceiling beams are carved to represent various musicians. The stained glass of the windows illustrates the four seasons and the months of the year, and under the windows is another beautifully carved oak bench. The window surround depicts a vine and various creatures and includes a scroll with the

31. Harman and Pevsner, p. 596.

6.17 Rochdale: Town Hall. Former Courtroom windows depict judges in scarlet robes. Photograph taken in 2011.

motto 'In Vino Veritas' in a humorous acknowledgement of the purpose of the room, which was and is mainly entertaining.

The west wing of the building originally housed facilities for the town's law and order and the fire services. Although salamanders and a phoenix decorated the Fire Engine bay[32], only the Magistrates' Retiring Room (later the Members' Lounge) and the Borough Court (later the Council Chamber) were elaborately decorated. The richest elements of the decoration in the Magistrates' Retiring Room are the carved oak doors and oak panelling with integral benches where the carving is at least as rich as elsewhere in the building. The panelled ceiling is decorated with the arms and monograms of past mayors. The walls between the panelling and the ceiling are now plainly painted, although they were originally covered in embossed leather. The windows contain small lights with a variety of motifs.

The courtroom (converted to the Council Chamber in 1980-81) was designed to be a suitably forbidding room with a high ceiling and windows above eye level, containing depictions relevant to the original purpose of the chamber. Most notably, the windows on the north side contain full-length portraits of King Alfred, Francis Bacon and Jeremy Bentham, all considered important in the legal and constitutional history of England. The south side of the chamber contains the public gallery with windows depicting the arms of Rochdale and Tudor roses in red and gold. The central window provides an appropriate backdrop to the former magistrates' bench below, containing images of three judges in their scarlet robes. Above the oak panelling is a frieze depicting crouching hounds, above which the walls, as well as the ceiling, are decorated with heraldic symbols relevant to the town of Rochdale and to the county of Lancashire.

32. Whitaker, p. 63.

A tower with a spire on such a civic building is a luxury afforded by few towns. Crossland's original drawings were for a striking but fairly modest tower, but it grew taller as Crossland added stage after stage, 'rather like an ambitious child with a set of building blocks, until it reached a prodigious height of two hundred and forty feet'[33], topped by a gilded statue of St George and the Dragon. At this height, Rochdale gave its population of 38,000 five feet more than Manchester provided for its population of nearly 339,000. Only one municipal building in Britain was higher.[34] Rochdale's tower, alongside its magnificent Town Hall, made an enormously strong statement of civic confidence and pride in an ancient town rapidly growing through wealth generated by the textile industry. At the opening of the building, Crossland must have taken great pleasure in the physical space of his extraordinary building, as well as in the congratulations and praise that were showered upon him. He must also have allowed himself an inward smile of satisfaction in having left a little of himself in the decoration of the building in the representation carved into perpetuity in a corbel of the Mayor's Reception Room.

## St John the Evangelist, Newsome, near Huddersfield

Such magnificent projects were seldom the lifeblood of an architect. Crossland understood this well and was entirely pragmatic about the commissions he accepted: large or small, church or secular, they all paid an income. In the same year that Rochdale Town Hall was officially opened, and despite now having his office in London, Crossland accepted a new church commission near Huddersfield. This was a church for the outlying community of Newsome. The first moves to build a church had been in 1869 from among the working people of the area, but it had been difficult to raise sufficient funds among the small and far-from-affluent local population. An anonymous donation of £1,000 (later learned to be from local industrialist and dignitary Thomas Brooke of Armitage Bridge[35]) and the provision of a site and a further £500 by Sir John Ramsden made the project viable. At first sight, this was perhaps a surprising commission for Crossland. It lacked any prestige, was to be low cost, and needed to be supervised from afar. It revealed, though, his philanthropic side, as this now well-established and financially secure architect refused the small income he might have earned from the project and provided the plans and

---

33. Sharples, p. 4.
34. Cunningham, p. 281. Greenock Municipal Buildings, opened ten years later, had a spire five feet higher than Rochdale.
35. Crook, *Lectures*, p. 28.

specification without a fee.[36] In fact, this was easily done as he reused an existing design, offering Newsome the design originally made for St James the Great in Flockton and built 1866-67.

He advertised in June for masons, carpenters and joiners, plumbers, glaziers, slaters, plasterers and painters. His advertisements carried his London office address, but he arranged for drawings and bills of quantity to be available between 12 and 19 June, at the Ramsden Estate Offices, from Mr Phillips, the clerk of works for the project, although tenders were to be sent to the Reverend T. Lewthwaite of Lockwood, Huddersfield.[37] The foundation stone was laid on the site off Jackroyd Lane on 17 July by Mrs Thomas Brooke of Armitage Bridge. At this time, £3,511 had been raised towards the cost, and it was estimated that between £800 and £900 still had to be raised. The initial plan was that the church would provide 500 spaces for worshippers[38], but it seems that the size of the church was reduced after the original planning, reflecting the funds available, as the completed church had 410 sittings at a cost of about £3,000.

Newsome was therefore both one of Crossland's smaller and cheaper churches. When completed, unsurprisingly, it bore a marked similarity to the Flockton church with nearly the same number of sittings, and, as at Flockton, it had a low-cost bell-cote rather than a tower. The roof had hammer beams,

the style much favoured by Crossland and used in small, as well as large, buildings. There was a minimum of decoration, and the windows were plain, but, as with Flockton, the budget allowed for a stained glass east window, similar to that at St Thomas, Sutton-in-Craven (1868-69). As a cost-saving expedient, the capitals were plain mouldings with no carving, although a decorative plaster frieze with vine leaves and tendrils was afforded.[39]

6.18 Huddersfield, Newsome: the Church of St John the Evangelist, 1872. Crossland reused his designs for the church at Flockton, providing them for Newsome without a fee. Photograph taken in 2017.

36. Law, Part 5.
37. *The Huddersfield Chronicle and West Yorkshire Advertiser*, 10 June 1871, Issue 1199.
38. *The Huddersfield Chronicle and West Yorkshire Advertiser*, 22 July 1871, Issue 1235.
39. Whitaker, p. 114.

The church, for which Crossland also designed the reading desk, was consecrated by the Bishop of Ripon on 12 October 1872, dedicated to St John the Evangelist. Many clergymen were present to hear the bishop thank Crossland during the service for providing the plans without charge – but Crossland (by this time very busy with a new project some 200 miles away) was unable to attend the consecration and receive the gratitude personally. A response was given in his absence by Mr A.J. Taylor, his senior assistant in Huddersfield.[40]

## All Hallows, Almondbury

At the time of the consecration of Newsome church, not only was Crossland busy with his large new project, but he was also preoccupied a few miles away from Newsome with the restoration of Almondbury church. Almondbury was a large hillside village two miles to the south-east of Huddersfield. In medieval times, it was a centre of weaving and was larger and more important than Huddersfield, but in the nineteenth century Huddersfield's development had eclipsed it. A committee had been formed following a vestry meeting on Easter Monday 1870 to consider restoration of the fifteenth-century church in the village, and to draw up plans[41] (although Crossland had actually drawn up plans for this restoration some seven years previously as a result of an earlier restoration initiative). Located as it was on the other local estate belonging to the Ramsden family, he would have seen it as an important local commission, and one for which he would have had a sense of obligation. This time, in 1871, he put forward restoration proposals that included the removal of the box pews and galleries that had been installed in an earlier intervention.

Crossland was probably now the favoured architect of Sir John Ramsden, and Sir John was prepared to go to some lengths to make sure he secured his services, although Crossland no longer worked locally. In July 1871, the Huddersfield press reported that the Ramsden Estate had been unable to contact Crossland[42], such problems being indicative of working for a patron from an office about 200 miles away.

It is likely that Sir John Ramsden found the fact that Crossland was now based in London, and, no less, that he was a Fellow of the London-based Royal Institute of British Architects, compelling reasons to engage him to

40. *The Huddersfield Chronicle and West Yorkshire* Advertiser, 19 October 1872, Issue 1624, p. 3.
41. *The Huddersfield Chronicle and West Yorkshire Advertiser*, 23 March 1872, Issue 1444, p. 7.
42. *The Huddersfield Chronicle and West Yorkshire Advertiser,* 22 July 1871, Issue 1235, p. 7.

work for the Ramsden Estate. Ramsden's previous architects (Sir William Tite and Sir Edward Blore) had been based in London and a 'London architect' carried prestige. In any case, Ramsden himself spent substantial periods of time in London, when it would have been easy for him to meet his estate architect.

It seems it did not take long for Crossland's favoured position with the Ramsden Estate to engender some local antipathy towards him. This is suggested by the fact that, towards the end of 1871, his father was the butt of hostility in a reader's letter that appeared in the local press. This letter complained that Henry Crossland's election as councillor for the Fartown ward of Huddersfield had been secured in order to help his architect son.[43] Indignation was perhaps only to be expected now that, having abandoned the area of his birth for London, Crossland was clearly held in high esteem by someone as important as Sir John Ramsden.

Nonetheless, Crossland's work on restoring All Hallows, the Parish church of Almondbury was soon underway. As an initial step, Crossland was first commissioned to carry out a survey and write a report on his proposals for the restoration. He must have written such reports for most if not all his restorations, but this is the only one known to have survived. It is quoted in full, as it reveals a great deal about Crossland's attitude to working on medieval churches. The report was written in February 1872, sent from his London office and addressed to the Reverend Canon Hulbert, the incumbent of All Hallows:

> Carlton Chambers
> 4 Regent Street, London SW
> 13 Feb 1872
> The Rev Canon Hulbert
>
> Dear Sir
>      I now have the pleasure of submitting to you Plans for the restoration of your Church, and with them I beg to explain briefly the principles upon which I have based my plan of restoration. The first and most important principle on which I have acted is the conservation of every stone which bears upon its surface the stamp of really old work. The second and almost equally important principle I have acted upon is the adding to the existing Fabric such features as after a careful survey I have found to have been removed or destroyed by previous so called improvements at the hands of Churchwardens or others.

---

43. *The Huddersfield Chronicle and West Yorkshire Advertiser*, 28 October 1871, Issue 1319, p. 2.

Acting upon these two principles, with the very interesting and noble Fabric (such as your church is) to apply them to renders the task of restoration a very pleasing one and not too difficult.

### Floor Levels

Owing to the unusual elevation originally made of the Nave floor above the Chancel floor, and since that the elevation of the Churchyard, the first in consequence of the Nave being a century and a half later in date than the Chancel and in the second being the result of heaping up the graves, I have determined to lift up the Chancel high enough to give a proper number of steps from the nave floor level to the altar platform and also to lower the ground outside to allow of two steps up to the original nave floor level. This as will be seen on the Longitudinal section gives a very satisfactory result.

### Arrangement. Seats etc

The ground plan shews the arrangement of the Nave aisles and Chancel and aisles. The tower I propose to open out to the Church and make it answer as a Baptistry, at the same time opening up the Western entrance which is now practically useless.

### Existing Galleries

These I propose to remove altogether.

### Floor of Passages

These tinted red on the plan should be of Staffordshire tiles, those in the Chancel being encaustic laid on a bed of Concrete one foot thick over the whole area of the Church, 12 inches below the floor level, deeper excavations being made for the Trenches for the Hot Water pipes. This is the only way to prevent further dry rot in the floors and unhealthy effluvia arising from the soil.

### Seats, Stalls, Screen and Font Cover

These should all be made of oak, and of a design in character with the remains of the existing screen, which originally, no doubt, was a rood screen and which I propose to replace. Possibly equally valuable guidance may be given in the designs of the Nave Seats and Font Cover, by the turning up of some fragments of old work relating to them.

*Nave & Aisle Walls & Roof Ceilings*

Such portions of the Nave and Aisle Walls (also the Tower) and roofs or ceilings as require renovating I propose to do, removing any modern plaster from the Walls and making good the stonework.

*Chancel Roof*

This must be entirely new, and at present I have no data to work upon beyond surmise, in making a design. I shall however have no difficulty in making a design (such as I shew on the elevation) which will harmonize with the rest of the building.

*Character of Restoration of Chancel*

I may now explain the plan upon which I have acted. The date of the Chancel as it originally existed and the remains still left, namely the windows on the North and South sides and the walls they pierce is clearly late 13th century. The Walls are in such a state as to render it impossible to put a new roof on to them, and of such rough masonry as to be scarcely weatherproof. The Chancel altogether has been reduced in height when the present roof was put on.

*Chancel*

I propose therefore to rebuild the chancel altogether east of the North and South Chapels, carefully preserving the old windows but raising them to meet the altered floor levels, and in the absence of any true knowledge of the old east window, I propose a window of seven lights to replace the present comparatively modern and awkward triplet window which is clearly too small to light so long a Chancel and undoubtedly of a debased type.

*Inner Porch Doorway*

Curiously enough the only other early-English feature in the church is the inner Porch Doorway. I have found it the same in two restorations I have carried out namely the Parish churches of Birstall and Rochdale, both having the inner Porch Doors of an earlier date than any other portions of the Nave or Aisles. This Doorway I propose to restore carefully, and to replace its detached shafts in Purbeck Marble.

*External Alterations*

I find no difficulty in restoring the external portions of the Tower, the aisles and clerestory up to the present eaves of the roof, the windows, the Buttresses and the Walls shewing clearly that up to this point they have not been materially altered.

At this point, however (the eaves) I have found after a careful examination that originally cornices and embattled Parapets followed the lines of the roof as I have shewn them. These were no doubt removed when the roofs were stripped of the lead to make way for the stone slates which now cover them. Studying Photographs and my own sketches some years ago I could not make out why this Church should be so different to any other Parish Church of equal importance within a radius of 20 miles, in its lacking embattled Parapets and pinnacles, and I now find evidence of the cornice having been cut away and the hole for water conduit remaining and moreover in all cases the upper weathering of the Buttresses has been removed, upon which the small pinnacles would rest.

These important features I propose to restore, and if your funds will permit of it, I should recover all the roofs with lead. I have now only to repeat that the restoration of every part should be carried out scrupulously and every stone remaining in its original position carefully guarded from injury and every stone added ought to shew itself a younger member of the same family of stones and we may fairly hope that your now handsome old Church, grand in its decay, may not lose its dignity nor appear altogether new-born.

*Cost*

I estimate the cost of carrying out my plans at £4,000. If the roofs are recovered with Slates and the fittings of deal in place of oak, it will be £3,250.

*The Dartmouth Chapel*

Beyond carrying out the parapet restoration outside and making good the Walls and Arches inside, I have suggested little to be done to this Chapel feeling that without Lord Dartmouth's instructions I could not do more than suggest even these additions.

I am
Yours faithfully
(Signed) W.H. Crossland

*Heating Chamber*

This I propose to place under the east end of the Chancel and to enter it from the North side. The principle of Heating I should recommend is the combined one of Hot Water and Air.[44]

Forgiving Crossland for forgetting about the heating chamber until after he had signed the document, Crossland's overall approach was clearly to treat the ancient building with great respect and with as light a touch as possible. He was concerned to retain ancient masonry and windows, and to reinstate what had been removed or damaged by earlier interventions, while removing inappropriate previous additions, such as the galleries and 'modern plaster'. He looked among previous work for evidence of the original building, inspecting carefully, for instance, at the level of the eaves, where he found evidence of the original cornices and castellation. Where he found no such evidence, he used his knowledge of other ancient churches to recreate in an appropriate style, as with the chancel roof. He proposed rebuilding only where the ancient fabric had become too fragile to restore.

At the same time, though, Crossland was also required to modernise the church to render it appropriate for contemporary liturgical practice. For this reason, he proposed an enlargement to the fragile chancel (rather than simply repairs), the creation of a baptistery under the tower and bringing

6.19 (opposite, top, left) Almondbury: All Hallows, restoration 1876. The castellation followed Crossland's plan closely. Photograph taken in 2017.

6.20a and 6.20b (opposite, top and middle, right) Almondbury, All Hallows: the nave of the church viewed towards the font. The top picture was taken before Crossland's restoration and clearly shows the galleries and box pews. This image was taken in 2017 from an old photograph hanging at the back of the church. The lower picture is a present-day view of the nave looking towards the font, showing the result of Crossland's restoration. The removal of galleries and box pews created an open aspect within the church. Photograph taken in 2017.

6.21 (opposite, below) Almondbury: All Hallows. The nave cleared of galleries, looking towards the altar and showing the fine timber ceiling that Crossland retained. It has decorated bosses and dates from 1522. Photograph taken in 2017.

---

44. West Yorkshire Archives Kirklees, DD/RA/C/box 36, Crossland, W.H., *Almondbury, Report of the Proposed Restoration of the Parish Church Almondbury*, 1872, Copy.

ALMONDBURY PARISH CHURCH BEFORE RESTORATION 1873 - 1877
VIEWED TOWARDS THE FONT

the west door into use again. Overall, he drew up plans for some new walls, castellated parapets, a new porch, extensions to the fourteenth-century side chapels and a new hammer-beam roof to the chancel. He also, though, proposed the retention of much of the fabric of the old building, including an exceptionally fine timber nave ceiling dating from 1522.[45]

By late February 1872, Crossland had presented his report and supplied plans for the restoration of All Hallows. At a Vestry meeting on 16 March 1872, the plans were approved by Sir John Ramsden and other interested parties including the vicar and the various subscribers to the project. £2,500 had already been raised towards the work so it was resolved to apply to the Bishop for a faculty to carry out the restoration. Arrangements were also made for Crossland's plans to be exhibited.

In an interesting use of the fairly new technology of photography, a Mr Lord was commissioned to take photographs of the interior before work began, [46] both as a record and so that restoration work could be modelled on the original as closely as possible. A local dignitary, the Earl of Dartmouth, became a donor since he was a descendent of one of those interred in the Kaye Chapel in the church. His contribution was to pay for the restoration of his ancestral chapel, as well as contributing £100 to the general fund.[47] Crossland himself donated £11.9s.6d as a 'special donation to chapels and memorials'.[48]

In June 1872, Crossland (now described as 'of London') advertised inviting tenders from builders and contractors for work on All Hallows. He arranged for the plans, specifications and bills of quantity (erroneously detailing them to be for All Saints Church rather than All Hallows Church) to be available from Mr Phillips, the clerk of works at the Ramsden Estate Office, Huddersfield, with tenders to be submitted to Crossland himself by 17 July at his London office. He signed the advertisements 'W.H. Crossland, F.R.I.B.A., Architect, Carlton Chambers, 14 June 1872'[49], carefully detailing the attributes he perceived to be those of a successful practitioner.

45. Gibson, Keith and Albert Booth, *The Buildings of Huddersfield* (Stroud, 2005, reprinted 2009), p. 12.
46. *The Huddersfield Chronicle and West Yorkshire Advertiser,* 23 March 1872, Issue 1444, p. 7.
47. *The Huddersfield Chronicle and West Yorkshire Advertiser,* 24 February 1872, Issue 1419, p. 7.
48. West Yorkshire Archives Wakefield, WDP12/275, Hulbert, Revd. C A, *Almondbury Parish Church and Schools: A Sixth Biennial Report.*
49. *The Huddersfield Chronicle and West Yorkshire Advertiser,* 15 June 1872, Issue 1516; 22 June 1872, Issue 1522; 29 June 1872, Issue 1528; and 13 July 1872, Issue 1540.

Work began on the restoration in September 1872 under Crossland's supervision. In 1873, the British Archaeological Association visited All Hallows to view the restoration. Clearly, they were interested in the medieval details of the church, and, since Crossland's report was the only serious attempt to make an assessment of the church, they relied heavily on his detail for the architectural description that provided the information necessary for their visit.

The church reopened with a special service in March 1874, although work on the restoration of the chancel had not begun at that stage. Nonetheless, the Ramsdens and the congregation were generally complimentary regarding Crossland's achievements.

The chancel was largely rebuilt two years later, although Crossland retained a group of three East windows.[50] The work was completed in 1876 and includes Crossland's favoured hammer-beam roof. The work had been largely funded by Sir John Ramsden, and the fully restored church was formally reopened on 27 November by the Bishop of Ripon. The vicar, the Reverend Canon Hulbert, wrote a new hymn especially for the occasion.[51]

## Longley Hall

Between 1870 (shortly after Crossland moved to London) and 1875, Crossland was responsible for rebuilding the local home of Sir John Ramsden himself. Longley Hall at Dog Kennel Bank, Longley, is a short distance from Huddersfield town centre. Originally built in 1577, the hall was rebuilt in the eighteenth century, retaining its sixteenth-century character. In the 1860s, however, the Ramsdens had a new building constructed on a nearby site. Designed by William Burn and known as Longley New Hall, it was used as the Estate Offices prior to the opening of Crossland's new building in the centre of Huddersfield. Although Longley New Hall was only a few years old, Crossland's commission was to enlarge and rebuild this building,[52] essentially to construct a new Longley New Hall, providing suitable modern accommodation for the Ramsden family's visits to Huddersfield and a small office for the Almondbury part of the Ramsden Estate. Crossland also drew up plans for some alterations to the Old Longley Hall, the plans being signed by his chief assistant, A.J. Taylor.[53]

---

50. Harman and Pevsner, p. 90.
51. *The Huddersfield Weekly News*, 2 December 1876.
52. R.I.B.A., W.H. Crossland biographical file, unnumbered document.
53. Harman and Pevsner, p. 360.

6.22 Longley: Longley New Hall, 1875. The striking curved glass staircase window is prominent. Photograph taken in 2017.

In his work on Longley New Hall, Crossland demonstrated his 'ability to combine traditional manorial forms with novel shapes and new materials'.[54] He designed a large house of coursed local stone with a blue slate roof and ashlar surrounds to the window and door openings. He included particularly good detailing, including a varied roofline, some castellation of the roof parapets and a finely detailed entrance decorated with the Ramsden coat of arms. Inside, a tall carved wooden over-mantel above the stone fireplace in the entrance lobby was also personalised with the Ramsden family initials. Several of the principal rooms on the ground and first floor were provided with moulded ceilings.[55] While the service end of the house was plain, Crossland included one daring and particularly striking feature: a large staircase window incorporating curved glass set directly into the stone. Here and elsewhere, he made prominent use of newly available large panes of glass. The expensive window would have looked particularly modern and fashionable at the time, and the fact that the glass was curved would have provided a talking point for visitors to this Ramsden home and made a clear allusion to the Ramsdens' affluence.

Crossland's involvement included attention to some remarkably small details of the sort not normally considered to need the involvement of an architect (including, for instance, estimating for boarding and roofing felt to insulate the roof and the fine details regarding the installation of a

54. Crook, *Lectures*, p. 29.
55. www.britishlistedbuildings.co.uk/en-491936-longley-new-hall (accessed 30 January 2017).

private toilet for Sir John Ramsden[56]), but having achieved the status of architect to the Ramsden Estate, Crossland would not have wanted to turn down work or to displease his patron, even in the smallest detail.

## Other projects for Sir John Ramsden in Huddersfield

A number of small works in the Huddersfield area also occupied Crossland at this time. In February 1872, the National School at Lowerhouses, Longley (not far from Sir John Ramsden's local home), needed more space. Sir John provided the land for this, as well as a donation of £25, thereby enabling Crossland's improvements to begin.[57] In April of the same year, Crossland provided plans for kitchens and a laundry at the George Hotel in Huddersfield – a small and unglamorous project to extend to the building, designed by W. Wallen in 1850 and built alongside the station for the Ramsden estate in 1851. Crossland continued to receive an enviable number of commissions for the Ramsden Estate in Huddersfield, though clearly some of them were humble. He was pragmatic about the work he took on and, despite having won large commissions, did not spurn smaller projects that were offered to him, as they all assured him of an income.

In 1872, there were discussions on the subject of a new purpose-built post office for Huddersfield (to replace a building in New Street), but there were disagreements as to which site should be used, delaying the start of construction. An agreement in 1872 was for the construction to be to Crossland's plans on either of two sites. A site in Northumberland Street was finally agreed for the new post office and associated warehousing, and by November 1873, preliminary work for it was being pushed forward quickly. According to the local newspaper: 'it is understood [it] will be commenced, carried on, and completed by Sir John Ramsden with all possible speed.' The newspaper went on to make clear Crossland's integral position in the expansion of the Ramsden Estate: 'Mr W.H. Crossland, F.R.I.B.A., of London, Sir John's architect, has been entrusted with the preparation of the designs.'[58]

Crossland's absence in London posed something of a problem, so supervision of the work on the post office was entrusted to another Estate employee, Mr Richard Phillips, clerk of works to the Ramsden Estate.[59] The

---

56. West Yorkshire Archive Service Kirklees, DD/RA/C/26/2, Ramsden Estate papers.
57. *The Huddersfield Chronicle and West Yorkshire Advertiser,* 24 February 1872, Issue 1419, p. 7.
58. *The Huddersfield Chronicle and West Yorkshire Advertiser*, 29 November 1873, Issue 1970, p. 5.
59. *The Huddersfield Chronicle and West Yorkshire Advertiser*, 29 November 1873, Issue

6.23 Huddersfield: Post Office, Northumberland Street, 1875. The single-storey building is one of Crossland's least successful. It is dwarfed by the higher buildings on either side. Photograph taken in 2015.

drawings, specifications and bills of quantity were available from Richard Phillips at the Estate Buildings, but tenders had to be sent to Crossland at his office in London.[60] The new post office opened in 1875, a single-storey block (as preferred by the post office) in Gothic style, with a crenellated roof parapet. It was a small building, of a scale inappropriate for its position between the taller adjacent buildings and one of Crossland's least successful structures. Edward Law supposed 'that the problems of this building are not of the architect's making but with his brief'.[61]

In 1873 Crossland was also asked to prepare a design for a concert hall for Huddersfield, although, for unknown reasons, it was never built.[62] It may have been that at an early stage there were suggestions that a concert hall might usefully have been combined with other civic facilities in a town hall – a scheme that was later realised by another architect.

## Other works around Huddersfield

Crossland continued to take on 'bread-and-butter' work around Huddersfield. In 1872, he began working on another school for Huddersfield: this time it was the school that had been commissioned in 1869 and associated with his St Andrews Church on Leeds Road (which had been consecrated in August 1870). Using his London address, he invited tenders in advertisements in *The Huddersfield Chronicle and West Yorkshire Advertiser* on both 7 and 14 September. On this occasion, though, the whole tendering process was handled though the Ramsden Estate Office. Plans were available at the offices of Messrs Baker and Sons Solicitors, Estate Buildings, Huddersfield, between 16 and 25 September, on which

1970, p. 5.

60. *The Huddersfield Daily Chronicle*, 28 October 1873, Issue 1942.

61. Gibson and Booth, p. 104.

62. Linstrum, Derek, *West Yorkshire: Architects and Architecture* (London, 1978), p. 375.

date tenders had to be submitted to Mr Baker. Bills of quantity were available from Richard Phillips, clerk of works, at the Estate Buildings.[63] The estimated cost was £1,323.[64]

Between 1874 and 1875, Crossland was commissioned to design a parsonage for Newsome, which was to be connected to his new church there. It was to be 'plain but substantial' and 'in perfect harmony with the church'. This was a small commission for an architect by this time well established far away in London. However, it was on Ramsden Estate land and, as 'the Ramsdens' architect', Crossland would have felt under some obligation. Sir John Ramsden had provided half an acre for the building and £200 towards the building, which attracted several other benefactions. Crossland supplied the plans, although it is not known whether they were free of charge as those for the church had been.

The laying of the cornerstone on 20 June 1874 was celebrated by tea for over a hundred people in the National Schoolroom and by a procession to the church of schoolchildren led by vicar and churchwardens. A time capsule in the form of a bottle was placed in a cavity in the foundation stone, containing a copy of that day's *Huddersfield Chronicle*, details of the planning and building of the church and parsonage, and a note that the project (the complete church and church school project) was initiated by a meeting in February 1869. After the consecration, a procession returned to the school, and each child was presented with a large currant bun to take home.[65]

In February 1876, Crossland took on another apparently small project for a dwelling house in Portland Street, Huddersfield. Again, the advertisement was signed by Crossland at his London office, but the drawings and quantities were available from Richard Phillips, the clerk of works at the Ramsden Estate Buildings. This time, though, tenders were to be sent to William Scott Esq, MD, of Waverley House, who was probably the client.[66]

## Huddersfield town centre buildings

Work on the Ramsden Estate Building itself, though opened in 1870, was completed in 1873 or 1874. Crossland's final payment for the project brought his fees to £1,927, amounting to a 5% fee of the cost of around

---

63. *The Huddersfield Chronicle and West Yorkshire Advertise*, 7 September 1872, Issue 1588 and 14 September 1872, Issue 1594.

64. Law, Part 5.

65. *The Huddersfield Daily Chronicle*, 22 June 1874, Issue 2144, p. 3.

66. *The Huddersfield Chronicle and West Yorkshire Advertiser*, 5 February 1876, Issue 2652.

*£38,547*. Final payments for Rochdale Town Hall were also made in 1874. Other building activity in Huddersfield continued and must have been very difficult to manage alongside the huge project he had by then taken on, more than 200 miles away.

The Byram Buildings (see pages 103 and 106) were completed in 1875, and the Byram Arcade was probably commissioned in the same year with the intention of incorporating the Byram Buildings within the project. The Arcade was a speculative development, to consist of many small units, intended for use as shops on the ground floor with extensive cellar space below and offices on the floors above, with a large studio on the third floor. In this commission Crossland was to experiment with a newly popular building type: arcades were becoming favoured as quiet places for shopping, protected from the weather, but with natural lighting, thanks to a glazed roof. (See page 180.)

The cashier to the Ramsden Estate, Isaac Hordern, showed considerable interest in this development, and it was probably his proposal that the Byram Building and Byram Arcade should appear as one building rather than two connected buildings. The Byram Buildings exceeded their budget, which caused some annoyance to Sir John Ramsden, costing over £9,400, on which Crossland received £416 and expenses of just under £100. The building has five gables fronting Westgate, the crow-stepped central gable reminiscent of Rochdale Town Hall. Although in scale with the Estate Office, Crossland managed to fit in five generous floors. Most exciting, though, were the large windows on the ground and first floors, made possible by the newly available plate glass.

Richard Phillips, the clerk of works at the Ramsden Estate Buildings, was again the clerk of works at the Byram Buildings, and Crossland relied on him for showing potential contractors plans and specifications of buildings. Indeed, it seems that Phillips acted as clerk of works on several occasions for Crossland-designed building developments. This support and that of his chief assistant, Mr A.J. Taylor, was invaluable to Crossland in managing and supervising construction work in Huddersfield while he was in London. The co-operation of these two men was fundamental to Crossland's success in Huddersfield.

## Chapter 7

# The London office: competition success

Crossland had worked hard to make his name known and gained respect for his work in the West Riding. In addition, and from early in his career, this ambitious architect sought an entry to the architectural scene of the large cities, including the metropolis itself, through entering architectural competitions. It was therefore important to him to find time to prepare designs for carefully chosen architectural competitions, always looking to break into these larger markets.

Around the time he left Leeds and established himself in London, he found time to enter at least three competitions. Although he had been unsuccessful in the competition for a design for the Criterion Tavern in Piccadilly, London[1], he was among sixteen or so architects invited to enter the competition for the London Corn Exchange in 1870[2], for which he submitted a Classical design.[3] He was unsuccessful in winning this project too, but his growing reputation, largely earned from the then all-but-complete Rochdale Town Hall, at last began paying dividends. With a change in the tide of fortune, he won two major competitions in 1872. The first of these was for a new town hall for Birmingham. Birmingham Town Council almost certainly evaluated Rochdale's Town Hall before embarking on their project, and earmarked the large sum of £150,000 for it, which was very close to the final cost of Rochdale's stupendous Town Hall. Almost thirty designs were submitted. Crossland's success was reported back in Huddersfield, but in a tone that made it clear that Crossland was no longer regarded as a local architect:

1. According to Janet Douglas, this competition entry was in 1868, but according to John Elliott it was in 1871.
2. *The Bradford Observer*, 12 March 1870, Issue 2251.
3. Douglas, Janet, *William Henry Crossland,* unpublished notes of lecture delivered at Cannon Hall, Cawthorne, South Yorkshire, 21 April 2012.

the choice of the Council fell on Mr W.H. Crossland of London and Leeds. Mr Crossland is well known here as the son of Mr Henry Crossland, of Longwood House, and as the architect of the Estate-buildings, St Andrew's Church etc. We congratulate Mr Crossland on receiving such a contribution to his ability as is implied in his selection by the Town Council of Birmingham.[4]

Despite winning the first prize, though, Crossland's design for Birmingham was not executed and the commission instead went to a local man[5], as seems often to have been the case with such competitions. This outcome was fortuitous, as it turned out, since Crossland was also successful in winning the huge project that was the subject of the other competition. This other success was for a sanatorium at St Ann's Heath, Virginia Water, in Surrey, to be erected at the expense of the phenomenally rich entrepreneur philanthropist Thomas Holloway (1800-83).

Thomas Holloway had made his fortune from the sale of patent medicines, ointments and pills, by tapping into people's concerns regarding common ailments. His real talent was in advertising his products, wherever and whenever there was an opportunity to do so, both in Britain and in numerous languages in very many countries around the world. By 1863, he was spending £40,000 a year on advertising[6] – a truly enormous sum for the time. He was 'a man who spent every moment of his adult waking life preoccupied with money, with "getting and spending"'.[7] His understanding of marketing techniques was decades ahead of other businesses.

Despite making an enormous fortune from the sale of these products, the Holloways lived modestly, and Thomas Holloway never attempted to enter 'society', living instead as something of a recluse, 'with no close relationships beyond his wife (to whom he was devoted) siblings and in-laws'.[8] He lacked social graces and social confidence, and apparently never felt comfortable in the company of other wealthy people. He was well travelled, though, and took an interest in the buildings he saw on his travels. With his innate

---

4. *The Huddersfield Chronicle and West Yorkshire Advertiser*, 20 May 1871, Issue 1181, p. 8.
5. Douglas, lecture notes, 21 April 2012.
6. Gill, Annabel, 'Who'd Have Thought It, Pills Have Bought It!' in *Higher* (the magazine for the alumni of Royal Holloway and Bedford New College), issue 17, autumn 2012, pp. 22-23.
7. Bingham, Caroline, 'The Founder and the Founding of Royal Holloway College' in *Centenary Lectures, 1886-1986* (Egham, 1988), p. 1.
8. Hall, Michael, 'A Thames Valley château: Royal Holloway College, Egham, Surrey' in *Country Life*, 21 May 2014, p. 121.

understanding of advertising, he realised 'that architecture could enhance his standing' and so 'his business premises, first in the Strand and then New Oxford Street in London, were palatial'.[9]

The beginning of Holloway's idea for an asylum followed attendance (probably on the suggestion of his wife, Jane[10]) at a meeting in 1861 where the philanthropist Lord Shaftesbury had sought funding to build an asylum to care for those with mental illness among the increasing numbers of the middle classes. Lord Shaftesbury's appeal had a considerable effect on Thomas Holloway, and, although at the time his business affairs occupied him fully, by 1864 he was already trying to find a worthwhile cause to which he could devote his wealth.[11] Having made provision for members of his family, but with no children to whom to leave his money, he wanted to use his fortune for some philanthropic purpose (as well as, no doubt, for a public memorial to himself), and he turned his thoughts towards building a middle-class mental asylum. He recognised that there was a lack of mental health provision for the middle classes, reasoning that the upper classes were well able to take care of their own, and the poorest of society had something of a public safety net in the growing number of asylums established in the later part of the century. There was, though, he concluded, little provision for the middle classes – people like himself – and he thought to contribute to filling that gap.

Holloway took this project idea very seriously and made fact-finding visits with his brother-in-law and agent, George Martin, to several institutions.[12] He found these asylums austere, depressing and not conducive to the recovery of good health. He therefore resolved that his asylum would be different: 'spacious, comfortable and welcoming'[13] and 'an inspiration which would be copied by others'.[14] In February 1871, Holloway met with the Commissioners in Lunacy, who found his plans attractive and appropriate, and offered professional assistance in the provision of a 'model' building. In June of the same year, he bought Trotsworth Farm at St Ann's Heath, Virginia Water, in Surrey. This was not far from his own home, Tittenhurst Park, just over the county boundary at Sunninghill, Berkshire, where he and his wife, Jane,

9.  Hall, p. 122.
10. Bingham, *Lectures*, p. 11.
11. Harrison-Barbet, Anthony, *Thomas Holloway: Victorian Philanthropist* (Lyfrow Trelyspen, Cornwall, 1990, revised 1993, Egham, 1994), p. 42.
12. Harrison-Barbet, p. 44.
13. Harrison-Barbet, p. 46.
14. Blythman, Guy, *The Holloway Sanatorium* (Egham, 2014), p. 7.

and other members of their families were living by 1870.[15] He allocated
£300,000 for the construction of the asylum and the Trust Deed was
executed the same year.[16]

For Holloway, the elevated position of Trotsworth Farm was perfect
for the building he planned. 'It would be clearly visible to the travelling
public from the railway running close by and thereby become its own
advertisement.'[17] There were other reasons why the site was perfect for
his Sanatorium: it fulfilled the stipulations of the Commissioners in
Lunacy in terms of location and geology to permit the laying of drainage
and other essential services. It was also close to Virginia Water Station,
which would provide good transport links. Holloway initially wanted to
have the building constructed in an Italian style, modelled on the river
frontage of Somerset House. By October 1871 he had changed his mind,
following advice from E.W. Pugin, who suggested a 'Flemish' style, like
the Cloth Hall in Ypres. Holloway wrote to one of the Commissioners
in Lunacy:

> I think we have got things almost into a groove. You will see that
> I have gone into the grand old Flemish style. I know that your
> taste is classical and which I greatly admire, but perhaps all things
> considered the Gothic would be most appropriate, as we can get
> red brick in the neighbourhood and a large building in the Italian
> style ought, I believe, to have stone facings. T.H.[18]

Though swayed by Pugin's advice, the choice of Flemish style was
therefore largely practical, as red bricks like those used in Flanders were
readily available locally. However, Holloway also found the style attractive:
he particularly favoured a building modelled on the Cloth Hall, one of the
best known secular Gothic buildings in Europe, and a building he knew
from the time when, as a young man, he had stayed in the nearby town of
Roubaix. Designing a large building in brick was to be a new experience
for Crossland.

E.W. Pugin also recommended that Holloway should consult Edmund
Sharpe of Lancaster, an architect well acquainted with Gothic style.
Holloway put in a great deal of work himself in developing plans for his

15. Saint, Andrew and Richard Holder, 'Holloway Sanatorium: A Conservation
    Nightmare' in *The Victorian Society Annual*, 1993, p. 19.
16. Harrison-Barbet, p. 44.
17. Williams, Richard, *Thomas Holloway's College: The First 125 Years* (Egham, 2012),
    p. 7.
18. Surrey History Centre, *Thomas Holloway, Letterbook, 4.8.1869-19.2.1872*, 2620/9/5.

7.1 Ypres: The Cloth Hall, mainly thirteenth century.

Sanatorium. He had clear ideas regarding the provision he wanted for patients – ideas that were about a century ahead of contemporary thought. In working out how to bring his ideas to fruition, he personally sought advice from many experts. For architectural advice, he worked with, and paid fees to, two eminent architects. Professor Thomas Leverton Donaldson (1795-1885) was one of the most prominent members of the architectural profession: he was the first Professor of Architecture at University College, London, a co-founder of the Royal Institute of British Architects, being President in 1863-64, and was considered 'the father of the architectural profession'.[19] Thomas Henry Wyatt (1807-80) was President of the R.I.B.A. in 1870. Wyatt and Donaldson were also architects for the Commissioners in Lunacy.[20] In an address to the R.I.B.A. more than a decade later in 1887, Crossland noted that Holloway had a third advisor, George Godwin, the editor of *The Builder*, who provided architectural advice and who had designed a lunatic asylum himself in 1847. Holloway also sought the practical knowledge of Dr David Yellowlees, the superintendent of Bridgend asylum, on the arrangement of rooms in such an institution. It is evident, therefore, that Holloway had secured advice of the highest possible calibre.

Holloway's advisors suggested that the best design for the asylum would be achieved by putting the scheme out to competition – as was normal practice for large or prestigious buildings. Although Holloway had his own ideas with respect to design, he was no architectural expert and was happy to accept their advice, thinking to invite six or seven architects to compete. A competition among a group of pre-selected architects was proposed, and Edmund Sharpe probably suggested some of the 'Goths' (including Crossland) among those to be invited to compete.[21] The competition was launched in 1871.

19. Bingham, *Lectures*, p. 13.
20. Crossland, W.H., 'The Royal Holloway College' in *R.I.B.A. Transactions*, Second series, Vol 3, 1886-7, p. 141.
21. Saint and Holder, p. 20.

Crossland's by now impressive portfolio ensured that he was included when Holloway made his pre-selection of architects who were to be invited to enter the competition. Crossland realised that this was potentially a very large project, in which he would have to work not only with his patron, but also within the conditions laid down by the Commissioners in Lunacy for asylum provision. He therefore felt it was essential to talk with Thomas Holloway prior to entering the competition and managed to arrange a meeting with Holloway in which he was able to discuss details.[22] As a result, he concluded that the project was indeed too large for one architect, and he therefore 'did not feel inclined to go single handed into this competition'.[23] He persuaded fellow London architect John Philpot Jones (an Irishman who had previously worked for some time in Canada) of Whitehall Place and Edward Salomons (a better known architect who had previously worked with Jones), to join him in a partnership for the competition. They formed their partnership in 1870, none of them having any experience of working on asylums.

Edward Salomons (1827-1906) practised in Manchester where he had designed, with John Philpot Jones, the Reform Club in 1870. It is possible Crossland had met Salomons in Rochdale while working on the Town Hall, at which time Salomons was working on the town's theatre.[24] On Crossland's own admission, John Philpot Jones put in most of the work on the asylum design[25], drafting and working out the plan while Crossland drew the elevations in a style that bore a close similarity to that of Rochdale Town Hall. Working with other architects was out of character for Crossland, this being the only time in his entire career that he is known to have done so. It suggests that, with a considerable workload in Yorkshire, he had real misgivings regarding the scale of the Sanatorium project.

The competition brief was for a building that would accommodate 200 patients. It was to be in the Flemish style, on which a commission at the rate of 5% (including the competition prize money) was to be paid. Holloway's detailed specification included the dimensions and character of rooms and precise requirements on many details including the plumbing system. A particular requirement was that exuberance of ornament was to be strictly avoided, inside as well as outside. Although Holloway was nominally an Anglican, he distrusted clerics, and a chapel was not included in the specification since he considered that a 'Noble Hall' would serve both recreational and religious purposes. No dining hall was included,

---

22. Crossland, p. 141.
23. Crossland, p. 141.
24. Law, Part 3.
25. Crossland, p. 141.

as it was anticipated that patients would take meals in their day rooms. The competition submissions were to be estimated not to exceed a cost of £40,000, 'but as much less as may be' and the winner was to be prepared to make modifications to Holloway's satisfaction.[26]

The competition for Holloway's asylum took place in the spring of 1872 and was announced in *The Builder* at the end of June 1872.[27] Twelve architects had submitted thirteen designs (one of them sending two, to Holloway's annoyance)[28], working to the brief that had been provided by Holloway. As was usual practice, the entries were anonymous and identified by an unrelated title or 'motto'. Crossland and his colleagues used the motto 'Alpha'. Holloway called on his advisors Professor Donaldson and Thomas Wyatt to judge the entries and they placed 'Alpha' first, winning the first premium of £200[29], (the first prize). Thomas Holloway, in his first act in promoting his new venture, sent a short letter to *The Builder*, enclosing a copy of the award and suggesting 'that you may publish in your next number, if you think proper'.[30]

The result of the Sanatorium competition became a continuing comedy of errors in the pages of *The Builder* in the summer of 1872. Keen to report the winning design as quickly as possible, the publication reported, on 20 July, without checking the facts: 'We understand that the design submitted by Mr Alfred Smith has been selected.'[31] On 27 July, the same journal published Holloway's letter and the adjudication details, using the motto names for the competition entries. There was no mention of the competing architects' names, so the readers of *The Builder* (except for the owners of the mottos) had no idea who the successful architects were. Included also was detail, as presented to Thomas Holloway by the judges, of how the award was made, and it was apparent that none of the entries had fully satisfied the judges:

> We must state that although there is considerable merit and taste displayed in the several projects, and evidence of a great amount of time and care having been bestowed upon the preparation of the drawings, yet there is still not one of the designs which would not

26. Surrey History Centre, 2620/6/1, *Suggestions for a Proposed Lunatic Asylum at St Ann's Heath, Near Virginia Water Station*, 1872, p. 2.

27. *The Builder*, 29 June 1872, p. 502.

28. Saint and Holder, p. 20.

29. Surrey History Centre, 2620/7/2, *Building Purchase Ledger for St Ann's Heath Asylum, 1872*, p. 2. 'transferred to WHC's account March 1874, "being the premium paid to Mr Jones on 22/7/1872"'.

30. *The Builder*, 27 July 1872, p. 593.

31. *The Builder*, 27 July 1872, p. 570.

7.2 (left) Virginia Water:
Holloway Sanatorium,
Crossland's original design.

7.3 (below) Virginia
Water: Holloway
Sanatorium, the original
plan by John Philpot
Jones.

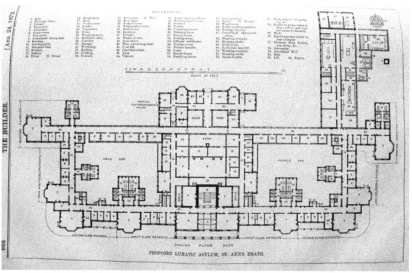

require more or less modification of plan and general arrangement
ere it could be carried into execution for practical working,
consequently we have selected that one as first which, with the least
alteration and no sacrifice of its own individual character would, we
believe, be the most suited to your purpose, and the least costly.[32]

The implication behind the report in this edition of 27 July was still that
the entry of Alfred Smith had won. In the following week's edition (dated
3 August), an apologetic explanation was given for the error of 20 July.
Nonetheless, bizarrely, it was Smith's design that was published – probably

32. *The Builder*, 27 July 1872, p. 589.

because the typesetting of the journal could not be changed at a late stage, and in any case, no engraving of the Crossland, Salomons and Jones design was available as a replacement:

> In our present issue we publish a view, illustrating Mr Smith's design. It is right we should say, however, that in doing this no reflection whatever on the referee's decision is intended: it is the result of a published mis-statement, which gave the first place to the design we have engraved; and we know nothing of the other designs. We propose in an early number to illustrate fully the design by Messrs Crossland, Salomons, & Jones, to which the first premium is really awarded.[33]

Doubtless, engravers had already been urgently set to work, but engraving was a slow craft and it was not until 24 August 1872, two months after the first announcement of the project, that the design of Crossland, Salomons and Jones was published, together with almost two columns on their winning entry, with much detail on the proposed facilities.[34] The designs were also displayed in the Conduit Street Gallery and in the Regent Street gallery of E. Freeman for a month between August and September 1872.

## Holiday in Canada

Crossland can have had little expectation of winning the Sanatorium competition, as, having submitted their competition entry and seen the opening of Rochdale Town Hall, he left responsibility for the Huddersfield projects with his chief assistant and took a holiday in Nova Scotia, visiting his brother, James. James Crossland had married a Huddersfield-born woman and emigrated to Canada and, by the time of his brother's visit, had lived there with his wife and children for several years. It is not known whether this was Crossland's first visit to his brother and family, but, in the early 1870s, regular services across the Atlantic Ocean were barely established and sailing to America or Canada for a holiday was undoubtedly an indicator of a successful and financially secure person. The journey could take anything from one to three weeks, depending on weather conditions, and second class as well as first-class passengers enjoyed a standard of opulence affordable by only the very few. Whether Crossland's wife, Lavinia, and daughter, Maud (then aged 11), went with him is unknown, but it seems unlikely, partly for reasons of cost, but also because of Maud's schooling.

33. *The Builder*, 3 August 1872, p. 609.
34. *The Builder*, 24 August 1872, p. 665.

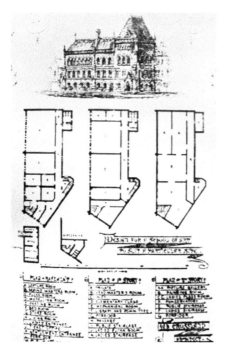

7.4 School of Art: Crossland designed this when he was in Canada in 1872. This drawing appears in *W.H. Crossland* by L.J. Whitaker (picture 51 between pages 43 and 44).

Even on holiday, Crossland seems to have continued to produce designs for buildings. He designed a School of Art and several other unidentified buildings, most likely during the time that he was on holiday in Nova Scotia. The School of Art design was in continental Gothic style, with, according to L.J. Whitaker, a 'plan typical of Crossland's mastery of planning'.[35] It had a corner detail at an oblique angle and an arcade of windows on the second floor that was 'almost Venetian and smacks of Ruskinian influences'.[36] So far as is known, neither the School of Art nor any of the other designs mentioned were ever built.

The result of the Sanatorium competition was telegraphed to Crossland in Canada in the summer of 1872. Some fifteen years later, in his address to the R.I.B.A. he recalled, 'When the adjudication was given in our favour I was up in the woods of Nova Scotia, thinking a good deal more of salmon and moose than of Sanatoria.'[37] John Philpot Jones summoned him back to London, where Crossland found his partner busily working on plans: 'in almost daily communication with Mr Holloway, submitting to him plans and views of designs in great variety'.[38] Jones had visited Dr Yellowlees (who had had some involvement in the judging of the competition) at Bridgend asylum, and Dr Yellowlees subsequently

35. Whitaker, pp. 180-81. Whitaker reports to have discovered by chance the undated design for the School of Art in a book entitled *The Angel in the Studio* by Anthea Callen. The drawing, with the title *Design for a School of Art to Suit a Particular Site* and signed 'W.H.C., Architect', was apparently first shown in a book entitled *Art Education* by Walter Smith and published in Boston, USA. It was referred to as one of several designs that could be adopted in the United States.

36. Whitaker, pp. 180-81.

37. Crossland, p. 141.

38. Crossland, p. 141.

assumed the role of consultant. Together with him, Jones had refined the plans, which, as Crossland recalled when he later addressed the R.I.B.A., 'were considered perfect' – a comment that must have been received by his audience as ironic in view of all the alterations that were to take place before the building eventually opened. He continued in his address: 'The plans had the entire approval of the Commissioners, and their architects Donaldson and Wyatt'.[39] The success of the triumvirate in this competition was to change the direction of Crossland's professional and private life completely.

## Development of the plans for the Sanatorium

There ended up being two different plans for the building. The first was the one that won the competition. Different accommodation was to be provided for the different classes of patient. First-class patients were to be accommodated nearest the centre in the main (south) part of the building. Fourth-class patients (those categorised as 'excited') were to be isolated in units at the extreme north-east and north-west, conveniently near the padded rooms. There was no central dining room in the plan, as the intention was that meals would be served in the day rooms.

The second plan was the result of further work between John Philpot Jones and Dr Yellowlees. Visually, it was much more like the Cloth Hall in Ypres than the original design and included major changes affecting circulation and storage space. The central block was enlarged to provide a dining room and some rooms lost their garden view. The axial corridors through the main block were removed, reducing some of the institutional atmosphere and allowing more day rooms to be provided. Access to public rooms became easier with day rooms and libraries becoming through rooms. Additionally, the laundry was removed from a wing at the north-east corner to a detached block on the south-east side, linked by a corridor.[40] Neither of these plans, as it turned out, gave the layout that was actually completed for the opening of the building.

Although not realised at the time, the removal of the corridors along the main façade made escape in the case of fire more difficult. The fast pace of Crossland's working life meant that he was 'unlikely to have found the time (or reason) to question the escape routes of the second plan'[41] being worked up by his colleague, John Philpot Jones. Work began on the asylum in 1873, the first brick being laid in May by Jane Holloway and

39. Crossland, p. 141.
40. Whitaker, pp. 199-200.
41. Whitaker, p. 200.

THE HOLLOWAY SANATORIUM, VIRGINIA WATER, WINDSOR.—Mr. Crossland, Architect.

7.5 Virginia Water: Holloway Sanatorium, revised design, *The Builder*, 17 July 1875.

7.6 (opposite) Virginia Water: Holloway Sanatorium, revised plan, *The Builder*, 17 July 1875. Axial corridors through the main block have been removed and a dining room added, together with other alterations.

the second by Holloway himself. Following the laying of the first bricks by the Holloways, there was a pause while the second plan was developed. However, work on the grounds was begun ahead of the building itself so that a start could be made quickly once the amended plan was finalised. So that there should be as little delay as possible with beginning the building, Holloway bought a brick-works and sold the bricks to his own builders[42], although bricks were also sourced from elsewhere. The main contractor was Sharpington and Cole, who began work on the site the following month with bricks coming from the Lawrence Brickworks at Bracknell. A railway siding at the brickworks allowed the bricks to be brought directly by train to the siding Holloway had built at Virginia Water Station.[43] An

42. Harrison-Barbet, p. 47.
43. Blythman, p. 9.

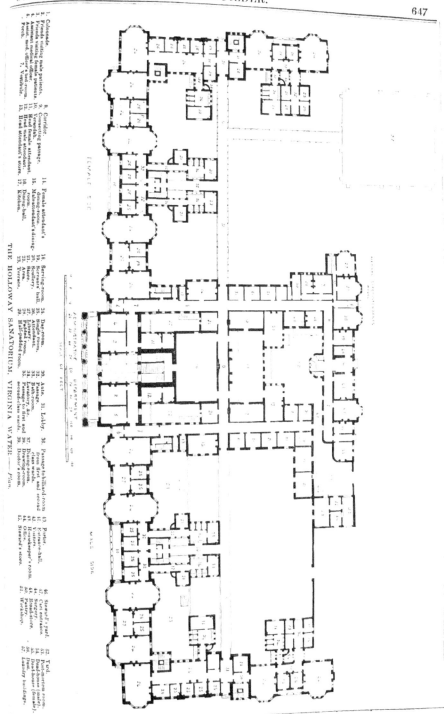

1. Colonnade.
2. Friends visiting male patients.
3. Friends visiting female patients.
4. Assistant medical officer
5. Assist. med. officer's bed-room.
6. Porch.
7. Vestibule.

8. Corridor
9. Connecting passage.
10. Verandah.
11. Head female attendant.
12. Head male attendant.
13. Head attendant's store.

14. Female attendant's dining-room.
15. Servant's hall.
16. Male attendant's dining-room.
17. Kitchen.

18. Serving-room.
19. Servant's hall.
20. Scullery.
21. Store.
22. Area.
23. Terrace.

24. Day-room.
25. Single room.
26. Attendant.
27. Library.
28. Padded room.
29. Half-padded room.

30. Attic. 31. Lobby.
32. Passage.
33. Bath-room.
34. Lavatory, &c.
35. Passage to first and second-class wards.

36. Passage to billiard-room
37. Dining-room.
38. Drawing-room.
39. Doctor's room.

40. Porter.
41. Entrance-hall.
42. Visitors.
43. Housekeeper's room.
44. Office.
45. Steward's store.

46. Steward's yard.
47. Cart entrance.
48. Surgery.
49. Dead-store.
50. Pantry.
51. Workshop.

52. Yard.
53. Post-mortem room.
54. Dead-house (male).
55. Dead-house (female).
56. Dust.
57. Laundry buildings.

FEMALE SIDE.

MALE SIDE.

ADMINISTRATIVE DEPARTMENT.

SCALE OF FEET.

THE HOLLOWAY SANATORIUM, VIRGINIA WATER.—Plan.

'Architect's Office' was set up for Crossland on the asylum site. Despite all this preparatory work, the project began slowly. Thomas Holloway put in a great deal of work himself, even after the project had been awarded to Crossland and his partners. He continued to seek advice on even very small details from Dr Yellowlees of Bridgend Asylum and a wide range of other experts in developing his ideas for the Sanatorium.

In June 1874, the logistics of Crossland's work scheduling between Surrey and the West Riding were thrown into utter confusion when his architect partner, John Philpot Jones, died unexpectedly on 1 June at the age of just forty-three.[44] Since Edward Salomons was probably never an active partner, Jones's modified plan, which was published in *The Builder* on 17 July 1875[45], was left in Crossland's hands. As Crossland noted in his speech to the R.I.B.A. in 1887, 'the carrying on of the work was intrusted [*sic*] to myself, Mr Salomons being at Manchester'.[46]

Having been anxious at the outset regarding the size of the project and having wanted to work with partners, Crossland must have had very considerable apprehensions as he took over his late colleague's plans and began to work for Thomas Holloway, supervising the work himself. His statement regarding the Sanatorium project, made at the beginning of his address to the R.I.B.A., suggests a decided lack of enthusiasm as he faced responsibility for the project alone: 'I should like . . . to explain how it fell to my lot to have to carry it out'.[47] Crossland must have begun to have more than an inkling that, with the death of Jones, this project was going to change the direction of his career and probably of his life, noting over a decade later in a remarkable understatement near the beginning of his R.I.B.A. speech: 'Then commenced a curious episode, and to me a new experience.'[48]

---

44. http://dictionaryofarchitectsincanada.org/node/179.
45. *The Builder*, 17 July 1875, p. 647.
46. Crossland, p. 141.
47. Crossland, p. 141.
48. Crossland, p. 141.

*Chapter 8*

# The London office: the big project

In 1873, when work on the Sanatorium buildings had barely begun[1], Thomas Holloway was, extraordinarily, already contemplating another huge project: a convalescent home for incurables. As with the Sanatorium, Holloway consulted the distinguished architect T.H. Wyatt regarding style.[2] Wyatt recommended French Renaissance, a style he favoured, at the same time lending Holloway several books and images of the style, including, in particular, an illustration of the château at Chambord in the Loire valley. According to Crossland, Holloway had casually mentioned the idea of the project to him and proceeded to ask Crossland's opinion on choosing a style of architecture similar to the Sanatorium.[3] He had also asked Crossland to provide illustrations of some existing buildings, the style of which Crossland considered suitable.

By this time, Crossland was beginning to believe that the Gothic style on which he had built his reputation was becoming less favoured – a view certainly shared with other architects at the time, who were trying to develop a style that 'combined the dignity and regularity of Classicism with the freedom and variety of Gothic'.[4] As he put it himself in talking of the awarding of the commission, he felt 'a return either to the purer Classical styles or to the Renaissance of the 16th century was certainly impending'.[5] Renaissance château styles were becoming popular among people of self-made wealth and were appearing in building journals. Holloway will have seen the designs and probably hinted to Crossland that he found them

1. Harrison-Barbet, Anthony, *Thomas Holloway: Victorian Philanthropist* (Lyfrow Trelyspen, Cornwall, 1990, revised 1993, Egham, 1994), p. 57.
2. Crossland, W.H., 'The Royal Holloway College' in *R.I.B.A. Transactions*, Second series, Vol 3, 1886-87, p. 142
3. Crossland, p. 142.
4. Crooke, J. Mordaunt, 'Mr Holloway's Château' in *Country Life*, 9 October 1986, p. 1122.
5. Crossland, p. 142.

attractive. Crossland therefore selected 'views of châteaux in the valley of the Loire, as well as that of Fontainebleau', which he gave to Holloway, 'placing Chambord first'.[6] As he recalled the occasion, he added that 'the effect on Mr Holloway was somewhat startling'.[7]

Holloway proceeded to discuss the nature of his second project with Crossland, saying he had been advised to hold another competition. He asked Crossland what he would do if he became a competitor, to which Crossland replied that he would visit Touraine in order to 'sketch and measure Chambord in the completest way; also such portions of the other châteaux as appeared to me useful in the study of the style and containing characteristics not found at Chambord'.[8]

Crossland can scarcely have expected Holloway's reaction when he asked, 'Will you do this Mr Crossland?' Crossland replied that he most assuredly would, whereupon Holloway patted him on the shoulder saying, 'My boy, you shall have the work; but mind, on the condition that you sketch and measure Chambord from bottom to top. No more competitions for me. I had too much trouble about the last.'[9] So, with this informal exchange, Crossland secured what was to become, by a very considerable margin, the largest commission of his career – 'the most important work of my life'[10], as he put it – and this at the same time as he was already committed to a large and complex project for the same client, as well as numerous projects around 200 miles away for his Huddersfield patron, Sir John Ramsden. Thomas Holloway had doubtless been impressed by Crossland's ability to manage a large project, not only at the Sanatorium, but also a few years earlier at Rochdale. It is not known whether his two patrons were aware of the existence of the other, although if they read the architectural press, they could not fail to have known. They might both have doubted whether their architect had the ability to deliver as he promised – but he did not let down either of them.

In 1873, Thomas Holloway was seventy-three years old, and childless and was anxious to spend his very considerable fortune on good causes (and his own grand memorials) as quickly as possible. In the same informal conversation when he offered his second project to Crossland, he asked how soon Crossland could start, to which Crossland replied, 'as soon as I could set matters quite straight at the Sanatorium I would start'.[11] So,

---

6.  Crossland, p. 142.
7.  Crossland, p. 142.
8.  Crossland, p. 143.
9.  Crossland, p. 143.
10. Crossland, p. 143.
11. Crossland, p. 143.

leaving supervision of the Sanatorium, probably, at that time, with John Philpot Jones, and the supervision of projects in and around Huddersfield to employees of the Ramsden Estate, at the beginning of September 1873[12] Crossland set off for Touraine, taking with him A.J. Taylor, his principal assistant from Huddersfield.

Thomas Holloway had announced his intention of joining them in France when the measuring and sketching had been completed, and in the middle of the month he duly arrived. Holloway kept a diary of the visit to the Loire, and it differs from Crossland's account given to the R.I.B.A. in 1897 in several details. Of the two accounts, Holloway's is more likely to be accurate, as it was written during the visit to France, while Crossland's was written some fourteen years later. Holloway suggests that he joined Crossland and Taylor when they had already been in Chambord ten days (not several weeks as Crossland suggested), making plans and drawings of the château. Holloway proceeded to join them in the work, checking through what Crossland had already drawn in order to begin to formulate his own ideas for his second large project – at that time an 'institution for incurables'.

There was plainly an unusually close rapport between Crossland and his wealthy self-made client, but Holloway nonetheless carefully checked the details of his architect's work when he arrived at Chambord:

> Mr Holloway, having spent two days in going round and through the building checking off our sketch-books, feature by feature, and finding only one bit of work missing, viz, a small dormer window on the east front which we could not get at easily – *but which had to be got at* before our work could be passed.[13]

Despite his age, and on his own admission finding it tiring, Holloway did a full day's work alongside Crossland and Taylor, much to Crossland's astonishment, forming clear ideas of how the dimensions of the château would be reduced to suit his purposes. Crossland began revising the plans during the last few days at Chambord, checking details of his work by revisiting the château. They spent around three weeks there, where they were joined also by George Martin[14], Jane Holloway's brother-in-law. Other châteaux were visited also, including Blois, Valençay, Amboise, Chaumont and Chenonceaux, as well as, on the way home, Fontainebleau

---

12. Bingham, Caroline, 'The Founder and the Founding of Royal Holloway College' in *Centenary Lectures, 1886-1986* (Egham, 1988), p. 15.

13. Crossland, p. 143.

14. Harrison-Barbet, p. 51.

8.1 (top)
Château de
Chambord, north
west facade.

8.2 (bottom)
Château de Blois.

and Versailles. Of all the châteaux they visited, it was the château at Chambord that most impressed Crossland, 'in the elegance of its design and the beauty of its sculpture'.[15] According to Crossland, they decided there in the Loire valley that 'our building' should be similar, with 'red brick and stone dressings', the idea for brick probably derived from their visit to the château at Blois – and because they already had an assured source of bricks back in Surrey.

They returned home through Paris, where Crossland went shopping for architectural books and photographs that would be useful in designing Holloway's second building. They left France for London at the beginning of October, but not before visiting a hospital and school that provided ideas for the Sanatorium. In particular they were persuaded against having any gas at the Sanatorium. Crossland plainly enjoyed this trip to France, stating in his address to the R.I.B.A. in 1887, that the work 'was of much too pleasant a character to be hurried'.[16]

15. Crossland, p. 143.
16. Crossland, p. 143.

Sometime between the autumn of 1873 and the spring of 1874[17], Holloway changed his mind for his second institution, almost certainly at the suggestion of his wife, Jane, from a hospital for incurables to a college for the higher education of women. Jane Holloway was certainly credited with the change of plan in contemporary newspaper reports.[18] The education of women 'was one of the great Liberal causes of the age and, in so far as anything is known about Holloway's politics, it is clear that he allied himself with the radical Liberalism common among his fellow businessmen'.[19]

Curiously, though, on return from France, Holloway put aside plans for his second institution for a while, as he focused his attention on the Sanatorium. However, on 12 May 1874, he purchased, for £25,374, the ninety-four acre Mount Lee Estate, about one mile from Egham, about two miles from the site of the Sanatorium and only a few miles from his own home. He allocated £150,000 for the cost of the construction of his College. The hilltop site meant that, in the same way as the Sanatorium, the College would be its own advertisement – clearly visible from some distance away and in particular from the railway line from London.

Crossland was kept very busy supervising work at the Sanatorium, particularly after the death of John Philpot Jones in June 1874, as well as working on the plans for the College. He was to spend around two years following the visit to Touraine working on the College plans, elevations and fine details, during which time he went back to France and Belgium, checking details. He used motifs from all the châteaux visited in the Loire, but most particularly from the château of Chambord. He drew substantially on the ground floor plan of this large château and more generally for the elevations and overall style.[20] The most famous detail of the château at Chambord, the double staircase, was apparently deliberately omitted from the design for the College[21], probably because there was restricted space available in his planning for the staircases.

Crossland worked on a number of ideas for the College, drawing on a variety of sources and not simply the châteaux visited in France. So, just a few months after the Mount Lee purchase, on 24 August, he wrote to Holloway from his home at 12 Park Village West, ostensibly to thank

17. Bingham, Caroline, *The History of Royal Holloway College 1886-1896*, (London, 1987), p. 35.
18. *The Leeds Mercury*, 26 June 1886, Issue 15044.
19. Hall, Michael, 'A Thames Valley Château: Royal Holloway College, Egham, Surrey' in *Country Life*, 21 May 2014, p. 122.
20. Whitaker, p. 5.
21. Whitaker, p. 5.

Holloway 'very much' for the £500 he had received. In the same letter, though, he informed Holloway that he had been working out 'sketchily' a plan for the proposed College, based upon 'the Castle Howard Plan, as far as the general appearance of the elevation is concerned'. He continued, 'Your suggestion as to the arrangement of *closed and open Corridors* will I think work admirably but the whole will require to be on a more extended scale than at Castle Howard'.[22] He sought also to assure Holloway that he was gearing up for the College project, as well as working on details of the St Ann's Heath Asylum, saying he was proposing to get his 'staff of assistants' together as quickly as possible at the offices at St Ann's Heath 'to get out not only the grand College Scheme but also the interior details for the Asylum'. 'These latter are far advanced and will soon be ready for your consideration.'[23] Reading between the lines of Crossland's reassurances, Crossland and his assistants were finding it difficult to manage the workload.

It seems that the construction of the asylum had been held up due to an insufficient supply of bricks. However, work on the twenty-two acres of grounds continued, and the brick supply problem was remedied during the summer of 1874. Despite the fact that Holloway would have seen progress for himself on his regular visits to the asylum site, this same letter of August 1874 informs Holloway that 'the whole central portion of the building is advancing satisfactorily and I see no reason why the main roof should not be on before the winter, now the red bricks are coming in so much faster'.[24] This was not to be, though, as attention shifted to the planning of the College.

Crossland was required by Holloway to write to a Mr James Beal, an auctioneer, land agent, journalist and reformer of his acquaintance. Holloway wanted Crossland to provide Beal with details of the Sanatorium and to inform Beal that Crossland was to build a Ladies College at Mount Lee. Crossland was to include that 'the founder intends that there shall be nothing like it in Europe'.[25] Beal duly wrote an article that appeared in *The Times* on 29 October 1874, as well as an article for *Building News*, in which he referred to the proposed institution as the 'Ladies' University' – probably the first time the term was used, and a description that Holloway then preferred. Beal was to go on to be supportive of Thomas Holloway as his plans for the College developed, acting 'as a kind of public relations agent

---

22. Royal Holloway Archive, GB/131/1/3, letter dated 24 August 1874.
23. Royal Holloway Archive, GB/131/1/3, letter dated 24 August 1874.
24. Royal Holloway Archive, GB/131/1/3, letter dated 24 August 1874.
25. Harrison-Barbet, p. 51. Much detail of the development of the College is sourced from this publication.

for Holloway over the College and, to some degree, over the Sanatorium as well'.[26] From the end of 1874, Holloway 'launched himself into a near frenzy of activity'[27] working on plans for the College.

It seems likely that there was a dispute, or at least a misunderstanding, between Crossland and Holloway regarding payments to Crossland and whether or not expenses were included in Crossland's fees. With the matter apparently settled, Crossland was at pains to reassure his client that he fully understood the terms of his employment. In a letter to Holloway from his Regent Street office dated 30 October 1874, a year after returning from the trip to the Loire, Crossland wrote that he would not claim expenses for himself and his clerk for the trip to Chambord 'to be made use of in designing and carrying out a Building for a Home for Incurables, which you had then in contemplation'.[28] Nor would he claim for visits within the UK 'in gratitude for your kindness to me'.[29]

Holloway had little knowledge of academic life and knew he needed advice. He prevailed upon his friend James Beal, who was acquainted with several educationalists and politicians, to arrange a meeting with people who would advise him. Accordingly, in the early part of 1875, Beal invited several politicians, including David Chadwick and Samuel Morley, and eminent educationalists including some of the growing number of female academics (Millicent Fawcett, Maria Grey, Elizabeth Garett Anderson and Emily Davies), as well as Sir James Kay-Shuttleworth to Holloway's offices in London's Oxford Street. At the meeting, Holloway was honest about his personal lack of relevant knowledge, but explained his plans for the College. Despite the advice from some of them, Holloway was adamant that the College would be a 'university', not a teacher training college or a high school. He also wanted the College to be secular and ultimately to be able to confer degrees.

Crossland was introduced to the eminent gathering and, at Holloway's request, presented his initial plan for the College. Since Holloway's change of plan from a hospital to a college, Crossland had made considerable changes to his original draft and the scheme presented was based on the château at Chambord more loosely than had been originally intended. It also included elements drawn from the Louvre in Paris, as well as the palace at Fontainebleau and the Loire châteaux of Blois and Azay-le-Rideau.

26. Saint, Andrew and Richard Holder, 'Holloway Sanatorium: A Conservation Nightmare' in *The Victorian Society Annual*, 1993, p. 18.
27. Harrison-Barbet, p. 51.
28. Royal Holloway Archive, GB131/1/4, letter dated 30 October 1874.
29. Royal Holloway Archive, GB131/1/4, letter dated 30 October 1874.

In 1875, there was much excited activity, involving the high-calibre experts that Holloway had enlisted, as ideas for the college were developed. Planning the College became a major preoccupation for Holloway. He advertised both the Sanatorium and the College as he advertised his pills and ointments, sending notices about the two institutions to newspapers all over the world, many of which printed them verbatim.[30] Holloway had become very well-known by this time, both through his ubiquitous medicinal products and through the many newspaper articles about his two philanthropic institutions. Undoubtedly some of his celebrity rubbed off on Crossland as plans for the two buildings in Surrey became topics of society conversation. Crossland himself came to be described as 'a well-known architect'.

Holloway's informal committee of prominent advisers was willing to play its part in the development of what they clearly saw as a pioneering institution. Women's education was very much the topic of the moment, with both Girton and Newnham Colleges in Cambridge being established in the second half of the nineteenth century and operational in the early 1870s. Thomas Holloway's plan to build a College for women therefore attracted much interest, but he found that some of the female academics had their own ideas and suggestions. After all the work in the Loire and many months of careful drafting, Crossland was frustrated at being told that he and Holloway were not planning the College in the most appropriate architectural style and that the predominant style of Oxford and Cambridge colleges would be more suitable. Crossland must have worried at the potential scale of redesigning and replanning that seemed to lie ahead, although his anxiety may have been alleviated somewhat by his brother's return from Canada to work with him. By 1875, James Crossland had joined him as his assistant[31] on the Sanatorium project, an arrangement that lasted for about two years, helping in particular with measuring up.[32]

With no higher education behind him, Holloway was easily swayed by the ideas of the female academics and felt that he should visit Oxford and Cambridge to make his own judgement. In 1875, he duly took Crossland and three assistants, including James Crossland, with him to Cambridge to draw up a design 'embodying as nearly as possible all the characteristics of the larger colleges'.[33] Holloway clearly had great confidence in Crossland,

---

30. Royal Holloway Archive, RF/126/1, *Press Cuttings Book, 1876-1900*.
31. R.I.B.A., W.H. Crossland biographical file, letter from Edward Law, 21 September 1986, and reply.
32. Surrey History Centre, 2620/7/2, *Building Purchase Ledger, St Ann's Heath Asylum*.
33. Crossland, p. 144.

as, in planning the trip to Cambridge, he asked Crossland to bring his plans with him to share with the heads of colleges, saying that he knew that Crossland 'can do anything in the way of designing and planning that is necessary'.[34]

The physical appearance of his planned Ladies' University was to serve as its own advertisement and (though unstated) as his memorial, and so it was of critical importance to Holloway. As he wrote to one of his prominent academic advisers: 'I propose that the "Ladies University" at Egham, should be of its kind a grand imposing building that it may not by an insignificant style dishonour its name. – You are aware that nowadays, it is necessary to fill the eye.'[35]

The trip to Cambridge lasted around four weeks, during which time they visited each college several times, and eventually Holloway selected Trinity College as his model. However, since the gate was too large, he chose a smaller one at St Johns as well as items from other colleges to use as models.[36] The design was then 'thoroughly worked-out'.[37] Holloway developed a cold and fever in Cambridge, marking an end to the visit, and they returned home on 29 March. With his recovery, Crossland observed that Holloway seemed to lose interest in the ideas of the female academics who favoured Oxbridge college designs and the intended visit to Oxford never took place. Although the basement plans of the College had already been established, Crossland took the opportunity to persuade his client to return to Renaissance styles for the rest of the building. A suggestion from Millicent Fawcett was retained, however: each student should be provided with two rooms.

One of Holloway's advisors, accountant and politician David Chadwick, Member of Parliament for Macclesfield, had brought to the Oxford Street meeting in early 1875 a Reverend William Hague, one of the trustees of Vassar College in New York State, who happened to be on a visit to England. Vassar College in Poughkeepsie had opened ten years previously and the visitor made a considerable impression on Holloway, who arranged a second meeting before the man's return to America. Holloway subsequently asked George Martin to include an information-gathering visit to Vassar College during his planned visit to America in April of the same year. Vassar College was the only example of the kind of institution that Holloway envisaged. He admired much of what he learned about the American college and went on to take several ideas from it.

---

34. Harrison-Barbet, p. 56.
35. Harrison-Barbet, p. 54.
36. Harrison-Barbet, p. 56.
37. Crossland, p. 144.

Since John Philpot Jones had been responsible for much of the design of the Sanatorium, Crossland had doubtless expected that his partner would shoulder much of the supervision of the construction. His unexpected death at the beginning of June 1874 meant that, when construction on the Sanatorium began again, to the second plan, the entire responsibility for supervision inevitably fell on Crossland. The project demanded ever more of Crossland's time, and he quickly learned that Thomas Holloway was a client with exacting standards who visited the site almost daily and interested himself closely in the development of the building, checking even small details on the large project. Holloway was prepared to spend a great deal of money, but was meticulous in ensuring it was spent carefully, taking 'immense care over the building, personally supervising every detail, both internally and externally'.[38] Crossland recalled at the 1887 R.I.B.A. meeting:

> Mr Holloway, who possessed amongst his other many good traits, one of looking into everything which was going on, and especially into those things which had the appearance of being hidden away, found some dozen men occupied in cutting bricks of an ornamental character, at a cost, as he put it, of twopence or threepence each brick. I happened to be on the ground at the time, and was soon cross-questioned as to whether some other material could not take the place of these ornamental bricks. I suggested Portland stone, which was eagerly adopted, and this change of material necessitated a change in the character of the design. Although the working and detail drawings were all made, they had to be set aside, and, as Mr Holloway would not allow the works either to stop or slow off, I had to make detail [sic] drawings of windows, doorways etc, hap-hazard, and trust to the general effect turning out satisfactorily.[39]

## Bereavements

The fervour of activity was brought to a sudden stop on 26 September 1875 when Holloway's beloved wife, Jane, died suddenly from bronchitis. She was sixty-one and her unexpected death dealt him an enormous blow from which he never really recovered. She had been at his side for nearly four decades, a constant support for a man who scarcely missed a day's work. He remained in deep mourning for about three weeks and stayed at home at Tittenhurst Park, ignoring his business interests and the development

38. Chapel, Jeannie, *Victorian Taste* (London,1982, second impression 1993), p. 10.
39. Crossland, pp. 141-42.

of the Sanatorium. By the end of October, he reluctantly returned to his business affairs and decided that the College should be built as a memorial to Jane. His enthusiasm for detail was gone though, and Crossland assumed an increasing responsibility for the architectural details.

In a tragic parallel, Crossland's own wife, Lavinia, died less than four months after Jane Holloway on 17 January 1876 at Boulogne in France.[40] Her age was given as thirty-seven years and eight months (although she was actually one year older). Her death, at home ('*en son domicile*') was registered at the town hall in Boulogne two days later and a compliant transcript produced (as was normal practice) in April of the same year. The registration was made not by Crossland, but by a businessman named Edmond (or Edward) Noakes and Jean-Baptiste Gallet, a teacher. This suggests that Crossland was not with his wife at the time of her death. Indeed, the report implies that Lavinia Crossland was living ('*demeurant*') in Boulogne, rather than simply on holiday. The circumstances of her being in France without him are unknown, and her relationship to the men registering her death is not given, although, with some lack of clarity, her death notification suggests that one of them was related ('*un parent*'). That she was married to Crossland is, however, made quite clear ('*épouse de William Henry Crossland, Architecte*'). Certainly, Crossland's workload would have made it difficult to spend much time with his family, and Lavinia may have chosen to take an extended break away. The cause of her death is not recorded in the report, and no record has been found of where she was buried in what turned out to be a temporary interment. The intriguing wording on her final grave in London suggests that her initial burial was at Boulogne. (See page 168.)

Crossland and Holloway were doubtless some support for each other in their bereavements, but it was an unequal relationship. Crossland must have felt singularly alone as he faced the supervision of two huge projects in Surrey, without the support of an architect partner that he had felt so necessary and without the personal and private support of his life partner.

Despite personal tragedy for both architect and client, work on the Sanatorium and planning for the College had to continue. By April, Holloway had drafted the Foundation Deed for the College[41], which was to be known as Holloway College. It was to provide the best education available for women of the middle and upper classes, and it was to be largely self-supporting. In the light of his wife's untimely death – and, very likely, also affected by Lavinia Crossland's untimely death – Holloway must

40. www.thegenealogist.co.uk, Recordset RG35. The account of Lavinia Crossland's
    death is handwritten in formal French and parts are difficult to read.
41. Harrison-Barbet, p. 58.

have felt his own mortality and appointed trustees for his planned College: George Martin (husband of Jane Holloway's youngest sister) and Henry Driver (younger brother of Jane Holloway), both generally referred to as Holloway's brothers-in-law, as well as accountant, politician and Member of Parliament, David Chadwick. On 8 May 1876, he conveyed to them the ninety-four acres of land at Mount Lee in Egham.

Following the drawing up of the Deed of Foundation, however, there was a delay of more than three years before building began. The reason for the delay is not known, but Jane Holloway's death took with it much of her husband's energy and enthusiasm. Responsibility for the details he previously managed himself passed to his appointed trustees. Crossland's energy and enthusiasm was doubtless similarly affected by his own wife's death, and he must have welcomed the unexpected extra time to work on his plans and designs for the enormous project, continuing to work on the college plans for a further two years.

Work on the Sanatorium progressed. The large project had got off the ground quickly, the joinery contract having been awarded in July 1875 to W.H. Lascelles, a well-known firm. But, after that, it seems 'progress was apparently slow and he [Holloway] was becoming impatient'.[42]

He was impatient too with Crossland when he asked for more money in October 1876. It seems, however, that he forwarded Crossland £1,000 'on account', telling Crossland that there would be no more money 'until something happens' at the Sanatorium.[43] Crossland acknowledged this advance from the architect's office at the Sanatorium in a letter dated 18 October 1876 and assured Holloway that, following the payment of £1,000, paid on account, he would make no charge for plans etc., nor for payments to his brother, James, and to his assistant, Taylor. He reiterated in the letter that his commission was 5%, including his own travelling expenses and those of people employed by him. He also mentioned in the letter that the concrete foundations of the Sanatorium were then being put in.[44] Crossland must have been relieved and grateful to have received the advance in October 1876, as he made sure 'something happened', managing to have the roof of the Sanatorium in place by August 1877[45], though much internal work remained to be done.

It seems that up until Crossland's request for an advance in 1876, payments to him had been somewhat haphazard, as, at about the same time, Holloway also insisted that financial arrangements with Crossland

42. Harrison-Barbet, p. 60.
43. Harrison-Barbet, p. 60.
44. Royal Holloway Archive, GB131/1/5, letter dated 18 October 1876.
45. Blythman, Guy, *The Holloway Sanatorium* (Egham, 2014), p. 9.

should be properly scheduled. At around this time too, Thomas Holloway seems to have changed his mind with respect to decoration at the Sanatorium. Having originally stated that a plain interior was appropriate for the purpose of the building, he now decided it should be made visually attractive and interesting. Indeed, to make his Sanatorium distinct from other sanatoria, the decoration was to be lavish. It was his view now that the decoration itself could help heal a temporarily damaged mind and that it was important 'above all things to avoid leaving a dimmed intelligence opposite to a blank wall'.[46] Several artists, including students from the South Kensington School of Art, were commissioned to decorate the entrance hall, staircase, great hall and patients' dining room. However, decoration by craftsmen naturally took a considerable time. The decorative scheme was carried out from 1877 into 1878 and seems to have been one factor in the delay in completing the building.

As Holloway began to refocus his energies on the College, it is likely that Crossland, of necessity, probably did the same, beginning to withdraw from close supervision of the Sanatorium once it was structurally complete. With the focus change of both patron and architect, any previous urgency in the project was diminished. With sole supervisory responsibility for the Sanatorium, Crossland must have been relieved that the huge College project had been delayed. Nonetheless, with further large projects in Huddersfield and several smaller projects elsewhere in Yorkshire, Crossland was undoubtedly extremely busy.

## Ruth

At some point during the 1870s, a young woman called Eliza Ruth Hatt came into Crossland's life, although details of where and when they met are not known. This young woman was to play a huge part in Crossland's life in the following years.

It is unknown whether they met while Lavinia was alive or whether they met when Crossland was already a widower and seeking some solace after his wife's untimely death.

Born Eliza Ruth Tilley on 29 January 1853 in Surbiton, she was one of six children. Her father, Mark Tilley, was 'a gentleman's gardener and dairyman', and her mother, Ruth, was a dressmaker. Her childhood home was Battersea, south London, and on 2 December 1869 she married John Benjamin Hatt at Christ Church, Battersea. She was just sixteen and he

46. Surrey History Centre, 2620/6/22, *Holloway Sanatorium, St Ann's Heath, Virginia Water*, pamphlet, apparently written just before the opening of the Sanatorium, unattributed and undated, p. 6.

was twenty-two. Her husband, who was also a dairyman, probably worked with her father and may have been employed by him. Their son, Benjamin Tilley Hatt, was born in Hook, near Kingston, some nine months later towards the end of 1870. Any happiness in their marriage may have been short-lived, though, as at the time of the 1871 census, Eliza was staying with her parents as a visitor, with her son but without her husband. Oddly – and suggesting that her marriage was already over – her four-month-old son was recorded as being the son of the head of household.[47] Crossland may possibly have met her as early as this, when her marriage seems to have already broken down. He called her Ruth and they formed a close relationship.

On 28 August 1877, Ruth gave birth to her second son. The boy was given the name Cecil Henry Crossland Hatt, betraying the fact that Crossland was the child's father. Whether Ruth's husband, John Hatt, knew of the relationship with Crossland and of the birth of Cecil, or whether their marriage had broken down completely by the time of the child's birth is not known. Whatever the circumstances, Crossland's domestic outgoings increased with the birth of his son.

For practical purposes, it seems certain that Ruth's marriage to John Hatt had ended by 1881, as her husband was living near Guildford and working as a porter in the Guildford Union Workhouse.[48] He is unlikely to have seen much, if anything, of his own son, Benjamin, at least from then on. Since divorce at this time was difficult and expensive, working-class people were more likely to decide to live apart and simply allow their lives to go in different directions. No evidence has been found that Ruth and her husband divorced.[49]

Despite earlier assurances that he would not ask for more advances, Crossland ran short of money during the summer of 1877 and requested a further £1,000, on account, on 3 August. He probably asked for the money in a conversation with Holloway, and the experienced businessman asked him to put his request in writing. Crossland's letter is therefore written in the light of an agreement having already been made. In it, he restated the financial arrangements as he understood them regarding his fee: in addition to his 5% commission, he was entitled, he wrote, to +1% for 'the measuring up of the work from time to time making altogether 6%, so that my entire commission on the £127,000 will amount to £7,620'.[50] He acknowledged

---

47. https://ancestryinstitution.com.
48. https://ancestryinstitution.com.
49. Law, Part 3. No decree absolute has been found in the Divorce Registry between 1871 and 1892.
50. Royal Holloway Archive, GB131/1/6, letter dated 3 August 1877.

that the monies he had already received 'inclusive of the sum you advance me today' were £8,500. 'I have been paid by you £880.00 in excess of any commission that is due at the present time.'[51] Crossland understood that this overpayment to him would be transferred to the College account, and the agreement between Crossland and Holloway was recorded in the building account book at the Sanatorium. The account book also showed that he had already received £8,200 with respect to the Sanatorium project and £300 regarding work towards the college building at the Mount Lee Estate.

The advance that Crossland had asked for in 1877 almost certainly related to his private life. It is likely that supporting Ruth and his infant son in addition to renting an expensive home and office and supporting his seventeen-year-old daughter, Maud, was causing Crossland financial difficulties. His request to Holloway for more money probably resulted from trying to support his dependents properly in separate homes. Crossland was grateful to Holloway for bailing him out, and the following day wrote to him with thanks 'for the great favour you have done me that I cannot refrain from adding to it the expression of my deepest gratitude for your great kindness to me in my time of need, which I beg you to accept'.[52]

In December 1877, *Building News* published an illustration of the intended college – essentially the design Crossland had shown to Holloway's eminent advisers in 1875. It clearly showed details – 'dormers from Blois, chimneys from Chambord and turrets from Azay-le-Rideau'[53] – from the Loire châteaux that Crossland had recorded in his sketchbooks, but the College as finally built looked very different. It is likely that changes to the design were made gradually, even after the building had begun, to achieve the design that was finally constructed.

The years 1876 to 1878 were years of great emotional turmoil for Crossland, not only because of the death of his wife at the beginning of 1876 and the birth of his illegitimate son in August 1877. He also suffered the deaths, in quick succession, of two more people close to him – and all at the time when he had to be focused on several projects in Yorkshire, as well as the two enormous Surrey building projects, either of which would have been a considerable challenge for any capable and dedicated architect.

On 22 October 1877, two months after Cecil was born, Crossland's father died at the age of seventy-one. He was buried at Christ Church, Woodhouse, Huddersfield. Crossland's brother, James, was executor of

---

51. Royal Holloway Archive, GB131/1/6, letter dated 3 August 1877.
52. Royal Holloway Archive, GB131/1/7, letter dated 4 August 1877.
53. Williams, Elizabeth, *An Architectural History of Royal Holloway College in Egham, 1874-87*, Surrey Archaeological Collections, volume 77, 1986, p. 100.

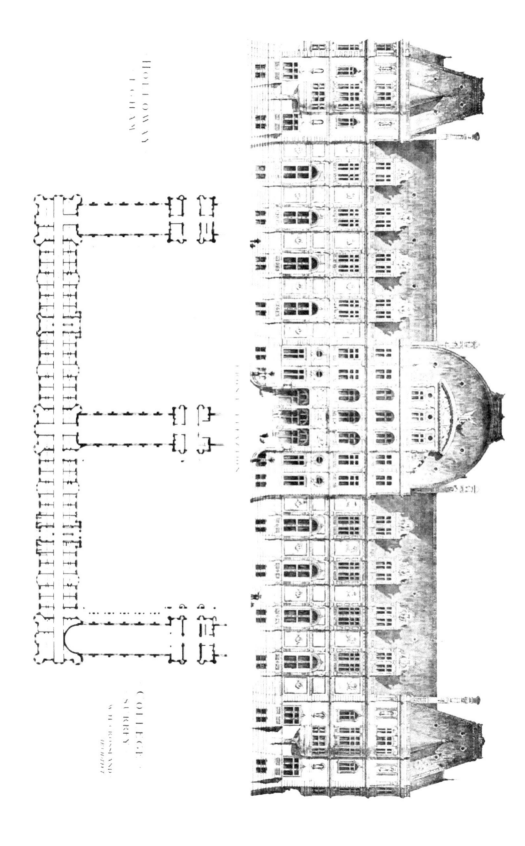

8.3 (opposite) Egham: Holloway College, the original design for the College, Mount Lee, Egham, *Building News*, 21 December 1877. It combined elements sketched at the Louvre, Fontainebleau, Chambord, Blois and Azay-le-Rideau.

their father's will. In naming James executor, their father probably felt that James would have more time to deal with his affairs than his busy younger son. It is possible that he disapproved of the relationship with Ruth and for that reason too may have left responsibility for his affairs to James. In his will, he also left James the family home, Longwood House, Netheroyd Hill, near Huddersfield. Soon afterwards, James returned to Huddersfield, made Longwood House his home and took over running their father's business of stone merchant[54], from which time he probably no longer worked as assistant to his brother. It must have been useful for Crossland, though, to continue to have a base near Huddersfield when working on projects in and around the town since the commissions for the Ramsden Estate continued to come in. The following year, in 1878, Crossland began the Byram Buildings and Arcade in Huddersfield for Sir John Ramsden.

Six months after his father's death, on 27 March 1878, Crossland's master died. It is likely that Sir George Gilbert Scott had been mentor and professional father figure to Crossland ever since his time as pupil in Scott's office in the 1850s, and he probably felt Scott's death almost as keenly as that of his father. Scott's funeral was a grand affair. Queen Victoria sent one of the royal carriages to take part in the funeral procession, and prominent figures were among the pall-bearers, including Charles Barry the younger, then President of the Royal Institute of British Architects, and representatives of institutions such as the Royal Academy, the Ecclesiological Society and the Society of Antiquaries. Crossland probably joined his funeral procession to Westminster Abbey, together with members of the nobility and high-ranking churchmen, as well as other former pupils, assistants and fellow architects. Scott was recognised in a eulogy as the most famous builder of his generation, and Crossland knew it had been his great good fortune to have been trained by such an acclaimed architect, and will have paid his respects in deep sorrow.

It seems that despite enjoying a comfortable income, Crossland was generally short of money. His domestic responsibilities and social aspiration probably required a level of expenditure he could ill afford. In May 1878, he went to Holloway again for money. A letter on 4 May acknowledged previous payments on account and acknowledged a cheque for £300 paid

---

54. https://ancestryinstitution.com.

into his Coutts & Co account 'by way of a loan . . . which I promise to pay when required by you'.[55] In another letter, just over a month later, he thanked Holloway for a further £320, paid into his Coutts & Co account. The letter also carefully detailed both the dates of previous correspondence regarding payments and the total amount received, 'making in all two thousand five hundred pounds that I have received from you on account of my commission at 5%'. There was more than a whiff of distrust here, particularly as Crossland concludes, 'I have taken a copy of these letters.'[56] It suggests that Crossland suspected Holloway would look for reasons to underpay him. It is clear, though, that Crossland's own behaviour in requesting several advances only served to irritate Holloway and to complicate the financial arrangements between his client and himself. A letter from Crossland to Holloway in August of the same year acknowledged a further £300 on account and stated that he had now been paid £2,810; it showed the same suspicion, again detailing all previous payments, with their dates.[57] It seems that the suspicion rapidly disappeared, though, as a receipt just three days later, which brought Crossland's total payments to £3,000, rather surprisingly added, 'My commission for the same being 5 per cent and no more, which includes extras of every kind and nature.'[58] Over the ensuing years, Crossland receipted his payments from Holloway 'for professional services' personally and in his own hand. In each receipt Crossland was careful to state the total amount he had received from Holloway, although he plainly thought it no longer necessary to review all previous receipts. Added to a receipt of November 1878, he wrote, 'I have no claim whatever upon Mr Holloway for any commission on the Sanatorium, the same having been entirely settled to my satisfaction'[59], suggesting that payment for the original asylum project was complete by then.

Soon after Lavinia's death, and despite all the work on his desk, as an act of personal remembrance, the grieving Crossland designed a memorial sculpture of a mourning angel. He secured the services of Ceccardo Egidio Fucigna (whom he had first met as assistant to John Birnie Philip while working at Akroydon) to carve the statue. Fucigna produced a high-quality marble statue, decorated with swags, scrolls and drapery, and there was an account of it in the journal *The Athenaeum*. In 1877, a cast of the sculpture was exhibited at the Royal Academy. It was displayed with an

---

55. Royal Holloway Archive, GB131/1/8, letter dated 4 May 1878.
56. Royal Holloway Archive, GB131/1/9, letter dated 17 June 1878.
57. Royal Holloway Archive, GB131/1/11, letter dated 23 August 1878.
58. Royal Holloway Archive, GB131/1/12, letter dated 26 August 1878.
59. Royal Holloway Archive, GB131/1/13, letter dated 30 November 1878.

8.4 London, Highgate Cemetery: the Crossland and Monach grave, 1879. The memorial 'Lux Perpetua' was designed by Crossland in memory of his wife and carved by C.E. Fucigna. Lavinia Crossland was the first interment in the grave. Photograph taken in 2014.

accompanying text: '"*Lux Perpetua*": part of a monument to the late Mrs W.H. Crossland – C.E. Fucigna.'[60] The statue was not given a home until nearly two years later on 19 May 1879, when Crossland, with his father-in-law, Robert Monach, purchased a large plot in Highgate Cemetery, at the cost of thirty guineas.[61] Theirs was a larger burial space than the average plot and was to be the Crossland and Monach family vault. The joint ownership was recorded on the kerb of the tomb they had made, describing it as the family vault of Robert Monach and W.H. Crossland. Crossland arranged for Lavinia to be reinterred at around the same time, the first of several interments in the family vault. Some of the dedication is now illegible, but it makes clear that his wife died in France about three years earlier. The

60. https://www.myheritage.com/research/record-90100-441655148/notices-and-critiques-on-the-paintings-in-the-royal-academy (accessed 20 November 2016).
61. Law, Part 3.

dedication is simple and unemotional: 'In memory of Lavinia Cardwell wife of William Henry Crossland F.R.I.B.A. of London Born 27 May 1837 Died 17 January 1876 . . .ed from Boulogne . . .er'.[62]

An engraving of the monument was published in *The Builder* in February 1882, with a commentary:

> MONUMENT IN HIGHGATE CEMETERY
> This monument was executed in London by Signor Fucigna for Mr. W.H. Crossland, architect, in memory of his late wife. It is executed in Sicilian marble on a red granite plinth, the whole resting on a landing of blue granite. The figure is rather larger than life, and a cast of it was exhibited at the Royal Academy. The architectural portion of the monument was designed by Mr. Crossland.[63]

---

62. Some of the inscription on the tomb is now illegible.
63. *The Builder*, 4 February 1882, p. 129.

# Chapter 9

# The Egham office

9.1 Egham: Holloway College, the silver trowel designed for the ceremonial laying of the first brick of Holloway College. It includes Crossland's name as well as that of the patron and the builder. Photograph taken in 2016.

On 30 July 1879, the building contract for the College was agreed with Messrs Thompson of Peterborough, a firm with considerable relevant experience from working on Glasgow University and Selwyn College, Cambridge. Mr John Thompson undertook to complete the building in four years from the signing of the contract at the cost of £257,000 (exclusive of fittings and furniture), on which Crossland was to be paid a commission of 5% (£12,850)[1], to include all his expenses. The contract did not include several essential works, including the engine house and underground tunnel to the college building, terracing and the lodges. Nonetheless, it was an enormous fee, and Crossland would have expected further small fees for the additional works. Thomas Holloway's health did not allow him to attend the start of the building of the college, so the first brick was laid by George Martin on 12 September 1879, accompanied by considerable ceremony. The occasion was commemorated with a silver bricklaying trowel, engraved with the names of the patron, the architect and the builder.

Crossland had begun the huge project earlier that year by building a bungalow for himself on the Mount Lee estate. This small home was the only home Crossland ever built for himself. Bungalows were a new type of

1. Chapel, Jeannie, *Victorian Taste* (London, 1982, second impression 1993), p. 11.

dwelling at the end of the 1870s: the style, often complete with a veranda, was a development of the type of home that those in the colonial service had built for themselves in India, and they were to become popular in England from the end of the nineteenth century. That Crossland chose to build his home on the Mount Lee site in this style demonstrates that he was abreast of new trends in domestic architecture, and it was one of the first bungalows built in Britain. As well as the brick-built bungalow, a wooden drawing office was also built for the Architect's Department, 'where the clerks and draftsmen made plans and worked out in detail every bit of ornament, plan and elevation'.[2]

9.2 Egham: Holloway College, Crossland's bungalow on the Mount Lee estate, 1878. This photograph was taken in about 1895, the year after Crossland finally relinquished the bungalow. It shows a mature and homely building with a veranda, the supports of which are covered in climbing roses. It was surrounded by a luxuriant garden.

Crossland moved his office from London to Egham in 1879, solely to be permanently on the site of the huge college project to which he was committed. 'It was Mr Holloway's express wish that Mr Crossland should be on the spot at all times to supervise the progress of the building'[3], even though a site agent, George Grey, was also employed by Holloway. The bungalow was to serve as both his home and his office and allowed him to supervise the construction of the college at close quarters. It became the 'Architect's Department, The Holloway College, Mount Lee, Egham, Surrey', as his own professional notepaper made clear. For how long after moving to the bungalow Crossland was to maintain his Carlton Chambers office in Regent Street is unknown, but Holloway's insistence that he lived on the College site, quite apart from the cost of running two offices in tandem, suggests it was not for long.

From the laying of the first brick of the College in 1879, construction progressed quickly. It is likely that building began with the pavilions at each corner of the building with the long façades between them added once the pavilions had taken shape.[4] Dates marked on bricks in the fifth-floor dormer

2.  Powell, M.J., ed., *The Royal Holloway College 1887-1937* (Royal Holloway College, 1937), p. 17.
3.  Powell, p. 17.
4.  Williams, Richard, *Thomas Holloway's College, The First 125 Years* (Egham, 2012), p. 12.

gables on both the east and the west sides of the building make it clear that the skyline was in place by the end of 1881[5], and building journals at that time were reporting that the building was nearing completion.[6] Plasterwork in the library and museum was begun in late 1882, and, according to several contemporary accounts, the building was ready in 1883, well within the stipulated time of four years.[7] There was, though, a delay of around three years in opening the College, for which there is no clear explanation.

The fast growth of the building was made possible by an enormous workforce that had been recruited. At the busiest period of construction, Crossland was overseeing up to 900 workmen, recruited from as far away as Birmingham, including stonemasons, bricklayers, carpenters and several other trades that were on the site. Their workshops and sheds stretched the length of the site along the Great Western Road[8], and the scale of Crossland's responsibility was of a size rarely assumed by an architect. Extensive plant and machinery were employed on the site enabling, among other processes, the cutting of mouldings 'by machinery of the most ingenious kind'.[9]

Obtaining materials for the site was laborious, as they had to be hauled from the station at Egham to the College construction site. 'The contractor brings all his materials on the ground by traction engines, two of which he has constantly at work between the railway station at Egham and the site, which are about a mile apart.'[10] Holloway tried hard to establish a private railway station to enable materials to be brought into the site by rail, but Lord Field of adjacent Bakeham House would not sell the land between the College site and the railway. Had Holloway been able to purchase, the arrangements for services to the College would have been rather different:

> He would have made a private railway station there with all the additions of sidings and goods sheds and the engine house, boiler house, electrical department and carpenter's shop would have been there. The expense of cartage would have been saved and there would have been a depot for stores upon the College estate immediately adjoining the railway with its own branch tracks.[11]

5. Williams, R., p. 10.
6. Williams, Elizabeth, 'An Architectural History of Royal Holloway College in Egham, 1874-87', *Surrey Archaeological Collections*, volume 77, 1986, p. 100.
7. Williams, E., p. 100.
8. Williams, R., p. 10. The Great Western Road became the present A30.
9. Royal Holloway Archive, RF126/1, Scrapbook, *Builder's Weekly Reporter*, London, 16 September 1881.
10. Royal Holloway Archive, RF126/1, Scrapbook, *Builder's Weekly Reporter*, London, 16 September 1881.
11. Powell, p. 17.

In 1880, some twelve months after the building in Egham began, Crossland had to find and appoint a sculptor for the project. He returned to Ceccardo Egidio Fucigna, by this time a well-established sculptor, whom he had first met on the Akroydon project in the late 1850s and who had carved the statue for the Crossland and Monach vault at Highgate Cemetery. As he was to relate to the R.I.B.A. meeting some seven years later:

> I was fortunate enough to secure the services of the late Mr Fucigna, who had been engaged with the late Birnie Philip on the half of the podium of the Prince Consort's Memorial, under my old master Sir Gilbert Scott. He proved himself, in every respect, to be the man of all others the best suited to my requirements. Clever, unambitious, devoted to his art, willing to live, like myself, on the works, and to give the whole of his time to them. He was a member of the Academy of Ferrara, and had studied Renaissance art in Florence and Rome. No comment of mine is needed to show the stamp of his ability, and when I add that his modesty was equal to his talent, it will be understood that I had secured an able coadjutor.[12]

Fucigna had also worked with William Burges at Castell Coch outside Cardiff so was well acquainted with flamboyant artistic decoration. In 1875, on the death of his master, he had taken over John Birnie Philip's studio.

## Complex personal lives

Holloway's requirement that Crossland lived on the College site, probably rent-free, was to have benefits for Crossland. The Egham bungalow provided a home where he and Ruth could live quietly together. It is not known for how long after Lavinia's death Crossland retained his opulent home near Regents Park, but there is no record of him living at any other address until he moved to the Egham bungalow. By the time of his daughter Maud's marriage in 1880, Maud was living elsewhere. Her address on the marriage certificate was 82 Charlotte Street, which, so far as is known, was never one of Crossland's addresses. It may have been a lodging house for single middle-class women. What seems certain is that, even as a young unmarried woman, she was no longer living with her father and therefore the tenancy of 12 Park Village West had almost certainly been relinquished well before this time.

Maud was nineteen when she married and she married well. Her husband, William Stanton Lart, a young architect with an Oxford degree, was her senior

12. Crossland, W.H., *The Royal Holloway College*, R.I.B.A. Transactions, Second series, Vol 3, 1886-87, p. 145.

by nine years. Their marriage took place on 20 May 1880 at the Parish Church of St John, Fitzroy Square, London. Her husband's father was described as 'a gentlemen', whose home was 1 Langham Place, a prestigious address in Westminster. It seems that Maud and William went to live in Windsor, as their daughter Dorothea Maud Lart was born there in December 1881.

By 1881, Crossland was spending most of his time on the College, supervising from his bungalow and the drawing office opposite. The census on 3 April 1881 recorded him living at the bungalow with two female servants, a female visitor and his wife, Elizabeth R. Crossland.[13] Despite the error in her first name, this was clearly Ruth, who was evidently by this time living with him as his wife. It is unlikely that they were married, even though both Crossland and Ruth were described as 'married' in the census (more correctly, he was a widower and she was married, but to someone else), and Crossland is included on the Tilley family tree as 'spouse' of Eliza Ruth Tilley. By this time, Ruth had probably been separated from her husband for some time, but would have known or assumed that he was still alive, making marriage to Crossland impossible without a difficult and expensive divorce. Crossland undoubtedly regarded her as his wife and she became known as his wife at the College site where she was certainly referred to as Mrs W.H. Crossland and where she took a full part in life there. An early history of the College states that she 'became very popular in the neighbourhood. The Garden Parties given by Mrs Crossland at the Bungalow were a feature of the summer season.'[14]

Surprisingly, their four-year-old son, Cecil, was not with them at the time of the 1881 census. Whether they kept him away from the site for reasons of safety or for reasons of propriety is not known. Cecil was, at that time, living with his maternal grandmother together with his elder half-brother Benjamin and an uncle at 61 Trinity Square in Margate, Kent. This address was a lodging house, the other occupants noted in the census being the lodging house keeper, a woman named Elizabeth Main, and her daughter and grandson.[15] It seems that Cecil's time in Margate was more than a short stay, as a few days before the census, on 27 March 1881, he had been baptised there. Inexplicably, on the baptism register, as well as the baby Cecil and his mother, Ruth, the only other household member mentioned was Ruth's husband, John Benjamin Hatt, from whom she was seemingly estranged and who was certainly not the child's father. The census details of a few days later record John Hatt as working in Guildford, some ninety-five miles away, while Ruth was with Crossland in Egham.[16]

---

13. https://ancestryinstitution.com.
14. Powell, p. 17.
15. https://ancestryinstitution.com.
16. https://ancestryinstitution.com.

In the absence of any more information, one can only speculate on the actual situation. It seems more than possible that Ruth was trying to create a record of a legitimate birth for her second son and that she invented some explanation for the child's father not being present at the baptism. It is hard to imagine that, had John Hatt attended the baptism, he would have agreed to a fabrication that named him the father of another man's child, particularly when one of the child's names was that of his true father.

Whatever the reason, it seems clear that Crossland set up home on the College site with Ruth, but without either Benjamin or Cecil, who lived in Margate, where they were cared for by Ruth's mother. Ruth could have visited relatively easily by train, and it would have been convenient to sometimes use her mother's address as her own, as at the time of Cecil's baptism.

## Work on the Sanatorium

During 1881, while Crossland was supervising work on the College from his bungalow, he was commissioned to design a chapel for the Sanatorium. Thomas Holloway distrusted formalised religion, although he undoubtedly had his own faith, as made clear by his instructions with respect to religious teaching at the College, which was to be: 'such as to impress most forcibly in the minds of the students their individual responsibility and their duty to God . . . [as he had] . . . witnessed the hand of God in all things'.[17]

As at the College, Holloway had stipulated that the Sanatorium should be non-denominational. He had also stated that there should be no chapel or chaplain at the Sanatorium, even though a chapel was a legal requirement for such an institution. His intention was that any religious observance would take place in the hall.[18] It appears, though, that he bowed to the requirements of the Commissioners in Lunacy by agreeing, late in the planning, to have a chapel added as a separate building.

Engrossed as he was in the huge College development, Crossland somehow found time to visit several Oxford college chapels with George Martin for inspiration in developing the design for the chapel[19], resulting in a design that was in 'a more diluted gothic style'[20] than the main building, reflecting Crossland's later architectural style and taste.[21] It seems Crossland

17. Harrison-Barbet, Anthony, *Thomas Holloway: Victorian Philanthropist* (Lyfrow Trelyspen, Cornwall, 1990, revised 1993, Egham, 1994), p. 92.
18. Saint, Andrew and Richard Holder, 'Holloway Sanatorium: A Conservation Nightmare' in *The Victorian Society Annual*, 1993, p. 22.
19. Surrey History Centre, 2620/7/2, *Building Purchase Ledger for St Ann's Heath Asylum*, p. 17.
20. Jeannie, Chapel, Victorian Society notes for the Society's visit, 1980, p. 3.
21. Saint and Holder, p. 22.

was asked to design little more than the basic building, though at a cost of £12,500 (on which Crossland was paid 5% plus £50 for the plans, making £675 in total).[22] It was built between 1882 and 1884 by John Thompson, the contractor for the College building. The high budget meant it was a finer building than most of Crossland's church commissions in Yorkshire. It was reported as 'barely finished' when the Sanatorium was opened the following year, and there was still no proper arrangement for services as late as 1887[23], suggesting that, despite complying with the requirements of the Commissioners in Lunacy, neither Holloway himself nor his trustees had much enthusiasm for the chapel.

While the afterthought chapel was being constructed, starting in 1882, work on the main Sanatorium building continued. The internal decoration was well advanced by this time, prompting a comment in *The Builder* that the building would open soon and that 'such a combination of rich colouring and gilding is not to be found in any modern building in this country, except in the House of Lords'.[24] As it turned out, there was much still to do before the Sanatorium opened for its first patients. Meanwhile, independently of those employed to carry out the decoration[25], Holloway himself had commissioned life-sized portraits of several famous historical figures to hang in the Great Hall.

## *Parallel projects*

Building at the College continued at a breath-taking pace in parallel to work on the Sanatorium – and, indeed, in parallel to Crossland's work in Huddersfield. Both Surrey buildings were constructed in red brick, which was readily available locally. Most of the bricks for the College as well as the Sanatorium came from the Lawrence Brickfield in Bracknell, although some were sourced from elsewhere. The bricks for the College were brought directly from the brickfield itself to Egham Station, from where they were transported up the hill. This was labour-intensive and Holloway must have much regretted being thwarted in buying the land below the Mount Lee Estate, where he had hoped to install his own private rail sidings for the huge College construction project. In all, some 7.5 million bricks were brought to Egham for the College. The Sanatorium took around 5 million bricks, and by the end of the two huge projects, the Lawrence Brickfield in

---

22. Surrey History Centre, 2620/7/2, *Building Purchase Ledger for St Ann's Heath Asylum*, p. 187.
23. Saint and Holder, p. 25.
24. Quoted in Chapel, *Victorian Taste*, p. 10.
25. Saint and Holder, p. 22.

Bracknell was virtually worked out. Sand came from a sandpit in the nearby village of Englefield Green, requiring less than a mile of transportation. So great was the demand for sand in the building of the College that, by the time it was completed, the sandpit was also virtually worked out.[26]

The major advantage of Crossland living on-site at Mount Lee, as Thomas Holloway well understood from the outset, was that he could supervise and control all aspects of the construction of the College closely and continuously. So, when bricks were delivered to the site, he ensured that they were separated into top quality and inferior quality. The top quality only went for the construction of the College building and the rest were used to build the mile-long perimeter wall.[27] Any difficulties with payments to Crossland during the building of the Sanatorium seem to have been resolved for the building of the College and Crossland received regular payments, which were often receipted with the addition of a friendly 'with compliments and best thanks'.[28]

By 1882, with deteriorating health, Thomas Holloway had passed responsibility for overall supervision of both the Sanatorium and the College projects to his brother-in-law, George Martin, and Crossland himself assumed a much greater responsibility for the details of both projects. The Sanatorium building was completed during 1882, and there was an expectation that the first patients would be welcomed in the autumn of that year.[29] However, the opening was delayed for a considerable while. Nonetheless, Holloway's two buildings had aroused great interest, and a visit to both was made in June by the Architectural Association. With Holloway indisposed, Crossland hosted the visit, which was reported at length in *The Builder*. Of the Sanatorium, the journal wrote:

> The Sanatorium, as Mr Crossland pointed out, consists mainly of what are really two terraces of houses, one terrace on either side of the Recreation Hall. Each house is arranged for a family or household of ten persons, besides attendants, and communications between the houses will only be by pass-doors for convenience of supervision. The stairs are arranged in short flights, and without well-holes, for obvious reasons.[30]

Ruth assisted in hosting the visit. After inspecting both buildings, 'the members sat down to an excellent cold collation in a tent tastefully

---

26. Williams, Richard, lecture, Thorpe Village Hall, Surrey, 24 October 2016.
27. Williams, Richard, lecture, 24 October 2016.
28. Royal Holloway Archive, GB131/1/19, example letter dated 25 September 1883.
29. Whitaker, pp. 200-01.
30. *The Builder*, 10 June 1882, p. 719.

decorated and arranged under the especial supervision of Mrs Crossland'.[31] It is apparent, therefore, that by this time Ruth was playing a full role as Crossland's wife on the College site.

Aware of his failing health, Holloway arranged for the execution of the Foundation Deed of the College on 11 October 1883, which formalised his wishes regarding the kind of institution his college was to be. He also recorded credit to his wife, Jane, with the words, 'The College is founded by the advice and counsel of the Founder's dear Wife, now deceased.'[32]

9.3 (top) Egham: Holloway College, plan for semi-detached cottages, 1883. Crossland turned the plan for the right-hand cottage into a detached dwelling for the lodge at the main entrance to the College.

9.4 (bottom) Egham: Royal Holloway College. The lodge at the main entrance to Royal Holloway, University of London was derived from Crossland's plan of 1883 for semi-detached cottages. Photograph taken in 2016.

He specified that the College should be non-denominational, but that it should be run as an orderly Christian household, and he wished the education provided to reflect the most advanced contemporary educational values. Just five years after London University had opened its degrees to women, his most aspirational desire was that his College should be able to confer degrees – a wish he did not live to see fulfilled.

Holloway had now put in place all the measures for his institutions to function as he intended, even if he was unable to continue to manage the projects himself. The work was not complete, though, and practical details still had to be addressed. So, during November 1883, Crossland and Holloway considered auxiliary works to the College, including a lodge for the main gates of the College. Crossland produced designs for a number of cottages, one of which was chosen for the lodge.[33]

A particular issue in completing the project was the terracing at the southern end of the college site.

31. *The Builder*, 10 June 1882, p. 719.
32. Bingham, Caroline, *The History of Royal Holloway College 1886-1896* (London, 1987), p. 35.
33. Royal Holloway Archive, RHC AR/511/3, ground plan of cottages, 1883.

Crossland had prepared a model for Holloway's consideration, with a central flight of steps leading down from the college building. Holloway's response was to leave out the central steps and there followed from Crossland a long, deferential, but cleverly persuasive letter to Holloway, encouraging him to change his mind. The problem with which Crossland was grappling was the steep slope on which the College was built, and he asked Holloway to reconsider his scheme: 'considering the great depth we have to deal with [it] appears to me the only one possible'.[34] He asked Thomas Holloway to recall the châteaux in France 'which we have made our model for this building where similar treatment of Terrace walls to the one I have shown almost is universal, even where the grounds were more confined and the view less beautiful'.[35] He pointed out that it 'adds to the palatial appearance' of the château. He continued in a markedly subservient tone:

> I offer these few remarks, Sir, not as desiring to oppose your views but as suggestions which I hope you will deem worthy of consideration. Furthermore I would desire to say that the other Terrace design will form a very noble addition to the building although it may not be so strictly in character with the style of it. I hope you may not find my letter tedious but should you do so, pray excuse it on the grounds of my great desire that such a commanding terrace as this will be should be worthy of the magnificent view which it will command.[36]

It seems that Crossland's persuasive attempt to change Holloway's mind fell on deaf ears, as central steps were not included in the final scheme. Instead, and surely more expensively, steps at the two corners of the terrace were constructed.

## Work in Yorkshire

Even while Crossland was supervising work on the Sanatorium and engaged on the work for the College at Mount Lee, remarkably, he continued to honour clients in Yorkshire. Although only a few years old, his church in Sheffield, St Marks, Broomhill, was closed for some weeks in 1878 for cleaning, painting and decoration. At the time, it was described as 'one of the plainest and yet neatest churches in the town' with an 'almost total absence of colour' and the only decoration in the carved reredos.

---

34. Royal Holloway Archive, GB131/52/2, letter dated 16 November 1883.
35. Royal Holloway Archive, GB131/52/2, letter dated 16 November 1883.
36. Royal Holloway Archive, GB131/52/2, letter dated 16 November 1883.

The congregation wanted something to make their church distinctive. In particular, they wished to have the chancel decorated to distinguish it from the rest of the church. Crossland, 'of London', as the architect of the church, was asked to provide a design, and he duly obliged, presenting the congregation with 'a most elaborate design', which was executed by J. & J. Rodgers of King Street, Sheffield. The local newspaper reported on the reopening of the church on Sunday 29 September 1878 with the comment: 'The work has been most faithfully and ably carried out, and the effect so far as the chancel is concerned is brilliant and imposing.'[37]

Crossland also received a call for help from Rochdale. Dry rot had been discovered in the wooden spire of Rochdale Town Hall and the Town Council wrote to Crossland about it. In a letter dated 3 March 1883, from 'The Holloway College, Mount Lee, Egham, Surrey', he agreed to superintend the restoration of the spire by visiting the work when required to do so. Although the development of dry rot can hardly have been his fault, he was prepared to do this for no fee, charging expenses (rail fares and out of pocket expenses) only. Circumstances changed, however, as the spire of the Town Hall was destroyed by fire on 10 April 1883, while work was in progress to remove the spire timbers affected by dry rot. Crossland's exceptionally tall tower had never been particularly popular in the town, so it seems that its destruction provided the opportunity for a change. The town council of Rochdale must have thought better of asking Crossland to design a brand new tower since he was now so preoccupied elsewhere. Some while later, Alfred Waterhouse was commissioned to do this and his tower was duly built.[38]

Even more remarkably, while engaged on the two huge projects in Surrey, Crossland took on further projects for Sir John Ramsden in Huddersfield. Sir John must have been pleased with his architect (Crossland was known as architect to the Ramsden Estate), as a series of commissions followed, developing the area between the Estate Offices and the parish church, including the Byram Building site. Over 200 miles away from Huddersfield, Crossland was, however, fully occupied (at least in Thomas Holloway's eyes) with the two large buildings in Surrey. This meant that A.J. Taylor, his long-time assistant in Huddersfield and Richard Phillips, the clerk of works at the Ramsden Estate Buildings were critical to the success of the new projects in Huddersfield.

From around 1877, Taylor had begun working out of the Ramsden Estate Buildings in Huddersfield, managing Crossland's projects for the Ramsden Estate. A local office in a fine building of Crossland's own

---

37. *The Sheffield & Rotherham Independent*, 30 September 1878, Issue 7497, p. 3.
38. Sharples, Joseph, *Rochdale Town Hall: An Illustrated Guide*, Rochdale Metropolitan Borough Council, undated, p. 4.

design was a perfect advertisement for Crossland, and an assistant with Taylor's experience provided a manageable solution for the busy Crossland. However, despite the several commissions from the Ramsden estate, it seems that the volume of work Taylor now had for Crossland in Yorkshire was no longer a full-time job. Under 'Business Services' among the classified advertisements, Taylor advertised his services in February 1877 and several more times through to late March, plainly looking for more work: 'A.J. Taylor, Building Surveyor, for ten years the Chief Assistant of W.H. Crossland Esq., architect. 27 Estate Buildings, Huddersfield.'[39]

Clearly, Crossland's reputation in the Huddersfield area was an asset for Taylor to exploit, and he believed using Crossland's name and making mention of their long-standing collaboration in his advertisement provided an enhancement to his own standing. Equally, though, Crossland depended on Taylor. Without Taylor working on Crossland's behalf in his office in the Estate Buildings, Crossland could not have managed his Huddersfield projects from London.

The first new project for Sir John Ramsden was the design of the arcade, which became known as the Byram Arcade (see page 134), which had probably been commissioned two years earlier. It was to be designed around the earlier Byram Building, effectively encasing it and creating one larger building with a range of facilities. There had been, though, a delay in beginning this project until later-commissioned projects were begun.

These later commissions were three more building projects for the Ramsden Estate, which would complete the development of the large area between the Estate Buildings in Railway Street and the Parish Church at the junction of Byram Street and Kirkgate. The Bulstrode Building (later known as Kirkgate Building), may have been commissioned as early as 1878, but construction seems to have been delayed because of issues regarding compensation for the buildings that had to be demolished for the construction. Compensation to the value of £27,635 was paid to those whose homes and premises were demolished for the Kirkgate project.[40]

In respect of these projects, Crossland advertised in 1879. In *The Huddersfield Chronicle and West Yorkshire Advertiser*, he sought tenders 'for all or any of the trades in the erection of shops, offices and warehouses, in continuation of new buildings now in course of erection in Byram Street and Kirkgate, Huddersfield, for Sir John William Ramsden, Bart'.[41] The signature

---

39. *The Huddersfield Chronicle and West Yorkshire Advertiser*, 24 February 1877, Issue 2981 (and subsequent editions).
40. Law, Part 6.
41. *The Huddersfield Chronicle and West Yorkshire Advertiser*, 11 October 1879, Issue 3802.

on the advertisement indicated that Crossland was in London, but it was at Taylor's office in Huddersfield that drawings and specifications were to be made available and from whom quantities could be obtained between 18 and 27 October 1879. On this latter date, sealed tenders were to be submitted to Crossland at 27 Estate Buildings, indicating that he viewed Taylor's premises in the Ramsden Estate Building also as his own office. At the same time as the call for contractors for the Kirkgate development, Crossland also sought revised tenders for the earlier-commissioned Byram Arcade in Westgate.

Crossland's location was given in the advertisement as 'London SW', which seems to have referred to his Egham office since he is not known to have had an office in south-west London. He may well have wanted to keep from Sir John Ramsden the fact that he was actually living on the site of his huge project for another patron, and, significantly perhaps, and certainly unusually, the advertisement gave no office address. Both his home and office postal addresses at the time were The Bungalow on the Mount Lee Estate. There seems no doubt that he supervised these projects for the Ramsden Estate for the most part from the bungalow on the College site, corresponding with his assistant, A.J. Taylor, and leaving much day-to-day management in his hands.

Crossland also corresponded and negotiated with Isaac Hordern, Sir John Ramsden's cashier in Huddersfield, over the construction of the buildings in the Kirkgate area. Although not qualified, Hordern had considerable architectural ability, and in Crossland's absence in Surrey, he sought to influence the planning of the Kirkgate buildings. He sent several suggestions to Crossland, often accompanied by a small sketch.[42] Hordern had considerable confidence in his own ability, and his ideas often prevailed, but these architectural interventions by an unqualified person irritated Crossland, and he sometimes needed to remind Hordern that he, Crossland, was the architect:

18 Nov 1878
Dear Hordern,
Kirkgate Buildings
I have considered your notes on this plan and so far as I think them desirable I shall embody them in my amended plans.
   You appear to forget that the staircase being double have apparently a greater width than a single one has. I think four feet enough.
   Yours always,
   W.H. Crossland[43]

42. West Yorkshire Archive Service Kirklees, DD/RE/48, Ramsden Estate papers, 1876.
43. Law, Part 7.

It seems Hordern was undeterred, and in February 1879, he was still making notes regarding the Kirkgate buildings 'on looking over the tracings sent down by Mr Crossland'.[44] He also drew up and signed his own scheme for the Byram Arcade. It seems that, overall, Hordern succeeded in having considerable influence over the Kirkgate buildings. He was anxious that Huddersfield should be perceived to be in the vanguard of architectural taste, and he sought to ensure that the styling of these buildings moved away from the Gothic of the Estate Buildings towards the Renaissance and Queen Anne revival styling that was becoming popular. Plainly, this suited the busy Crossland well, as he was able to reduce his creative workload by applying to the Huddersfield buildings motifs developed for the Sanatorium and the College.

The Bulstrode Building, the Somerset Building, Waverley Chambers and the Byram Arcade on the Kirkgate site were similarly styled and constructed more or less in parallel, beginning around 1881. They are particularly striking buildings in a prominent position and, as a group, make a strong and confident architectural statement. They were built of sandstone ashlar with slate roofs, and Crossland gave them eye-catching details, particularly at roof level. These included high ornate chimneys, tall sash windows, steeply pedimented dormer windows and much decoration. The sculptural work was of a particularly high standard benefitting from Crossland's appointment of the sculptor Fucigna to the College project in Egham. Fucigna produced the sculptural designs for all four buildings including classical Greek motifs, as well as references to the Ramsden family and Huddersfield's industry, particularly the textile trade.[45] The carving was carried out by local sculptor Samuel Auty, working from Fucigna's models. The resulting decorative detail was more and of a much higher quality than that found generally on commercial buildings at the time and doubtless therefore cost more than comparable buildings. There was some annoyance on part of Sir John Ramsden that Crossland allowed cost increases on several occasions[46], but overall he was pleased with Crossland's significant contribution to the dramatic improvement of the centre of Huddersfield.

The Byram Arcade, enclosing the Byram Building, was completed first, probably late in 1881. Tall and galleried, it blended well with the Estate Buildings, as did the other three similarly styled buildings. The central space of the Byram Arcade was covered by a rectangular pitched glazed roof supported by an iron frame between the second and third floors. Most

---

44. West Yorkshire Archive Service Kirklees, DD/RE/48, Ramsden Estate papers, 1876.
45. West Yorkshire Archaeology Advisory Service, WYHER/12845, Waverley Chambers.
46. Law, Part 7.

of the units opened onto the galleries around the central light well. The awkward shape of the site challenged Crossland as did its slope, which had a difference in height of six feet across the 100-feet-wide façade[47], and was possibly a cause of the delay in beginning the project. Crossland managed to conceal the slope with the shop display windows becoming gradually taller towards the east. The arcade itself, though, was somewhat cramped, lacking the grandeur of arcades of the same period in other towns and giving shoppers little space in which to browse. The stonework of the building, as of all four buildings, was of high quality. The crow-stepped gable was reminiscent of both Rochdale Town Hall and of the Sanatorium in Surrey that was being built at the same time. The four-centred entrance arch to the arcade spanned the frontage of one commercial unit and a spacious entrance passage hid the arcade inside. Across the entrance Crossland placed a heraldic design incorporating a lion and a griffon, with the Ramsden coat of arms and a scroll declaring the name of the arcade.[48]

The Somerset Building at 10 Church Street was built as an office and retail development with shops on the ground floor and offices on the upper floors. Waverley Chambers was located at 5-9 Kirkgate and 1 Wood Street, a prominent corner location by the Market Place, on Kirkgate. The building was designed as a three-storey hotel with a basement and an attic, ground floor retail units and a small yard at the back.[49] Waverley Chambers took its name from Sir Walter Scott's Waverley novels and was used as a temperance hotel. Both buildings were completed in 1883.

The Bulstrode Building was a larger building, opposite the ancient parish church, on the corner of Byram Street and Kirkgate, a major thoroughfare through the town centre. It occupied an entire town-centre block, with Wood Street to the west and Church Street to the north, and provided ground-floor retail units on the inside as well as the outside. The main entrances were at the Kirkgate and Church Street ends, with an additional entrance on the east side. Wide staircases from Kirkgate and Church Street led to the first floor, where there was a covered arcade with large rooms each side for offices or warehousing. The upper floor comprised a balcony with gangway bridges and was also intended for offices or warehousing. Completed by 1885, the Bulstrode Building was the last of the group to be finished.

There were similarities in the interiors of all four of these buildings. Crossland developed the glazed roof plan of the arcade, bringing light into both the Bulstrode and Somerset buildings with a central glazed atrium, and in both buildings he arranged offices on the upper floors around the space

47. Whitaker, p. 177.
48. Whitaker, pp. 173-78.
49. West Yorkshire Archaeology Advisory Service, WYHER/12845, Waverley Chambers.

9.5 (above) Huddersfield: the Byram Arcade, 1881. The Ramsden arms were placed over the entrance. Photograph taken in 2017.

9.6 (below, left) Huddersfield: the Byram arcade, 1881. The interior was somewhat cramped and lacked the grandeur of arcades of the same period in other towns. There was little space for shoppers to browse. Photograph taken in 2015.

9.7 (below, right) Huddersfield: Waverley Chambers, 1883. The three-storey building was used as a temperance hotel. Photograph taken in 2015.

9.8a and 9.8b (top and middle) Huddersfield: the Bulstrode (later Kirkgate) Building, 1885, *The Builder*, 6 January 1883, p. 12 and the same building in 2014. This is the largest of Crossland's four Renaissance and Queen Anne revival style buildings in the centre of Huddersfield.

9.9 (bottom) Huddersfield: the Kirkgate Building, detail. Bullseye windows, keystones carved into heads and an exciting skyline reveal a marked similarity to details on the College in Egham that was being completed at the same time. Photograph taken in 2014.

created under the atrium. His designs combined practicality and a pleasing appearance by means of attractive balustrading to the galleries around the atrium and elegant steel trusses supporting the roof. The addition of scrolled cast-iron balustrades in the Bulstrode Building enhanced the appearance of the two main cantilevered staircases.

Together, these four buildings completed the Ramsdens' redevelopment of the frontage to the New Town. They were the last significant commercial development by the Ramsden Estate in Huddersfield town centre and Crossland's last buildings for the town. Together they constituted a group of Huddersfield's best commercial buildings. The years 1860 to 1890 saw more new building in the centre of Huddersfield than at any other time, much of it on a grand scale, and, among all the new buildings, those by Crossland were particularly important.[50]

## Meanwhile, in Surrey . . .

Meanwhile in Surrey, the College was substantially completed by the end of 1883, and the Sanatorium too was finished, fully furnished, insured and ready to open. To celebrate reaching this momentous point in the protracted Sanatorium project, it was arranged that an engraving of the Sanatorium should appear in the *Illustrated London News* at the beginning of January 1884. All that remained to be done before the Sanatorium could open was the appointment of a medical superintendent and staff. It was therefore a devastating blow for Crossland and for everyone associated with the two projects when, on Boxing Day 1883, the wealthy patron died of congestion of the lungs. He was eighty-three.

Crossland had already become accustomed to Thomas Holloway being a more remote figure. Holloway had lost much of his enthusiasm for work when his wife died in 1875, and instead of his daily scrutinising visits to the Sanatorium construction site, at the College site Crossland became used to Holloway simply driving past. Indeed, he is known to have actually visited the College building site only four times, delegating day-to-day supervision to Crossland and overall control to George Martin. Nonetheless, as the instigator and paymaster of the two grand projects, Holloway had remained central to the development of both. Holloway had planned his succession by making his brothers-in-law George Martin and Henry Driver trustees (and requiring them to add the name of Holloway to their surnames by deed poll) and therefore responsible for the completion of the building schemes in his absence.

50. https://historicengland.org.uk/listing/the-list/list-entry/1415452   (accessed   21 November 2016).

THE HOLLOWAY SANATORIUM FOR MENTAL DISEASE, AT VIRGINIA WATER.

9.10 Virginia Water: Holloway Sanatorium, 1885, engraving, the *Illustrated London News*, 5 January 1884. This was published to celebrate the anticipated imminent opening of the asylum.

There was never any doubt that Crossland would be fully paid, but Holloway's death must have been profoundly distressing for Crossland as he surveyed the two enormous buildings, into which he had put so much of himself, which now had no patron. Although he had always been deferential towards Holloway, they had had a good working relationship. They had spent private time together, especially when gathering inspiration for the college in Touraine, and Holloway was more than satisfied with his architect, as Crossland was proud to recall in his 1887 address to the R.I.B.A.. According to Crossland, Holloway seldom praised anyone but 'on his third visit to the College after its completion, he once again, after six years, patted me on the back and said, "Well done, Mr Crossland, I am more than pleased."'[51] Crossland was also happy to acknowledge that he learned useful business skills from Holloway, recounting to the same R.I.B.A. meeting: 'The late Mr Holloway was a client who sent me to school, a man who (quoting Holloway's own words) "always worked with his head, never with his heart."'[52] Crossland attended Holloway's funeral along with the building contractor, John Thompson, at the Church of St

51. Crossland, p. 148.
52. Crossland, p. 148.

Michael and All Angels at Sunninghill, Berkshire, where Jane Holloway was already buried. Soon afterwards he designed a fine but simple tomb for the Holloways in the eastern section of the churchyard. Two other family members were later also interred there. Holloway's pithy epitaph read 'He, being dead, yet speaketh.'

Crossland recognised that it had been his great good fortune to gain the patronage of Thomas Holloway, who had encouraged him to broaden his architectural knowledge by visiting Touraine and studying the châteaux there. It 'enabled Crossland to soar to the highest levels with his Royal Holloway College'[53], and Crossland probably wondered what a future without Thomas Holloway held for him.

Despite the death of Holloway, work at both sites continued, under the competent and energetic supervision of George Martin-Holloway. He quickly appointed a medical superintendent for the Sanatorium: Dr Sutherland Rees-Phillips, who came from Wonford House Hospital, Exeter. To Crossland and the trustees of the Sanatorium, who all expected it to open imminently, Rees-Phillips brought a shocking revelation in quickly informing Holloway's trustees that the plan of the Sanatorium would be unacceptable to the Commissioners in Lunacy, so the building would never be granted the necessary licence to function as a Sanatorium.

9.11 Sunninghill, Berkshire:
Church of St Michael and All Angels,
the Holloway tomb, designed by Crossland
in 1884, in the eastern section of the
churchyard.
Photograph taken in 2012.

Despite this advice, an application for a licence was made to the Commissioners in Lunacy. As Rees-Phillips had predicted, it was refused. Regulations had changed since the beginning of the construction and new legislation required that all rooms occupied by those with mental illness should open into a corridor from which a staircase should lead directly to the outside of the sanatorium.[54] The alterations made by John Philpot Jones in consultation with Dr Yellowlees of Bridgend Asylum in drafting the second plan meant the residential wings for the patients did not have corridors. Instead, generous

53. Whitaker, p. 249.
54. Crossland, p. 142.

apartment-like suites of rooms were accessed directly from staircases behind them, possibly anticipating that patients would bring their own servants.[55] Crossland explained in his R.I.B.A. address that new Acts of Parliament and new fire regulations had been adopted since the original design: 'Dr Yellowlees and Mr Jones had planned a building on altogether different principles.'[56] The stark reality was that the Sanatorium was obsolete before it had even opened. It was clear alterations had to be made if a licence was ever to be granted.

During 1884, Charles Dorman (1837-1901), architect to St Andrews Hospital, Northampton, was appointed to be architect to the Sanatorium. The influence of Dr Rees-Phillips in this appointment is clear, since he looked to St Andrews Hospital as a model for the modernised Holloway Sanatorium.[57] It is unlikely, though, that Dorman ever went to live in Surrey for anything more than a prolonged stay to supervise work at the Sanatorium.[58] Modest payments to Dorman, of 78 Abingdon Street, Northampton, were entered in the Building Purchase Ledger for the Sanatorium in 1885 and 1886, but with no detail of what they were for.[59] At this time there were no entries for Crossland in the 'General Account'. It seems clear, therefore, that Crossland had little responsibility for the necessary alterations. However, from stylistic similarities to other Crossland buildings (such as the staircases, which are similar to those at Rochdale Town Hall), it is likely that Crossland carried out some new design work, probably without a fee. Charles Dorman then most likely oversaw the implementation of the alterations and structural interior work that was required for licensing, and for which he received much praise. The Annual Report of the Sanatorium for 1886 complimented him: 'for the fertility of resource which overcame most successfully the difficulties in the original construction, which had been pronounced by some asylum experts as irremediable'.[60]

---

55. Blythman, Guy, *The Holloway Sanatorium* (Egham, 2014), p. 12.

56. Crossland, p. 142.

57. Saint and Holder, p. 24.

58. *The Builder*, 7 September 1901, p. 217. Charles Dorman's obituary stated that he had come from Uppingham to Northampton, where he began his business in 1882. Described as a Northampton architect and taking his son into the business in Northampton in the late 1890s, he was responsible for several prominent buildings, especially in Northampton.

59. Surrey History Centre, 2620/7/2, *Building Purchase Ledger for St Ann's Heath Asylum*, p. 78.

60. Egham Museum, The Joy Whitfield Collection, Box 476b, 'Holloway Sanatorium, Annual Report 1886', cited by Andrew Saint in *The Holloway Sanatorium, Virginia Water*, Draft Report, October 1993, p. 7.

Crossland and Dorman met the considerable challenge of restoring corridors and repositioning staircases, returning the design to something similar to Crossland and Jones's original scheme. Alterations were also made to the sanitary arrangements, including the installation of a new system of flush closets and a complete revision of the water system. A new gasworks and other new facilities were installed. Despite Dorman's important contribution at alteration stage, Crossland always regarded the Sanatorium as *his* project. When he visited with the designer Charles Robert Ashbee after completion, he took great pride in it, regarding it as 'his' achievement and did not feel that the design defects that had to be remedied for licencing were his fault.[61]

The smaller buildings on the site were also designed by Crossland, including the lodges at the entrances and several cottages. He designed the terrace in front of the Sanatorium building and the landscaping for the whole site, as well as two pairs of fine gates. Holloway had been anxious that the grounds, as the building itself, should be of high quality and had exhorted Crossland to work to his highest standard, modelling the landscaping on the gardens of the Crystal Palace at Sydenham. The grounds were probably completed before the Sanatorium, and, as with the building itself, they were to attract the criticism of the Commissioners in Lunacy, and substantial alterations were implemented from the late 1880s. By this time, though, Crossland's involvement with the project was over.

Soon after Thomas Holloway's death, Crossland and Ruth left their home on the College site and returned to live in London. Crossland had enjoyed living in a rural environment and wrote of his pleasure in having the Mount Lee Estate at his disposal and Windsor Forest nearby, in which to pass his spare time.[62] He maintained his office there and doubtless continued to visit the College site frequently, which was an easy journey by rail from Waterloo Station to Egham. He had lived four and a half years on the site, supervising the building of the College, but seemingly felt that the internal fitting did not necessitate him being there continuously. Moreover, with Thomas Holloway dead, there was no longer his patron's insistence that Crossland lived on the project.

In 1884, Crossland began renting a property in Bloomsbury – 46 Upper Bedford Place.[63] This house was on the Duke of Bedford's land, developed by John McGill in the 1820s. This housing project followed Thomas Cubitt's development of Bedford Place, to the south of Russell Square, as

---

61. Saint and Holder, p. 25, citing the Ashbee Journals.
62. Crossland, p. 145.
63. Upper Bedford Place is now known as Bedford Way and has been redeveloped with
    buildings that form part of University College, London.

an upper middle-class suburb. The property had been the childhood home of the designer and architect C.R. Ashbee[64] (who accompanied Crossland on the visit to the Sanatorium after its completion). It seems, therefore, that Crossland knew the Ashbee family on a personal level, and he became the tenant when the Ashbee family tenancy came to an end.

Crossland chose his new home carefully. Bloomsbury was well known not because its residents were wealthy or fashionable (as in the West End), but because they were artists or intellectuals. Indeed, other architects, including Sir William Tite and Richard Carpenter had been residents of Upper Bedford Place before Crossland. Since 1826, this area of London had also been the home of University College, the nucleus of the then-radical London University. It had accommodated the British Museum since 1847, housed in Robert Smirke's fine classical building. It attracted professional middle-class people like doctors, lawyers, writers and publishers, as well as architects, artists and philosophers. Crossland felt at home among such people.

He was able to visit the two Surrey building projects by train when necessary, and he and Ruth enjoyed the return to London society.

During the same year, 1884, Crossland had to cope with another death among those intimately involved in the Egham project. Ceccardo Fucigna, his sculptor, died with a small amount of work still incomplete at the College. Crossland will have been relieved that Fucigna's assistant, Boldini, completed the work, but his artistic skill was inferior to his master's: the difference in their talent being particularly evident in the apse of the chapel at the College. Crossland must

9.12 London: Bedford Place, Bloomsbury. Crossland's home from 1884 in Upper Bedford Place was one of those demolished to build the present University College. The street design was similar to this nearby street. Photograph taken in 2017.

have been much saddened by the death of this craftsman whom he much respected and with whom he had worked so well.

---

64. http://www.ucl.ac.uk/bloomsbury-project/streets/upper_bedford_place.htm (accessed 9 January 2017).

## *Opening of the Sanatorium*

The Commissioners in Lunacy finally officially licensed the Holloway Sanatorium on 12 June 1885. It was formally opened just three days later on 15 June by Edward, Prince of Wales with the Princess of Wales (later King Edward VII and Queen Alexandra) in a special ceremony, at which the Royal party was hosted by George Martin-Holloway, and at which Crossland was one of those presented to the Prince.[65] The opening ceremony took place in the recreation hall, known as the Great Hall, which was decorated with displays of flowers, and the ceremony was followed by a lavish banquet in the dining hall. The building was much acclaimed for the high standard of comfort offered to the mentally ill.[66] In all, it had taken thirteen years to complete. The final cost had risen from the initial estimate of £207,359 to £320,000.

By a considerable margin, the Holloway Sanatorium was the most impressive and lavishly appointed of the institutions built in the nineteenth century for those with a mental illness and was intended to provide 'freedom combined with active surveillance . . . worthy of its liberal-minded founder who so earnestly desired that no expense or trouble should be spared in rendering it all that he wished, as a means of restoring health'.[67] Although the design of the main building was based on the thirteenth-century Ypres Cloth Hall, and externally was certainly reminiscent of the famous Flanders building, the completed building was less Gothic than its inspiration. In the alterations for licencing and in several other aspects, it was different from the competition design.[68] Crossland had elaborated and varied the design to add interest and to reduce the appearance of an institution, including, among other details, a variety of window designs. Both internally and externally, it was built to an extremely high standard.

The long façade of the Sanatorium is broken by the forward-projecting Great Hall block with the main entrance underneath and a dominating tower rising behind. The tower contained a tank for the supply of water throughout the building, which could also be used in the case of fire. The use of Portland stone dressings in replacement of brick decoration (an early change required by Holloway) gave the building a 'brightness and

---

65. *The Times Digital Archive* (accessed 18 February 2017), 'The Holloway Sanatorium' in *The Times*, 16 June 1885.
66. Whitaker, Abstract (no page number).
67. Surrey History Centre, 2620/6/22, *Holloway Sanatorium, St Ann's Heath, Virginia Water*, pamphlet, apparently written just before the opening of the Sanatorium, unattributed and undated, pp. 6-7.
68. Saint and Holder, p. 21.

9.13 (top, left) Virginia Water: Holloway Sanatorium. This palace for the insane eventually opened on 12 June 1885. Photograph taken in 2013.

9.14 (top, right) Virginia Water: Holloway Sanatorium, entrance cloister. Photograph taken in 2013.

9.15 (bottom, left) Virginia Water: Holloway Sanatorium. The entrance hall was restored in the 1990s. Photograph taken in 2017.

9.16 (bottom, right) Virginia Water: Holloway Sanatorium. Brightly coloured grotesques and animals decorate the entrance hall. Photographs taken in 2013.

sharpness of line that was unexpected from the competition drawing'.[69] Some external features, such as stair blocks forward of the main façade (as at Rochdale) and the turrets, were added when the licence stipulations required stairs for patients.[70]

A large cloister under the Great Hall protects the main entrance, which leads to the exuberantly colourful entrance hall, where every surface is painted or stencilled with grotesques, animals and naturalistic patterns, using bright colours and much gold.

The staircase, as at Rochdale Town Hall, leads to a half landing from which a double flight reaches the generously proportioned rectangular Great Hall, matching Rochdale Town Hall in grandeur. There is a stage at one end and, as at Rochdale, a magnificent hammer-beam roof and stained glass in every window. Most of the wall surface and the ceiling are covered in a riot of decoration, including plants, animals and medieval scenes. Around the walls hang the life-sized portraits that Holloway commissioned without liaison with the artists who decorated the walls, and, in the view of many, the paintings detract from the overall decorative scheme. The portraits are of people considered by Holloway to have made Britain great, including Queen Victoria and Prince Albert, Queen Elizabeth I, King Alfred the Great, Admiral Lord Nelson, the Duke of Wellington and, of course, Holloway himself. Crossland's genius is also recognised in a portrait, alongside one of George Martin-Holloway in a decorated double frame painted onto the wall at the opposite end of the hall from the stage.

The other main room, the former dining room (now a swimming pool), also has a hammer-beam roof and was originally decorated with panels in the style of Watteau paintings. The patients' rooms were luxuriously appointed and modern facilities were provided for the care of patients.

The chapel, which had been commissioned from Crossland in 1882, after the main building was substantially complete, was finished in 1884. Later described as 'bare and cheerless'[71], there is an apse raised a step above the nave floor, but no chancel. The oak benches, stone pulpit, altar rails, reredos, lectern and stained glass were added a few years later, by which time Crossland was no longer architect to the Sanatorium.

Thomas Holloway was a man who seldom voiced his opinions, but he had been well pleased with the building, suggesting that it would immortalise Crossland. Holloway may have voiced his satisfaction with

---

69. *The Builder*, 24 August 1875, p. 643.
70. Whitaker, p. 207.
71. Egham Museum, The Joy Whitfield Collection, Box 476d: the view of the Commissioners in Lunacy in 1899, cited by Andrew Saint in *The Holloway Sanatorium, Virginia Water*, Draft Report, p. 7.

9.17 (top) Virginia Water: Holloway Sanatorium. The Great Hall has a striking Crossland 'signature' hammer beam roof. Photograph taken in 2017.

9.18 (bottom, left) Virginia Water: Holloway Sanatorium. Stained glass and wall decoration in the Great Hall. Photograph taken in 2013.

9.19 (bottom, right) Virginia Water: Holloway Sanatorium. A double portrait of W.H. Crossland and George Martin-Holloway is on the back wall of the Great Hall. Photograph taken in 2017.

9.20 (below) Virginia Water:
Holloway Sanatorium. Crossland also
provided the dining room (now the
residents' swimming pool) with a very
fine hammer beam roof. Photograph
taken in 2017.

9.21 (right) Virginia Water:
Holloway Sanatorium Chapel, 1885.
Photograph taken in 2017.

the building, but payment to Crossland scarcely bore this out. The final
cost of the Sanatorium was about £320,000, including endowments, and
Crossland received £7,620 as a fee – a commission that amounted to 3.5%
of the cost of the asylum. This low rate of commission derived from an
agreement Holloway seems to have extracted from Crossland in 1877,
at a time when Crossland was having financial problems and had asked
Holloway for several advances. Crossland's requests for money irritated
Holloway, and he was determined to protect himself against such requests
getting out of hand. A note written into his Building Purchase Ledger for
the Sanatorium on 3 August 1877 records the rate of commission as 6%,
but on terms that protected him against paying Crossland more in the
event of increasing costs – which, as it transpired, were considerable. The
details of the agreement were specific:

> Mr William Crossland has in consideration of a cheque for £1,000,
> being given to him this day, agreed by a letter bearing this date . . . that
> he will consider and agree that the sum of £127,000 shall be fixed at
> which his Commission as Architect, and for measuring up the work
> by himself or his brother or others employed by him, shall stand

and that whatever payments may have to be made to contractors or others hereafter, he shall not be entitled to receive any commission for the same. So that his commission at 6% on £127,000 is £7,620.

Mr Crossland is debited on a/c of the Mount Lee Estate with £300, so that the whole amount he has now received is £9,500, therefore he is overpaid £1,880, which will now stand to the debit of the Women's College Account, hence £580 will have to be carried from here to the debit of the Women's College Account.[72]

A commission of 3.5% was a disappointing reward for a prestigious project that occupied Crossland for about twelve years and helps to explain his need for all the Yorkshire projects he juggled over those twelve years.[73]

## The College

Once construction had begun in earnest, the College was built in about six years, a memorial to Jane Holloway, as Thomas Holloway had directed. Like the Sanatorium, it was built to an exceptionally high standard, using English bond bricklaying and tuck pointing throughout the building, Portland Stone dressings and much ornamental sculpture. Its glory was its magnificent skyline.

9.22 Egham: Royal Holloway College, 1886. English bond bricklaying and expensive tuck pointing was used throughout the College building. Photograph taken in 2019.

72. Surrey History Centre, 2620/7/2, *Building Purchase Ledger for St Ann's Heath Asylum,* 3 August 1877, p. 206.
73. The Sanatorium was taken over by the National Health Service in 1948. It closed in 1981 and remained empty and deteriorating until 1995 when a development company was granted permission to develop the grounds, with the condition that the main structure was restored. High-class housing was built in the grounds and the side wings of the main building were converted to town houses. The whole project took five years with the restoration requiring much detailed conservation work. The entrance hall, staircase and great hall were restored to a very high standard as public areas, returning them as nearly as possible to their original glory. The dining hall became a swimming pool and the chapel became a badminton court, although many original features were retained. The site is now known as Virginia Park. Access to the restored areas is limited to pre-booked groups, as well as pre-booked visits during Heritage Open Days.

It was one of the largest buildings erected in Britain during the 1880s, and one of the few buildings of such high quality constructed in the late nineteenth century.[74] Unlike any other building of the time, it startled critics.[75] Holloway had been obsessed with style and ostentation, which had caused Crossland much frustration. The College plans were changed some four times. For Crossland, it was a similar experience to the Sanatorium, where, when the building was already underway, Holloway ordered a change from ornamental cut brick to Portland stone on the grounds of economy. Crossland had to fulfil Holloway's wishes without slowing down the work on the building itself even though the alterations meant a change in the character of the design.

The final College building is in a Renaissance style drawing on a variety of sources. The building displays influences from the various Loire châteaux that Crossland visited with Thomas Holloway in 1874 and from elsewhere. Though originally intended to be based on the château at Chambord, the similarity in the final building is undoubtedly less than originally planned. As Crossland refined and embellished his design for the College, combining style elements from different times and different places, it was said:

> that there is to be observed a considerable amount of originality, both as to plan and detail, and a kind of English feeling has been introduced into the style, which assimilates it to our wants, our climate and our local traditions. So much so, that Mr Crossland may be said to have gone forward a good stride on the road to the creation of a new style, but yet with careful steps avoiding the snares and pitfalls which beset the architect who too boldly breaks with ancient traditions.[76]

Crossland achieved an eclecticism truly of his own time such that the College embodied exactly what late nineteenth-century architects said they were looking for: a Victorian style.[77]

The College plan is straightforward: two quadrangles with a central spine. The focal point is the colossal ornate tower over this central block, capped with a huge stylised crown, modelled on the crown over the central staircase at Chambord and bearing a marked similarity to the crown spire of St Giles Cathedral, Edinburgh.

---

74. Williams, Richard, lecture, 24 October 2016.
75. Whitaker, p. 244.
76. *The Graphic*, 26 June 1886, Issue 865.
77. Crooke, J. Mordaunt, 'Mr Holloway's Château' in *Country Life*, 9 October 1986, p. 1124.

9.23 (above) Egham: Royal Holloway College. The College was built on an unprecedented scale with a magnificent skyline. Photograph taken in 2013.

9.24 (left) Egham: Royal Holloway College. The ornate tower over the central block of the College building. Photograph taken in 2016.

Crossland based the interior design on corridors, a very different layout from existing university buildings for men at Oxford, Cambridge and elsewhere, where undergraduate rooms were arranged up staircases that opened off quadrangles or other spaces. It is doubtful that this 'English Collegiate' style would have translated well into a building of the vast dimensions of Holloway's College.[78] More importantly, the corridor design was more secure than the Oxbridge pattern, which was an important consideration in designing for a community of females. Crossland will also have designed with contemporary perceptions of female well-being firmly in mind. The prevalent view at the time was that women's constitutions were weak, and it was therefore supposed that their health could be damaged if they had to go outside into the open air to get to bathroom facilities.[79]

9.25 Egham: Royal Holloway College. Long, wide corridors characterise the College building. Photograph taken in 2013.

The College was constructed on an unprecedented scale, particularly in the context of the development of education for women. It was built for 250 women students when Oxford and Cambridge had only recently begun admitting a limited number of women, and the matter of higher education for women still caused controversy. 'Newnham and Somerville would fit into one of Royal Holloway's vast quadrangles, where they would be totally overpowered by its flamboyant architecture.'[80] The College measures 550 feet (about a tenth of a mile) in length by 376 feet, and its two quadrangles cover 'more ground than any other college in the world.'[81] Within its vastness, 'Crossland scores a triumph in the efficient grouping of well over 800 rooms fulfilling a variety of different purposes.'[82] The building has two six-storey north-south wings, but because of the slope of the land, the southern end has an extra storey. Crossland made a feature of the slope at this end

78. Hall, Michael, 'A Thames Valley Château: Royal Holloway College, Egham, Surrey' in *Country Life*, 21 May 2014, p. 122.
79. White, William, *Scenes from Student Life*, BBC Radio 4, 25 April 2016.
80. Hall, p. 120.
81. *The Leeds Mercury*, 26 June 1886, Issue 15044.
82. Williams, E., p. 119. The description of the College draws substantially on this article.

9.26 Egham: Royal Holloway College, the north wing, shortly after completion
in 1886. The chapel is to the left of the entrance arch and the picture gallery
(originally intended to be the recreation hall) is to the right.

by designing a substantial brick terrace (on the design of which he and
Holloway had disagreed) below the College building. The area below the
terrace is landscaped with lawns, flower beds and a small lake.

In Crossland's design, the three connecting wings housed the public
rooms. A chapel and a recreation hall were in the northern entrance wing,
with a magnificent clock tower over the entrance between them. The
dining hall and kitchens were in the central range, crowned by the huge
lantern tower, decorated with water creatures and winged lions, which
concealed the water tank. The large lecture theatre, library and museum
were accommodated in the southern wing, with a decorated lantern and
tower over the southern entrance gate (described by Crossland as the
'tradesman's driving gateway'[83]), balancing the bell tower in the northern
wing.

83. Williams, E., p. 119.

9.27 (top) Egham: Royal Holloway College, the north quadrangle, towards the middle wing. The corridor was glazed in the early twentieth century to provide a means of crossing from the east wing to the west wing indoors, without having to walk through the library. The statue of Queen Victoria was placed where it still stands, in the north quadrangle, shortly after the college opened. Photograph taken in 2019.

9.28 (middle, left) Egham: Royal Holloway College, the middle wing and the south quadrangle. The middle wing contains the original kitchens and dining room. Photograph taken in 2016.

9.29 (opposite, middle, right) Egham: Royal Holloway College, the south wing. A massive tower balances the tower in the north wing. The statue of Thomas and Jane Holloway was placed here in the south quadrangle shortly after the college opened. Crossland referred to these entrance gates as the 'tradesmen's driving gateway'. Photograph taken in 2016.

9.30 (opposite, bottom) Egham: Royal Holloway College, steps from the corner of the terrace at the southern end of the building. Crossland and Thomas Holloway disagreed on the siting of the steps descending from the terrace. Photograph taken in 2019.

The chapel, recreation hall and arches of the main gateway were designed with semi-circular headed double-height windows with heads carved onto the keystones, representing, among others, Jesus Christ, evangelists, prophets, biblical kings, virtues, elements, Minerva and Homer. From the outset, and in keeping with Thomas Holloway's liberal religious views, the chapel was intended to be non-denominational, and, as if to emphasise this, the carved heads decorating the quadrangle side of the chapel include Mohammed and Confucius. Holloway's wish had been for the college to be run as 'an orderly Christian household with a simple daily service, the reading of a portion of Scripture and a form of prayer approved by the governors'.[84]

The elevations of the residential wings facing the quadrangles are visually striking. Each is topped with a fine pediment above the main staircase carved by Fucigna and illustrating the foundation and purpose of the whole institution. As described by Crossland they are 'Commerce and Medicine, to illustrate the characteristics of the illustrious founder; Poetry and Science; Charity and Education; and a large portrait bust of the founder, supported by allegorical figures of "Surrey" and "Agriculture"'.[85]

The whole of each quadrangle is a supremely confident composition by an architect in complete command of his craft, blessed with a generosity of funding that enabled him to achieve what many architects could only

9.31 Egham: Royal Holloway College. This pediment includes an image of Thomas Holloway. Photograph taken in 2016.

84. Surrey History Centre, PX/56/74, obituary of Thomas Holloway, in *Illustrated London News*, 5 January 1884, p. 24.
85. Crossland, p. 147.

dream about.[86] The decoration of the whole building is a lavish eclectic mix of geometric and naturalistic motifs, many reinterpreted from what Crossland sketched at Chambord. A large number of different decorative motifs are used in the small panels above the windows of the east and west wings, including naturalistic designs of animals and birds, classical imagery including acanthus leaves and architects' instruments. There seems to be no theme behind this rich variety of designs, but Fucigna carved them all to a high standard and may well have chosen the subject matter himself.

The outline of the building is punctuated by dormers and gables, towers and turrets, both circular and octagonal, capped with conical and pepper-pot roofs, cupolas and lanterns decorated with fantastical creatures. These, as well as Italianate urns and other objects and an abundance of stone carving create a fairy-tale skyline, where there is always something new to beguile the observer. Looking closely, however, the limited number of designs used is surprising: Crossland applied the same design to all the chimneys, and there are only two dormer designs, one for the towers and another for the wings, despite the range of designs seen on his visits to the Loire area. It is tempting to suppose that with the discerning Thomas Holloway dead, simplification was one solution for Crossland in managing his many commitments.

Inside the residential wings, the rooms on every floor open on each side of an exceptionally wide corridor (ten feet wide) that runs the full length of the wing. This ensures the building is an integrated whole rather than a series of separate units, as is the case in Oxbridge colleges that were built on the staircase system. The staircases in the residential wings, on the footprint of a single room, are an example of Crossland's mastery of design: economical on space while fulfilling their practical function perfectly. They are structurally and stylistically an integral part of the whole building while not obscuring the vista along the corridor and decorated so as to be pleasing to the eye.

A clever, but very expensive, design feature was to keep the College's services away from the main building. To this end, the boiler house, laundry and other facilities

9.32 Egham: Royal Holloway College, a staircase inside the west wing of the College. Crossland demonstrated his mastery of design by putting the staircases in the residential wings on the footprint of a single room. Photograph taken in 2016.

86. Williams, E., p. 108.

9.33 (top) Egham: the boiler house, Royal Holloway College. Two very tall chimneys carried smoke away from the site. The building has been completely remodelled as performance space and a café. Photograph taken in 2019

9.34 (middle) Egham: Royal Holloway College. The slope of the hill was levelled with spoil from digging the foundations and from excavating the tunnel, creating a level sports ground. Photograph taken in 2019.

9.35 (left) Egham: Royal Holloway College. The grand north entrance leads into no more than the open air of the north quadrangle – no grand reception hall here. Photograph taken in 2013.

were constructed some 300 yards to the east of the college building and access was achieved through a tunnel. The huge amount of soil excavated was piled up with soil dug for the foundations alongside the west wing, levelling the slope of the hillside and creating a flat area for sports. *The Morning Post* commented:

> Throughout the vast establishment both gas and electric light are laid on, while arrangements for heating by steam are also perfected. For these purposes, large engineering works, in which are five huge boilers and the requisite machinery, have been erected in a low lying portion of the grounds and hence to the lower regions of the college will be conveyed by means of a subterranean tramway the provisions and all other necessities.[87]

In the boiler house, Crossland created an impressive building with a fine iron roof and two tall chimneys to carry the smoke away from the College building at a high level.

Nonetheless, and despite Thomas Holloway's apparent complete satisfaction, there were some major aspects of the design of this educational palace that, surprisingly, Crossland seems not to have thought through. The north entrance from the road is extraordinarily grand with a broad arched entrance under the clock tower, the chapel to the left and the recreation hall (which was to become the picture gallery) to the right – but it leads simply into the open air of the north quadrangle. What came to be used as the main entrance is a small and unremarkable door approximately in the middle of the long east façade, which leads to a small reception area and then simply into a corridor. This is a palace with no grand entrance hall or vestibule. Another issue was that the only indoor route between the east wing and the west wing was through the south cross wing and required using the library as a thoroughfare – a practice that caused considerable disturbance and which was stopped after a while.

The major rooms in the cross wings all have barrel-vaulted ceilings and are decorated with pilasters. The chapel, 'a kind of English translation of the Sistine chapel at Rome'[88] is a single-aisle church, and, in the style of medieval colleges, the pews face each other along the length of the aisle. Much of the decoration is of familiar biblical motifs, but the relief work was unusual in nineteenth-century churches.[89] The decoration is of a very high standard, mostly by Fucigna, with the exception of the south side of the apse ceiling,

---

87. *The Morning Post*, 21 June 1886, Issue 35569, p. 3.
88. *The Graphic*, 26 June 1886, Issue 865.
89. Williams, E., p. 115.

which was completed by Fucigna's assistant, Boldini, after Fucigna's death.[90] There remains in the Royal Holloway Archive a cartoon drawn by Crossland, one of the few pieces of his artwork to survive, showing statues of saints in niches along both side walls, but the niches were never filled.

9.36 Egham: Royal Holloway College, a drawing of the interior of the chapel by Crossland himself. It is one of the very few pieces of his artwork that survives. Each of the niches along the sides of the chapel has the name of a saint written above. However, the niches have always been empty. This drawing makes it clear that the intention was to fill them with statues.

Despite the empty niches, Crossland was very pleased with the final appearance of the chapel, including a long explanatory section about it in his address to the R.I.B.A. in 1887. He was particularly pleased with the mellowed fresco-like effect achieved on the groups of figures on the ceiling and in the apse: 'delicate in colour, somewhat in the manner of old ivories – that is, the colour is worked into hollows of draperies, etc. and rubbed off the more salient surfaces, thus avoiding heaviness. The general scale of colour obtained by these means is not unlike that of the Sixtine [*sic*] Chapel.'[91] Other painted decoration is by Clayton and Bell.[92]

---

90. Crossland, p. 147.
91. Crossland, p. 147.
92. Powell, p. 18.

9.37 (above) Egham: Royal Holloway College. The chapel is a single-aisle church in the style of a medieval college chapel with the pews facing each other along the length of the aisle. Photograph taken in 2013.

9.38 (below, left) Egham: Royal Holloway College. The library bookcases were purpose-made to fit this public room. Photograph taken in 2016.

9.39 (below, right) Egham: Royal Holloway College. Furniture was also purpose-made for the residential corridors. Photograph taken in 2013.

The original library and former museum in the south wing are divided into bays by stone arches. Massive oak bookcases and other furniture, produced by the main contractor, were purpose-made to fit these public rooms as well as the residential corridors.[93]

The College was formally opened by Queen Victoria on Wednesday 30 June 1886, twelve years after Thomas Holloway's purchase of the Mount Lee estate. 'On the day of the ceremony . . . crowds of people poured from the surrounding villages, and still more from London, into Egham, which was quite *en fête* with flags and a triumphal arch.'[94] Some 600 school children had been invited to swell the crowds and many distinguished people had been invited. The Queen drove over from Windsor, accompanied by several other members of the royal family and escorted by a detachment of the Life Guards. Arriving at 5.30, George Martin-Holloway, trustees and governors were presented to the Queen, as was Crossland and the builder John Thompson. The Archbishop of Canterbury led a short service in the chapel, after which the Queen looked at the decoration in the chapel and visited the Picture Gallery.

OPENING OF THE ROYAL HOLLOWAY COLLEGE FOR WOMEN BY THE QUEEN—THE ROYAL PARTY LEAVING THE CHAPEL AFTER THE RELIGIOUS CEREMONY

9.40 Egham: Royal Holloway College. This image of Queen Victoria admiring the decoration of the chapel appeared in *The Graphic* on 10 July 1886 to celebrate the opening of the College by the monarch.

93. Whitaker, pp. 233-36.
94. *The Graphic*, 10 July 1886, Issue 867.

According to the Court Circular published in *The Standard* two days after the ceremony, it was in the Picture Gallery that Crossland was presented to the Queen. It must have been with enormous pride that he offered her an album of his own work, consisting of a selection of illustrations of the college. John Thompson, the building contractor, presented the Queen with a golden key, set with diamonds.[95]

The Queen was then escorted to a dais in the upper quadrangle, where the band played 'God save the Queen', George Martin-Holloway presented an address and the Earl of Kimberley spoke to say, 'I am commanded by Her Majesty to declare this College open.' There followed loud cheers, a fanfare of trumpets, a blessing by the Archbishop, a rendition of 'Rule Britannia' and then the royal party left to return to Windsor, leaving other guests to enjoy refreshments and inspect the College building.[96] The Queen was pleased with what she saw at the opening ceremony and allowed 'Royal' to be added to the name of the College. Decorative details had been completed ahead of the granting of this honour, including the 'HC' cyphers on the lampposts, which still record the original name 'Holloway College'.

9.41 Egham: Royal Holloway College. The cypher 'HC' is for Holloway College. This detail was completed before the College was granted the use of 'Royal' in its name and remains on several street lamps to the present day. Photograph taken 2016.

The 'genius' of Crossland was celebrated in press reports of the opening and a plan of the College was printed in *The Builder* on 3 July 1886. The College building was not fully finished by the time of the opening and fitting out continued into 1887. Academic life finally began in October 1887 with the arrival of the first tutors and the first twenty-eight women undergraduates and their maids.[97] The academic staff and students were accommodated on the first and second floors of the west side of the building. Each student was allocated two rooms: a

95. *The Standard*, 2 July 1886, Issue 19335, p. 2.
96. *The Graphic*, 10 July 1886, Issue 867.
97. Williams, E., p. 115.

study with a view looking over the college grounds and a bedroom across the wide corridor, facing one of the quadrangles, while their maids were accommodated on the fourth floor. All the rooms were provided with solid practical furniture[98], some of which was built-in and custom-made to fit the rooms.

Late in the planning of the College, Thomas Holloway had decided to emulate Matthew Vassar, who had assembled a collection of paintings for his college in Poughkeepsie, New York State. Holloway began to buy pictures for the College in May 1881 and in about two years, formed a valuable collection of work by contemporary artists. The pictures were hung at the Sanatorium while the College was completed, and there were suggestions for a purpose-built gallery. In the event, this was never built. With nowhere else to display the paintings for the official opening, they were moved from the Sanatorium to the Recreation Hall at the College, Queen Victoria noting in her diary that the royal party were taken to the 'Picture Gallery'.[99] There the pictures remained, despite criticism regarding the lack of top lighting and that the pilasters interrupted the hanging.[100]

The final cost of the college was around £600,000, including the cost of the land and additions such as the lodges and terraces, the engine house and the underground tunnel taking services to the College building, furniture and the pictures for the Picture Gallery. In addition, an endowment of £200,000 was provided.[101] Remarkably, though, the construction work originally quoted at £257,000 (exclusive of fittings and furniture) was on budget. In his address to the R.I.B.A. in 1887, Crossland explained the unusual method by which this was achieved, 'after a plan which had been agreed upon between Mr Holloway and myself'[102]:

> By dividing the building into a number of blocks, lettered A to F . . . and again dividing these blocks into a series of sections bounded by each floor, it became easy, so long as the building was carried on level throughout (and this was stipulated in the contract), to ascertain from the priced quantities what amount was due to the contractor; also, in case of disputed quantities, everything being localised, the reference and proof were easily

98. Dennis, Graham and Richard Williams, *The Englefield Green Picture Book* (Egham, 1992), p. 32.

99. The collection of paintings at Royal Holloway, University of London is catalogued and described in *Victorian Taste* by Jeannie Chapel.

100. Alterations were made in 1903 on the advice of the artist Briton Rivière. Crossland had no involvement in the changes that were made.

101. Powell, p. 17.

102. Crossland, p. 144.

established. The outcome was that upon the original contracts,
and upon other contracts priced from the same bills, there have
been no extras.[103]

The Sanatorium and the College[104] together cost well over 1 million
pounds[105], 'the munificence of the benefactions being altogether without
precedent in this country.'[106] The Times reported, 'The mere money
expended on them surpasses in amount anything hitherto done by private
means.'[107]

---

103. Crossland, p. 144.
104. The College became part of the University of London in 1900. Royal Holloway,
    University of London, is today the flourishing provider of higher education
    that Thomas Holloway aspired to create. It has expanded beyond anything
    Holloway could have dreamed of, spreading down the hill towards Egham.
    Founders Building, as the original building is now known, remains the heart of
    the university. In 1965 the first male students joined, and in 1985 the College
    amalgamated with Bedford New College, bringing the student population
    to about 1,000. By the end of the 1980s, there were 2,500 students and the
    student population in 2018 was about 10,000. It is highly regarded across a
    broad spectrum of disciplines. Holloway would perhaps be particularly pleased
    to know that the largest department is the School of Management.
105. Worth more than £120 million in 2019.
106. *The Leeds Mercury*, 26 June 1886, Issue 15044.
107. *The Times*, 19 December 1883, Issue 31007, p. 3.

*Chapter 10*

# The thespian dream

While Crossland was heavily engaged on the Sanatorium and the College, Ruth undertook charitable work, beginning to develop the foundations of what was to be her own career. Up to the late 1880s, she involved herself in organising events for charities such as bazaars, concerts, fairs and dances, as well as hospital work and nursing the sick.[1] Crossland was gradually drawn into her interests, encouraging and actively supporting her. In 1884, they had moved from Egham back into London, renting 46 Upper Bedford Place in Bloomsbury, although the bungalow on the College site remained Crossland's office until 1894.[2]

On 31 May and 1 June 1884, around the time that they moved back to London, Ruth took part in a two-day charity event with members of the acting profession, organised by several titled and society ladies. It took place at the Royal Albert Hall to raise money for the Chelsea Hospital for Women.[3] Attendance was reported as very good, and those attending included foreign royalty in the person of Ismail Pasha, the Khedive of Egypt, and his suite. Among the sideshows and other attractions were a series of tableaux based on several of Shakespeare's plays, and Ruth ('Mrs W.H. Crossland') appeared in one based on Romeo and Juliet. Intriguingly, she appeared alongside a Mrs Lart, which was the married name of Crossland's daughter, Maud. There is no means of being certain whether this Mrs Lart was, in fact, his daughter, but it is not a common surname. Maud certainly remained on good terms with her father and may have also accepted his second life-partner to the extent that they became genuine friends – Ruth was, after all, only about seven years older than Maud.

---

1. *The Era,* 16 April 1892, Issue 2795.
2. Williams, Richard, *Thomas Holloway's College: The First 125 Years* (Egham, 2012), p. 9.
3. *The Morning Post*, 31 May 1884, Issue 34926, p. 3.

Such charitable work served to establish Ruth in London society, and Crossland became involved in charity work himself. He became the honorary secretary of the St John Ambulance Association, which had been formed less than a decade earlier in 1877. Surprisingly, in the days immediately before the opening of the College, he was busy selling tickets for another charitable event, with which he and Ruth were involved. The event was on 28 June 1886, just two days after the opening of the College, but the sale of tickets was announced in the press on 21 June, just when Crossland must have been busy checking final details to be ready for the grand opening. The charitable event was a prestigious three-day fundraising Hungarian Market and General Eastern Bazaar and was opened by the Princess Beatrice at Willis's Rooms in the St James area of London. Many eminent artists of the day took part, and those wanting tickets were directed in press advertisements to apply to Crossland, in his capacity as honorary secretary, at his home address in Bloomsbury, as an alternative to contacting specialist ticket agents.[4] At the event itself, in his capacity as honorary secretary, Crossland was one of the four men in the welcoming party who greeted Princess Beatrice and escorted her to the dais where she declared the event open. After this she visited the various stalls that had been set up, each with a motto in Hungarian across the top of the stall. These stalls were presided over by various ladies, some with titles, amongst whom was 'Mrs Crossland'.[5] Such an occasion was a perfect opportunity for both Crossland and Ruth to make new society acquaintances and to cement those already made.

While taking this exciting new direction in their lives, 1885 and 1886 were to be years of personal tragedy for Crossland and Ruth. Firstly, Crossland's brother, James, died in 1885. His death was registered in London, and it is likely he was staying with his brother at the time of his death. Surprisingly, since his wife and four children were presumably in Huddersfield, he was buried in the Monach and Crossland vault at Highgate Cemetery. His interment took place in May 1885 and was the second interment in the family grave. An inscription on the tomb describes him as 'of Dundas, Canada'.

In 1886, as Crossland himself was basking in the glory of the many accolades that came his way following the opening of the College, Ruth's first son, Benjamin Tilley Hatt, died tragically at sea, and his death was registered in Neath, Glamorganshire. He had enlisted in the Merchant Navy, but his life was cut short at the age of just sixteen. His was the third

---

4.  *The Morning Post*, 21 June 1886, Issue 35569 and 28 June 1886, Issue 35575; and *The Standard*, 21 June 1886, Issue 19325.
5.  *The Times*, 30 June 1886, p. 18.

interment in the Highgate Cemetery grave. The inscription added to the tomb, abbreviating his name to Ben, reveals that he died from exposure on the wreck of a barque named 'Earlscourt'. Although he had lived apart from his mother for at least some of his early life and had moved away for a life at sea by his mid-teens, his death affected Ruth deeply – it was said that her nervous system was 'completely shattered'.[6]

The young man's father, Ruth's estranged husband, may have been unaware of the death of his first son. He had made a new life for himself in Hampshire, his separation from Ruth being so complete that he almost certainly had no idea whether his wife was alive or dead and probably chose not to try to find out. Confident that he could risk bigamy, in February 1888 John Hatt married again, stating in the marriage register that he was a widower. Ruth almost certainly knew nothing of this marriage. He went on to have two further children and various occupations including a coal merchant and later a golf caddie. He lived until 1919 and is buried at All Saints Church, Fleet, Hampshire.[7]

As sadness coloured their private lives, Crossland's public life briefly sparkled. Following the opening of the Royal Holloway College, Crossland achieved something of a celebrity status among architects. He was invited to address the Royal Institute of British Architects in 1887 to discuss with other Fellows and Members the planning and processes behind the construction of the College. He spoke of his relationship with Thomas Holloway, living on the site of the great project and of his immense respect for craftsmen sculptors who work alongside architects in creating the decorative details of buildings. The address was then published in the R.I.B.A.'s Transactions. It gave considerable insight into Crossland's thinking and way of working and was to become the longest written statement Crossland left for posterity. He spent a substantial part of the speech in addressing the relationship between an architect and the sculptor who embellished an architect's buildings, concluding that the sculptor generally received insufficient recognition and remuneration. He discussed at length the sculptors Alfred Stevens and a Frenchman called Briant before describing the work of Fucigna, who had died while working at the College in Egham.

Small works at the College continued to demand Crossland's time. While the College was being fitted out in 1887, he advised on lighting the huge building. A few maintenance and 'snagging' jobs remained to be addressed after the arrival of the students, as well as the completion of small auxiliary buildings. A cottage close to the boundary wall was completed in 1887, for the use of the Head Gardener at the College. Despite its insignificance

---

6. *The Era*, 16 April 1892, Issue 2795.
7. https://www.ancestryinstitution.com.

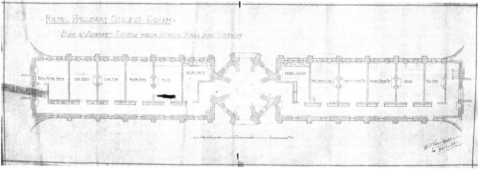

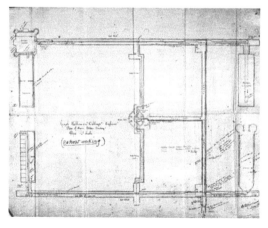

10.1 (top) Egham: Royal Holloway College, the Head Gardener's Lodge, 1897. Photograph taken in 2019.

10.2 (middle) Egham: Royal Holloway College, plan for alterations to Domestic Offices, 1887.

10.3 (bottom) 2 Egham: Royal Holloway College, plan for work on the heating system, marked 'as now working', 1888.

alongside the enormous College building, Crossland endowed the little building with considerable charm. Its part timber framing was emphasised with black and white painting, and the roof was decorated with several rows of scalloped tiles, reminiscent of the roof of his Lockwood gatehouse of 1863. The tall chimneys were particularly striking, their style derived from those of the College building itself.

Even with the College in use as Holloway had intended, there was new work on the site for Crossland. He drew up plans in 1887 for early alterations and improvements to the 'domestic offices' under the dining room and kitchen[8], and the following year he worked on a problem with the heating system, proposing alterations[9] and providing plans for these proposals.

Nonetheless, it seems that, following his dedication and enormous commitment to the two huge projects in Surrey, Crossland resolved to ease the pressure on himself and take a step back from such an all-consuming career. Despite Holloway's parsimony with respect to his fee for the Sanatorium, he had earned well from the Holloway and Ramsden projects and doubtless felt sufficiently financially secure to no longer have to follow every possible income opportunity.

He continued to take on some commissions, probably choosing those that appealed to him. In 1887, he was commissioned by Thomas Holloway's surviving relations to build a chapel in memory of Holloway at the church where Holloway's funeral had taken place. This was the ancient Church of St Michael and All Angels at Sunninghill in Berkshire, not far from Royal Holloway College and close to Holloway's home, Tittenhurst Park. The Holloway Chapel was built at the expense of the by then knighted Sir George Martin-Holloway and completed by 1889 with five windows dedicated to Holloway's memory. The chancel was rebuilt to Crossland's design at the same time, with the chapel and rebuilt chancel together forming an extension to the church.

In 1888, Crossland wrote to the governors of the college on notepaper of the Architect's Department, thanking them for relieving him from the grave responsibility, which had up to then rested upon him. This probably marked the point at which the building was accepted as fully commissioned, from which time Crossland would not be considered responsible for any future defects.[10] Nonetheless, he was retained as consulting architect, and he carried out a number of maintenance and small construction projects for the college in the following few years. This was in contrast to the management of snagging issues at the Sanatorium, where Crossland had

8. Royal Holloway Archive, RHC AR/511/3, 1887.
9. Royal Holloway Archive, RHC AR/511/4-7, 1888.
10. Law, Part 3.

10.4 Sunninghill: Church of St Michael and All Angels, rebuilding 1889.
Crossland added a polychrome memorial chapel to Thomas Holloway's memory
(on the left) and rebuilt the chancel. Photograph taken in 2012.

10.5 Sunninghill: Church of St Michael and All Angels,
Crossland's chancel. Photograph taken in 2012.

little involvement after around 1883, as the works in the years following its opening were carried out by Charles Dorman. Crossland selected six of Philpot Jones's designs of the Sanatorium to keep for posterity[11] and had the plans for the College bound into three volumes.[12]

## Introducing Charles Dorman to Huddersfield

Crossland's last recorded visit to Huddersfield was in March 1888, when he stayed with a Mrs Fairlamb at Woodhouse Hill, not far from the Crossland family home.[13] The visit may have been to introduce Charles Dorman to Sir John Ramsden, as, by 1890, Dorman was working for the Ramsden Estate, being described as architect to Sir J. Ramsden. He carried out work for the Ramsdens in the early 1890s, including work concerning the provision of drains at Crossland's Bulstrode Building.[14]

## Ruth's career

In easing the pressure on himself, Crossland was in a position to be more supportive of Ruth in her mental recovery following the death of her son, Benjamin, and in developing her career aspirations. She had apparently wanted to go on the stage from an early age, but had been discouraged from doing so by her family and instead focused her energies on charitable activities, in which she was very successful. Her son's death at sea in 1886 affected her profoundly, and it was suggested to Crossland that she should now be encouraged to go on the stage, in the hope that she might gain some relief from doing something she had so longed to do.[15] Organising this, as well as organising the care necessary for their son, must have posed a considerable challenge, but Crossland was prepared to support her.

By August 1888, Ruth had joined the theatre company of playwright and impresario Mark Melford for an eight-week engagement touring the provinces, and her acting career was taking off. She assumed the stage name Ruth Rutland and began to enjoy good reviews as Lady Josephine Blair, an aristocratic kleptomaniac, in *Kleptomania*, a farce written and directed by Mark Melford. Crossland almost certainly provided not only moral

11. Law, Part 3, citing a memorandum of 1887 in the records of the Sanatorium. These designs were almost certainly subsequently destroyed by Crossland.
12. Chapel, Jeannie, *Victorian Taste*, Royal Holloway College (London, 1982, second impression 1993), p. 11.
13. Law, Part 3.
14. Centre for Buckinghamshire Studies, D-RA/5/41, correspondence including letters from Charles Dorman, 1890-94.
15. *The Era*, 16 April 1892, Issue 2795.

support for Ruth, but also financial support in the costs arising from living away from their home in London and also in beginning to build up her collection of gowns and wigs for the stage.

Surprisingly for a newcomer, Ruth took the leading role and her name quickly became highlighted in advertisements for the play, indicating that in the space of just a few months she had become a leading actress. Reviews recognised her success. A large advertisement in *The Era* on 1 September 1888 featured 'Ruth Rutland', and reprinted excerpts from several reviews[16], including:

> Miss Ruth Rutland is a handsome, an imposing, a magnificent representative of the aristocratic victim to kleptomania, (*Hull Daily Express*) and Miss Ruth Rutland, a lady of stately figure and carriage, is thoroughly ladylike and unconscious as the fair pilferer and her costumes are exceptionally rich. (*Leeds Evening Telegraph*)

and

> Perhaps the best performance of all is that of Miss Ruth Rutland as the kleptomaniac, her grand stage presence and superb acting proving one of the greatest attractions. (*Leeds Evening News*)[17]

The *Leeds Evening Express*, quoted in the same advertisement in *The Era*, was evidently also impressed by her performance as the best in the company – but was also intrigued as to her real identity:

> Playgoers who visit the Grand Theatre this week to see Mr Mark Melford's funny, but risky, farce *Kleptomania* cannot fail to be struck with the strong claims to admiration of the ladies of the company, and particularly with the fine stature and commanding presence of the handsome lady who plays the peculating wife of the unfortunate Major-General Blair, whose costumes are much discussed by the feminine section of the audience. This lady figures on the programme as 'Miss Ruth Rutland' but that name, I believe, only conceals the identity of Mrs W.H. Crossland, a lady well-known in London society, and the wife of a prominent architect. 'Miss Rutland' has but just taken to the stage. Her figure would have rendered her invaluable, physically, in certain Gilbertian operettas such as Ruth in 'The Pirates', the Fairy Queen in 'Iolanthe', Lady Jane in 'Patience', and so on.

16. *The Era,* 1 September 1888, Issue 2606.
17. *The Era,* 1 September 1888, Issue 2606.

Also quoted in the same advertisement, the *Leeds Evening News* triumphantly stated:

> No! There can be no mistake about it. The charming kleptomaniac now appearing at the Grand as Miss Ruth Rutland must surely be Mrs W.H. Crossland, wife of the well-known architect. Her splendid appearance lends great power to the character, and her performance convinces one of the consoling fact that in the new society actress we have an acquisition to the stage. Isn't that so, Mr Mark?[18]

Ruth, as Miss Ruth Rutland, was therefore soon recognised as Crossland's wife. The tone of the recognition emphasises the fact that Crossland himself was also a well-known personality following the opening of his two masterpieces in Surrey. It is likely Crossland accompanied Ruth when on tour, at least sometimes. She needed his support as she tried to overcome the sorrow caused by the death of her Benjamin and as she embarked on her hazardous new career. In any case, he would otherwise have seen little of her. Whether their young son, then aged ten, also travelled with his mother is not known. It is more likely that he stayed with his grandmother, as he had done on previous occasions, while his mother was establishing her acting career.

Separation from Cecil was difficult for Ruth, though. When her first engagement with Mark Melford's company finished at the end of September, her rapid rise in the profession was seen as 'a sudden and pronounced success'[19], and she was rewarded with the offer of a two-year contract, which, according to the press, she was 'most reluctantly compelled to decline . . . owing to her presence in London being imperatively necessary'.[20] It is likely that having suppressed maternal instincts for eight weeks while touring Britain, she felt she had achieved a sufficient stature in her new profession to dictate her terms – and she wanted to see more of her young son. She was briefly described as 'disengaged' (or not currently working), and, for her fans, her home address – the Crossland home at 46 Upper Bedford Place – was provided in the newspaper report.

Ruth's gamble paid off, though, and she doubtless made better arrangements for seeing Cecil as she was soon re-engaged by Mark Melford, who must have found it difficult to contemplate the loss of his new star. Her re-engagement to play the same role of Lady Josephine was reported in November.[21]

18. *The Era*, 1 September 1888, Issue 2606.
19. *The Era*, 29 September 1888, Issue 2610.
20. *The Era*, 29 September 1888, Issue 2610.
21. *The Era*, 17 November 1888, Issue 2617.

The company endured an exhausting schedule of engagements in top provincial theatres (though not always, it seems, with a top-quality show) in places as far apart as Belfast, Glasgow, Leeds ('Brilliant success at the Leeds Grand – they laughed till they cried') Liverpool, Birmingham (where the play was taken too slowly and Ruth Rutland – perhaps unsurprisingly – was hoarse[22]), Brighton, Ryde (where the company kept the audience laughing, but a few more rehearsals would have been desirable[23]), Bristol, Plymouth and many towns and cities in between, including several return visits. Ruth enjoyed being in the public eye. Readers of reviews learned that Ruth Rutland was a woman with an imposing physique: 'The Juno-like figure of Miss Ruth Rutland was well adapted for the part of the stately Lady Blair'[24], and, since actresses were frequent instigators of new fashions and new hairstyles[25], in the way she coiffed and dressed herself, she took her place among those seen as trend-setters.

Ruth's name was often singled out and used as the headline in advertisements to attract attention to the play: 'Miss Ruth Rutland, Lady Josephine in Kleptomania'.[26] She spent fifteen months touring the provinces with Mark Melford's company. By the autumn of 1889, the impresario was happy to introduce her to the London stage, and it seems that she considered her grounding in the provinces to have been complete. A London production of *Kleptomania* was announced, with her name heading the bill ('Miss Ruth Rutland as Lady Blair'), suggesting she had made a considerable success on tour in her first role.

Ruth made her London debut in November 1889. Among the classified advertisements in the *Pall Mall Gazette*[27], *The Morning Post*[28], *The Standard*[29] and elsewhere was the announcement of her breaking onto the London scene at the Strand Theatre. She was described as a new society actress: 'KLEPTOMANIA. – Mrs W.H. Crossland's first appearance in London today at 2.30 in Kleptomania. Second matinee Monday next.'

She was well received with favourable reviews in the press:

> STRAND THEATRE – Miss Ruth Rutland (Mrs W.H. Crossland) made her first appearance on the London stage yesterday, in Mr Mark Melford's amusing farcical comedy, 'Kleptomania.' Miss

22. *Birmingham Daily Post*, 26 February 1889, Issue 9570.
23. *Hampshire Telegraph and Sussex Chronicle*, 29 December 1888, Issue 5611.
24. *The North-Eastern Daily Gazette*, 12 February 1889.
25. Goodman, Ruth, *How to Be a Victorian* (London, 2014), p. 115.
26. *The Era*, 30 March 1889, Issue 2636.
27. *The Pall Mall Gazette*, 7 November 1889, Issue 7688.
28. *The Morning Post*, 7 November 1889, Issue 36628, p. 4.
29. *The Standard*, 7 November 1889, Issue 20384, p. 4.

Rutland was well qualified by her handsome and stately figure, as well as by no little comedy talent. . . . Miss Rutland is evidently experienced in stage business, and her rendering of the character was graceful and pleasing. The audience gave the lady a very cordial reception and her first London performance may be pronounced decidedly successful.[30]

Her employer continued to keep Ruth well occupied. Within days, she appeared in the first London performance of another Mark Melford comedy, *Stop Thief!*[31], which was reviewed as being lightweight and needing more rehearsal, although 'Mrs W.H. Crossland' was praised.[32]

Meanwhile, Crossland was refocusing his career. It seems that, on the completion of the Kirkgate Buildings in Huddersfield in 1885, he had declined further work for the Ramsdens. Having passed to Charles Dorman (the Sanatorium architect he introduced to the Ramsdens) his mantle as architect to the Ramsden Estate, he began to look for projects in London.

In 1889, Crossland took on a commission in central London. Compared to Thomas Holloway's College and Sanatorium, this was a small project, but was the sort of work he had probably anticipated when he moved to London almost two decades earlier. To that extent, it must have held some excitement for him, small though it was, to be at last taking on a commission in the heart of the metropolis. The project was for Christie's, the fine art business, which had been granted a lease on No. 5 and part of No. 4 Bury Street, immediately adjoining one of the galleries at their existing premises in the St James area of London. The business commissioned Crossland to design a block of residential chambers and shops on the site, and the building was completed the following year.[33]

1889 also brought more personal sadness. Crossland's mother-in-law, (Lavinia's mother) and wife of Robert Monach who co-owned the Highgate Cemetery family vault, died. She was buried in the family grave in September.

Early in 1890, Ruth Rutland appeared in another Mark Melford production, *Nixie*, at Terry's Theatre in The Strand and afterwards at the Globe. She was then engaged by another theatrical producer, Mr Herbert Darnley, for the part of Mrs Sterndale in *The Solicitor*, which was staged in Liverpool. When former actress Violet Melnotte introduced the play to a London audience at Toole's Theatre, King William IV Street, Ruth Rutland

---

30. *The Morning Post*, 8 November 1889, Issue 36629, p. 5.
31. *The Era*, 9 November 1889, Issue 2668.
32. *The Era*, 16 November 1889, Issue 2669.
33. http://www.british-history.ac.uk/survey-london/vols29-30/pt1/pp295-307#h3-0007.

became a member of her company, and her comedy acting again received good reviews. She subsequently appeared in *The Two Recruits*, and at the end of the season transferred to the theatre company of Mr Willie Edouin, a comedian, actor and theatre manager, and she appeared at The Strand Theatre in *Private Inquiry, Turned Up, Daggers Drawn* and other productions.[34] Altogether, Ruth performed in five productions in 1890 and five in 1891.[35]

10.6 Playbill for 'Nixie'. Crossland's wife, Ruth Rutland, is featured as Mrs Belasys (seventh from top) in the cast list. The play opened at Terry's Theatre in the Strand and moved to The Globe.

Although Ruth Rutland moved between several theatre companies, she remained on close terms with her first employer and mentor. At the time of the 1891 census on 5 April, Mark Melford, described as an author, and his actress wife, Ethel Melford, were house guests of the Crosslands in their Bloomsbury house. Also making up the household were their son, Cecil (then aged thirteen), James E. Crossland, aged twenty-seven, Crossland's nephew (noted as born in Hamilton, Canada, and described as a naval

34. *The Era*, 16 April 1892, Issue 2795.
35. J.P. Wearing, *The London Stage 1890-1899: A Calendar of Productions, Performers, and Personnel*, https://books.google.co.uk/

officer), as well as a cook and a housemaid. Ruth was described as wife and actress, and, as in the previous census, her first name was recorded wrongly – this time as Edith.

Ruth was clearly a talented actress. She made a late entry into the profession because of family commitments, but quickly gathered a following of admirers. Such was their interest in her that when she became ill in 1892, the stage magazine *The Era* published a reassurance for her fans in March: 'Miss Ruth Rutland's dangerous illness has been a source of great anxiety to her numerous friends. We are glad to state, however, that all danger is now past, and that she is making satisfactory progress.'[36]

Less than a month later, it was announced that she was 'disengaged', and, for fans who might have wanted to contact her, addresses were provided, as was usual practice: both the Strand Theatre and the Crossland family home in Bloomsbury were cited.[37] The reassurances to fans had been either false, or, having made something of a recovery, Ruth suffered a serious relapse. Tragically for her fans and devastatingly for Crossland, she died of typhoid fever on 8 April 1892. Her death was reported in *The Era* on the Saturday following.[38]

Her death was sudden, at the age of thirty-nine – the same age as Crossland's wife, Lavinia, when she died – and Crossland's world fell apart, emotionally, socially and professionally. They had lived happily as husband and wife in a close, modern and forward-looking relationship for more than a decade and supported each other in their respective careers. She had been happy to live with him at The Bungalow, supporting him in his most challenging commission; he had been pleased to encourage and support her in her new career, which had helped Crossland himself remain engaged and interested during the personal anti-climax that followed the opening of the Royal Holloway College. For a few short years, Mr W.H. Crossland and Miss Ruth Rutland must have been something of a golden couple: he basking in the glory of his architectural masterpieces and she as a fast-rising star of the stage. Her death was truly a tragedy for Crossland, leaving him bereft of companionship, with his social standing diminished and a large question mark over his professional life.

Ruth was interred in the Crossland vault at Highgate Cemetery. Her short epitaph clearly suggested that she was married to Crossland. It carried more warmth than Lavinia's epitaph and made Crossland's feelings for her abundantly clear: 'Ruth, wife, companion, friend of W.H. Crossland. Born 29.1.1853, died 8.4.1892'.[39]

---

36. *The Era*, 19 March 1892, Issue 2791.
37. *The Era*, 9 April 1892, Issue 2794.
38. *The Era*, 16 April 1892, Issue 2795.
39. *The Era*, 16 April 1892, Issue 2795.

*Chapter 11*

# Into obscurity

Crossland's reason for living was lost when Ruth died. Her death made Crossland painfully aware of his own mortality, and he arranged for his will to be drawn up only six weeks afterwards and almost certainly as a consequence of Ruth's sudden death.

While Ruth's epitaph on the Crossland vault suggested that she was married to Crossland, his will suggested otherwise. In his will, Ruth's surname was given as Hatt, the name of the man she married at the age of sixteen, with no mention of the name Crossland. The solicitor who drew up Crossland's will is likely to have advised Crossland that exact and correct names had to be used. Such accuracy would have been of less importance to the census enumerator and to the Registrar of Births, Marriages and Deaths, where Ruth could be described as his wife, but such a statement in his will, if not true, could have jeopardised the bequest to his son.[1] In his will, Crossland's clear concern was to make provision for their son, then aged only fifteen, in the event of his own death before Cecil reached the age of twenty-one.

> This is the last Will of me William Henry Crossland of No. 46 Upper Bedford Place in the County of Middlesex, Architect. I revoke all former Wills and Testamentary dispositions. I devise unto William Stanton Lart and Walter Ledger who I also appoint Executors of this my Will all my interest in Grave No. 23297, Square 70 in the Highgate Cemetery which is now jointly vested in me and Robert Monach and I desire to be buried therein as also my child Cecil Henry Crossland son of Eliza Ruth Hatt deceased. And I devise and bequeath all my estate and effects whatsoever and wheresoever unto the said William Stanton Lart and Walter Ledger upon trust to apply the same for the benefit of the said

1.  Law, Part 3.

Cecil Henry Crossland Hatt during his minority and to pay or transfer the whole or remainder thereof to the said Cecil Henry Crossland Hatt on his attaining twenty one for his absolute use and benefit. And I confirm an Indenture of Settlement which I have already made in favour of the said Cecil Henry Crossland Hatt. In witness whereof I have to this my Will set my hand this twenty sixth day of May one thousand eight hundred and ninety two.

Signed by the above named William Henry Crossland as and for his last Will and Testament in the presence of us both being present at the same time who at his request in his presence and in the presence of each other have hereunto subscribed our names as witnesses.

Fred T Astin, solicitor, 61 Gresham House, Old Broad Street.
Thos. Godfrey of the same place, his Clerk.[2]

Crossland named as executors his son-in-law, William Stanton Lart, and Walter Ledger, whose relationship to Crossland is not known, but who, years later, presented one of the few remaining images of Crossland to the Royal Holloway College (see page xx). The security of his son was clearly paramount for Crossland. He made no bequest to his daughter, Maud, nor even made a mention of her in his will, despite apparently having a good relationship with her. This was probably because he knew that she had received a substantial inheritance from her maternal grandmother, while Cecil, still a minor, had no other provision for his welfare. Maud's husband's profession (he was an accountant and company secretary) would have also ensured a good income.

Early the following year, Crossland's father-in-law, Robert Monach, died. He had survived Crossland's mother-in-law by four years, and his death marked the end of Crossland's connection with Lavinia's family. In February 1893, Robert Monach was buried in the family vault he and Crossland had bought together in Highgate Cemetery.

Completely bereft following Ruth's death, Crossland still needed an income and continued working on small projects. Between 1892 and 1893, he drew up a plan to support the bank behind the Engineer's shop at the Royal Holloway College[3], and in 1893 he designed improvements in the ventilation of the kitchen at the College.[4]

2. Law, Part 3.
3. Royal Holloway Archive, RHC/14/3/2/1/6, 1892-93.
4. Royal Holloway Archive, RHC/14/3/2/1/7, 1893.

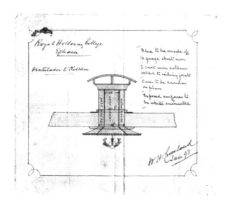

11.1 Egham: Royal Holloway College, design for ventilator to the kitchen, 1893.

Crossland's last building for the College was the swimming pool, a small building in the woodland below the south terrace, built with the same high standard of brickwork as the College building. It was completed in 1893.

Away from the College in 1893, Crossland also took on a new and challenging project, which helped to fill his empty life. This was the alteration, amounting to a complete conversion, of a property that was located between 62 Regent Street and 9 Glasshouse Street, in Regents Quadrant, close to Piccadilly Circus in central London. It was probably intended to be part of the overall redevelopment of Regent Street, which took place from 1895 into the first quarter of the twentieth century. Of the various properties with addresses on these streets, this was the only one that extended between the two streets, with a front entrance on both and with a very difficult angled footprint. In 1893, the premises were a bakery, with a bakehouse and shop and traded under the name of Petzrywalski's.

The building was of substantial size and Crossland was commissioned to design a conversion that was to turn it into dining premises – almost certainly a club – with the choice of dining options and rooms for hire that members would have

11.2 Egham: Royal Holloway College, Swimming Pool, later Jane Holloway Hall, now a fitness suite. This was Crossland's last commission for Royal Holloway College. Photograph taken in 2013.

expected. Crossland's plans provided: in the basement, a grill room, smoking room and saloon as well as a coal store, a beer store and a wine store; on the ground floor, two cafés and a saloon; on a mezzanine floor, a private room; on the first floor a private room, servants' hall and stores; and on the second floor, a scullery, stores and kitchen. Too few lavatories

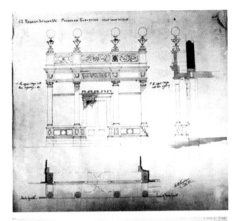

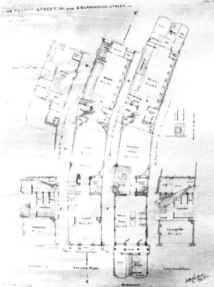

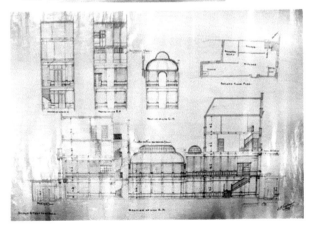

11.3 London: 62 Regent Street and 9 Glasshouse Street. This shows the floor plans for Crossland's planned alterations; the elevation of the proposed new Regent Street entrance and a section through the proposed refurbishment, 1893. Photograph taken in 2016 of LRRO1/2484 Land Revenue Records and Enrolments, Subject maps and plans, (plans and elevations for 62 Regent Street and 9 Glasshouse Street, London), 1893 at The National Archives.

were provided in the first plan and more were added at a later design stage. It was an awkward plan, largely because of the difficult shape of the site. With the kitchen located on the second floor, a great deal of movement would have been necessary for serving meals.[5] Crossland may well have been asked to amend the plan again, but no evidence of this has been found, and it is not known whether the conversion took place to Crossland's plans.

Meanwhile, in Marsden, near Huddersfield, a project doubtless long forgotten by Crossland (see pages 68-70) was beginning to take shape. A new church for the community was built in stages from 1894, mainly due to the efforts of the then incumbent, the Reverend Richard Buller, who was described as 'a man of unbounded energy and strong determination'.[6] It was built to Crossland's plans under the guidance of architect C. Hodgson Fowler of Durham, assisted by local Marsden architect James Kirk. Crossland's foundations, covered over in the late 1860s, were apparently unsalvageable and new foundations were laid in 1894. The nave and side aisles of a building seating around 600 worshippers were completed and dedicated in October 1895, at a final cost of about £10,000. It was dubbed the 'Cathedral of the Colne Valley'.[7][8]

Crossland may have read about the new church in the architectural press and in other circumstances would have been proud that his plans had eventually been realised. By 1894, however, two years after Ruth's death, Crossland had more pressing concerns. He had left the affluence of Upper Bedford Place and was living at 18 Great George Street, Westminster. Although this too was a prestigious central London address, close to the Houses of Parliament, he was almost certainly reduced to a small apartment – perhaps to just one room. He almost certainly had a

5. The National Archives, LRRO1/2484, land revenue records and enrolments, subject maps and plans (plans and elevations for 62 Regent Street and 9 Glasshouse Street, London), 1893.

6. http://www.achurchnearyou.com/marsden-st-bartholomew/ (accessed 15 September 2015) and www.marsdenparishchurch.org.uk/history.htm (accessed 15 September 2015).

7. http://www.achurchnearyou.com/marsden-st-bartholomew/ (accessed 15 September 2015) and www.marsdenparishchurch.org.uk/history.htm (accessed 15 September 2015). After more fundraising, the chancel, Lady Chapel and vestries were completed in 1899, and the church was finally finished when the tower and baptistery were added in 1911.

8. An alternative conclusion, that the church 'stands on foundations of a church by W.H. Crossland', is given in Harman, Ruth and Nikolaus Pevsner, *The Buildings of England, Yorkshire West Riding, Sheffield and the South*, 2017, p. 400.

short and therefore cheap lease, as the building was due for demolition to make way for new government buildings that were built in the early twentieth century.

Crossland had always enjoyed living well and always made his home in an affluent and fashionable area. He probably lived beyond his means for much of his working life, this being suggested in October 1876 by his request for an advance from Thomas Holloway. His outgoings almost certainly increased even further as Ruth built her career. If he travelled with her when she toured the provinces in 1888-89, he would have had to pay his own travel and hotel costs. He almost certainly subsidised Ruth's expenses.

The extravagant lifestyle Crossland had probably enjoyed over many years eventually caught up with him. On 8 August 1896, his business went into receivership[9], and, under the Bankruptcy Acts of 1883 and 1890, on 12 August he was subject to a Receiving Order.[10] Described as 'late of Upper Bedford-place, Russell-square, WC, architect and surveyor', all his assets were taken into the custody and control of the court to pay off creditors so far as was possible.

It is not clear who initiated bankruptcy proceedings. Although possible, it is unlikely that he made the move himself because of the repercussions that it would have had on his career. The most likely instigator was his landlord at Upper Bedford Place. If Crossland had accumulated substantial arrears on his rent, the landlord might well have observed that Crossland was working less than previously and therefore doubted whether the arrears would ever be paid.

Bankruptcy threatened Crossland with the greatest possible fall from grace. For a man who had contributed several important churches to the revival of the Established Church in Yorkshire, won the confidence of three wealthy patrons, designed many of the buildings that gave modern Huddersfield its character, designed three of the greatest secular Gothic revival buildings in England and slipped into the life of London society with apparent ease, the ignominy was scarcely imaginable. Bankruptcy in late nineteenth-century Britain was a social disgrace.

Bankruptcy proceedings could be protracted, but, remarkably, Crossland managed to salvage something of his reputation by coming to a satisfactory arrangement with his creditors in just three months. At eleven o'clock on Wednesday 18 November 1896, Crossland appeared before Mr Registrar Giffard in Court 1 at the Bankruptcy Buildings, Carey Street, Lincoln's

---

9. *The Morning Post*, 8 August 1896, Issue 38742, p. 6.
10. *The Times*, 12 August 1896, Issue 34967, p. 8.

Inn[11], and at this November court appearance, his bankruptcy was discharged. Having forfeited his assets to pay his debts, Crossland was now stripped of personal wealth – but he had saved himself from public disgrace and the shame of bankruptcy.

Nonetheless, even being brought so close to bankruptcy brought with it humiliation. Having virtually no money at all, he became something of a pariah in society. The Royal Institute of British Architects would not have required his resignation[12], but the cost of his Fellow's annual subscription was probably now beyond his means. Just a decade after praise had been heaped on him by fellow members of R.I.B.A. as they hailed his masterpiece, his association with the organisation lapsed and his name disappeared from their records. The last reference to him in the R.I.B.A. records is in the R.I.B.A. Kalendar of 1894-95, when he was listed as living at 18 Great George Street, Westminster. Thereafter, he simply disappeared from R.I.B.A.'s records, not being listed as retired.[13] Crossland almost certainly felt that his appearances in the bankruptcy courts brought shame not only upon himself, but also on the profession, and, even if his subscription was not an issue, he probably felt it was honourable to sever links with the R.I.B.A..

He could have returned to Yorkshire, but did not. He may have been too ashamed to return, or it may simply have been that he no longer had family or contacts to whom to return. He now also had no place in London society just a few years after being so warmly embraced. Yet he remained in London, probably to be near his children and such work as he had. It must have been some comfort to him that he remained on good terms with his daughter, Maud, and her husband, William Lart, who by now were probably living in London with their one daughter. His relationship with his son may have been less warm.

The Royal Holloway College retained him as architectural adviser on an annual basis until 1900[14], and he continued to report on the fabric of the building and carry out small projects for the college. After all, Crossland had designed the greatest modern college building in Britain, and, despite his changed circumstances, his skills were not in dispute and nobody knew the vast red-brick edifice better than he did. In December 1898, he

---

11. *The Morning Post*, 18 November 1896, Issue 38829, p. 6.
12. Personal correspondence between the author and the R.I.B.A. Information Centre, 3 June 2016.
13. R.I.B.A., W.H. Crossland biographical file, letter dated 6 September 1979 from The British Architectural Library to Elizabeth Williams at St Andrew's University.
14. Chapel, Jeannie, *Victorian Taste*, Royal Holloway College (London, 1982, second impression 1993), p. 12.

produced the specification of the work needed to set up five rooms as a botanical laboratory on the second floor in the north pavilion on the east side of the College.[15]

By the turn of the century, he had moved from 18 Great George Street, Westminster to 25 Abchurch Lane, a narrow medieval alley between Cannon Street and Lombard Street in the City of London[16] and had professional notepaper printed with this address. The College called on him to carry out a survey on the building and his report – seemingly his last work for the college – was sent in a letter from Abchurch Lane on 22 May 1900.[17] In the same year, the College became part of the newly formed University of London, and the survey commissioned from Crossland was almost certainly preparatory to this.

In the same year as the Royal Holloway College terminated its link with Crossland, his daughter Maud died at the age of only forty. Her death was on 8 March 1900, and she was interred in the family grave at Highgate Cemetery on 12 March. Crossland had had a good relationship with his daughter, and, as he grieved, he must have felt more and more alone.

The census in 1901 recorded that he had moved again and was boarding with the Whyand family – a woman of sixty-one and her two nieces, together with a female boarder near Regents Park in London.[18]

Crossland's son, Cecil, married in 1903, at the age of twenty-eight. By the time of his marriage, Cecil had reversed his last two names and was using Crossland as his surname.[19] He and his fiancée gave the same address, clearly suggesting a pre-marital relationship that would have attracted disapproval from most sections of society.

Cecil Hatt Crossland married Lucy Beryl Holland on 28 November 1903 at the Church of St Saviour, Paddington. Crossland may not have been present at his son's wedding, as the two witnesses who signed the parish register were Lucy's parents, Edwin and Emma Holland. The absence of Crossland's name as one of the witnesses might suggest a breakdown of the relationship between father and son, even though Cecil had taken his father's surname. Cecil's occupation on the marriage register was given as an actor; Lucy's father was described as a 'professor of singing'; and the occupation of Crossland himself was also, surprisingly and intriguingly, given as an actor.[20]

15. Royal Holloway Archive, RF126/1.
16. Abchurch Lane today remains a thoroughfare of medieval narrowness, but was redeveloped in the twentieth century with office buildings.
17. Royal Holloway Archive, RF126/1.
18. https://ancestryinstitution.com.
19. Crossland's son later reshuffled his names again. In the census of 1911, he was calling himself Cecil Henry Crossland and was described as a comedy artist.
20. https://ancestryinstitution.com.

It may be, therefore, that Crossland eked out an existence after his severance from the College by joining the acting profession. After leaving the employment of the Royal Holloway College and having relinquished his Fellowship of the Royal Institute of British Architects, Crossland probably felt the architectural profession was closed to him. He had followed Ruth as she sought to develop her career and became absorbed into the acting profession, welcoming members of the profession to his Bloomsbury home as house guests. He had seen his son follow his mother's career example in his own choice of career and then join, through marriage, a family that lived in the world of entertainment. The theatre had plainly become an environment to which Crossland could relate and in which he probably felt comfortable. The bohemian world of entertainment was altogether more accepting of unconventional lifestyles than the world of the generally well-heeled and more straight-laced patrons of architecture. Taking a common-law wife, living beyond one's means, bankruptcy courts and any other irregularities in Crossland's life would probably have been quickly overlooked and soon forgotten.

In her will, Crossland's daughter, Maud, left most of her estate to her daughter, but directed her trustees to pay an annuity of £104 to her father with the oddly worded caveat 'if in their discretion they thought fit'.[21] This seems to recognise that her father was living in much-reduced circumstances and hints at the fact that Crossland might have slipped from the rectitude of just a few years earlier. It may have been the fact that Crossland had joined the acting profession that prompted the terms of Maud's annuity provision. Whatever the circumstances that led to Maud's caveat, Crossland had to somehow find enough money to live. Even if Maud's trustees thought fit to pay the annuity, two pounds a week would have provided only the bare essentials of life and Crossland would have needed to find means to supplement this income. Small acting parts would certainly have been a way of doing this.

Cecil and his wife Lucy continued to live in the London area, where Cecil developed a career as a comedy artist. Assuming the relationship between father and son remained amicable, they gave Crossland the pleasure of another grandchild in 1905, when their daughter Beryl Joan Crossland was born.[22] Nonetheless, in financial circumstances far removed from the comfort of his earlier life, with his first and second wives both dead, his brother dead, his daughter dead, and his wealthy but comradely patron dead, Crossland's last years will have been colourless and purposeless. If he no longer had contact with his son, his life will have been truly bleak.

21. Law, Part 3.
22. https://ancestryinstitution.com.

Sometime in the early 1900s, Crossland moved again – to an apartment at 57 Albert Street, Camden. This was in the same street and just a few houses away from where he had lived in the 1850s when he was a pupil in George Gilbert Scott's office. It was also only a short distance from the opulent home in Park Village West that he rented when he first opened his office in London three decades earlier. The Albert Street property had once been a fine Georgian terraced house, but it had seen better times. Divided into several units, it was described as a lodging house. Camden was unfashionable at that time, and it was a poor home indeed for a man who had, for the most part, lived and worked at the most chic addresses throughout his life. It must have been a torment to be reminded of earlier, happier, successful times, and it is therefore something of a puzzle that he chose to return to live in this part of London. However painful, having lost everything else, he probably felt he would be more comfortable in an area he knew well, rather than somewhere completely new.

After the opening of the College, Crossland is known to have had taken personal possession of six of the designs of the Sanatorium by his one-time partner, John Philpot Jones. They 'were sent round to his house, 46 Upper Bedford Place, Russell Square [on] 2nd March 1887. These designs were stored away upstairs in the roof.'[23] Crossland also had plans of the Royal Holloway College bound into three large volumes. In 1906, the College asked him to deposit with their institution his copies of the plans of the building. Crossland replied that he could not oblige, as they had been destroyed, with more of his work, some years previously.[24] Tragically, in these dark years of his life, Crossland can never have considered what a loss the destruction of his life's work would be.

On 14 November 1908, Crossland died of a stroke in Camden.[25] He was seventy-three. The death certificate gave the causes of death as a cerebral haemorrhage and asthenia, the latter term meaning simply debility. The informant of his death was his landlord, C. Otto Dahl.[26]

Crossland's death was sudden. It is likely that none of the strangers around him in the lodging house at the time of his death had any idea of who he was and the social standing he had enjoyed up to some fifteen years earlier. Unless he had told them – and there was no reason why he should have confided in casual contacts – they would not have known that he had a family grave waiting for him at Highgate Cemetery. He had bought

23. Surrey History Centre, 2620/7/2, Building Purchase Ledger for St Ann's Heath Asylum, p. 10.
24. Law, Part 3.
25. https://ancestryinstitution.com.
26. Law, Part 3.

11.4 57 London: Albert Street, Camden. Crossland rented an apartment here from the early 1900s and died here in 1908. Photograph taken in 2017.

the plot with his father-in-law in 1879, prompted by the death of his first wife, Lavinia, and embellished it with a fine angel statue of his own design. Both his wives and his daughter, Maud, were already buried there, along with his brother, James, and his first wife's mother and step-father and his second wife's first son. In his will, he stated that it was his wish to be buried in this grave in Highgate Cemetery, but it is unlikely that he had a copy of his will with him at the lodging house where he was living: it would have been in safekeeping with a solicitor, probably Fred T. Astin of 61 Gresham House, Old Broad Street, who had witnessed the will. If he no longer saw his son on a regular basis, Crossland's funeral will have been arranged by strangers, and there would have been nobody to point out that he had a family vault waiting for him.

So it seems that, even in death, there was no respite from the ignominy brought by the brink of bankruptcy, as he was probably buried in a pauper's grave. Crossland left £29 2s 9d (£29.14p) – worth approximately £2,800 in 2016.[27] Although this would have been seen as riches by the poorest strata of society, it was an insignificant estate for a man whose dignified, coherent and inspired designs had earned him the patronage of wealthy people, a very substantial income, accolades most could only dream of, an entry to high society and personal fame.

Surprisingly, in a borough where records were already good, his burial or cremation seems not to have been recorded, and his burial or cremation place remains unknown. So the death of W.H. Crossland passed essentially unnoticed. It was the saddest finale for an architect who had soared to the top of his profession and who had been showered with praise for his achievements. In destroying so many of his designs, he did nothing to

27. https://www.measuringworth.com/calculators/ukcompare/relativevalue.php.

help later generations understand and appreciate his work. He must have known, though, that his best buildings were among the finest buildings ever constructed in England and that he got as near as any architect to creating a nineteenth-century style of architecture in his confident and eclectic mix of earlier styles and motifs. Over some of the most exciting decades British architecture has ever known, when the built environment was utterly transformed, despite the anonymity of his later years, the contribution of William Henry Crossland was truly significant.

W.H. Crossland. This engraving appeared in *Building News*, 7 February 1890, accompanying an incomplete list of his commissions.

# Architectural commissions by W.H. Crossland

| 1855-56 | Huddersfield, Cowcliffe and Netheroyd Hill Church of England Sunday School |

## Halifax office

| 1859-63 | Huddersfield, St Thomas' Church, Bradley |
| 1860 | Manchester, Assize Court (unsuccessful competition entry) |
| 1861 | Leeds, Mechanics Institute (unsuccessful competition entry) |
| 1861 | Huddersfield, school, Hillhouse (demolished) |
| 1861 | Elland, pair of houses (demolished) |
| 1861 | Elland, terrace of three houses, one with shop (demolished) |
| 1861-63 | Halifax, houses at Akroydon |
| 1861-63 | Almondbury, Nettleton's Almhouses |
| 1861-65 | Copley, St Stephen's Church |
| 1862 | Elland, terrace of three houses, one with shop (demolished) |
| 1862 | Elland, mansion (demolished) |
| 1862-63 | Huddersfield, Christ Church, Moldgreen |
| 1862-63 | Huddersfield, parsonage house, Hopton, Mirfield |
| 1862-65 | Ossett, Holy Trinity Church |
| 1863 | Hawnby, near Helmsley, All Saints Church (restoration) |

## Leeds office, 17 Albion Street

| 1863 | Huddersfield, gatehouse to Woodfield House, Lockwood |
| 1863 | Leeds, house in Cookridge Street |

| | |
|---|---|
| 1863 | Leeds, terrace of houses in Belle Vue Road |
| 1863 | Leeds, eighteen cottages at Armley Hall for the Leeds Model Cottages Society |
| 1863-70 | Birstall, St Peter's Church (rebuilding) |
| 1864 | Elland, hotel |
| 1864 | Huddersfield, Bankfield House, Taylor Hill (demolished) |
| 1864-71 | Rochdale, Town Hall (successful competition entry) |

## *Leeds office, 23 Corn Exchange*

| | |
|---|---|
| 1864-68 | Far Headingley, Leeds, St Chad's Church |
| 1865 | Elland, two houses with shops |
| 1865 | Huddersfield, St Thomas' Church, Bradley |
| 1865 | Huddersfield, St Bartholomew's Church, Marsden (plans: built 1895) |
| 1865 | Leeds, rectory, Methley |
| 1865 | Lockington, near Beverley, St Mary's Church (restoration) |
| 1865-66 | Elland, St Mary's Church (restoration) |
| 1865-66 | Middlesmoor, Pateley Bridge, St Chad's Church (rebuilding) |
| 1866 | Broughton-in-Craven, All Saints' Church (restoration plan: built 1873 to plan altered by unknown hand) |
| 1866 | Masham, St Mary's Church (restoration) |
| 1866-67 | Staincliffe, Dewsbury, Christ Church |

## *Leeds office, 25 Park Square*

| | |
|---|---|
| 1866 | Manchester, Manchester Exchange (unsuccessful competition entry) |
| 1866-67 | Flockton, St James the Great Church |
| 1867 | Leeds, Christ Church, Armley (unexecuted) |
| 1867 | Womersley St Martin's Church (restoration) |
| 1867-68 | Hoylandswaine, St John the Evangelist Church and school (attribution) |
| 1867-69 | Kellington, St Edmund's Church (restoration) |
| 1868 | Huddersfield, Rishworth Lodge, Ripponden |
| 1868 | Huddersfield, semi-detached houses (West Mount and Marshfield), Edgerton |
| 1868 | London, Corn Exchange (unsuccessful competition entry) |

| 1868 | London, Criterion Tavern (unsuccessful competition entry) |
|------|-----------------------------------------------------------|
| 1868 | Ripon, St John's Church, Bondgate (rebuilding) |
| 1868 | Ripon, St Mary Magdalen Church (replacement) |
| 1868 | Rochdale, landscaping, river wall and parapets |
| 1868-69 | Sutton-in-Craven, St Thomas' Church |
| 1868-69 | Kildwick-in-Craven, St Andrew's Church (restoration) |
| 1868-71 | Sheffield, St Mark's Church, Broomhill and vicarage (attribution) |
| 1868-74 | Huddersfield, Ramsden Estate Office |
| 1869 | Staincliffe, Dewsbury, vicarage for Christ Church |
| 1869-70 | Huddersfield, St Andrew's Church, school and vicarage (vicarage not executed) |

## London office, 2 Carlton Chambers, 4 Regent Street

| 1870-72 | Rochdale, St Chad's Church (restoration) |
|---------|-------------------------------------------|
| 1870-75 | Huddersfield, Longley New Hall and alteration plans for Old Longley Hall |
| 1871-72 | Huddersfield, St John the Evangelist Church, Newsome |
| 1872 | Birmingham, Council Offices (successful competition entry, unexecuted) |
| 1872 | Huddersfield, Lowerhouses, Longley, National School (improvements) |
| 1872-76 | Almondbury, All Hallows Church (restoration) |
| 1872-1885 | Virginia Water, Holloway Sanatorium (successful competition entry) |
| 1873 | Huddersfield, George Hotel, kitchens and laundry |
| 1873-75 | Huddersfield, Post Office |
| 1874-75 | Huddersfield, Newsome vicarage |
| 1875-81 | Huddersfield, Byram Buildings and Byram Arcade |
| 1876 | Huddersfield, house on Portland Street |
| 1877 | London, memorial for Crossland and Monach tomb, Highgate Cemetery |
| 1877-1885 | Huddersfield, Kirkgate Buildings |

## Egham office

| 1878 | Egham, bungalow |
|------|-----------------|
| 1879-87 | Egham, Royal Holloway College |
| 1881-83 | Huddersfield, Somerset Building |

| 1881-83 | Huddersfield, Waverley Chambers |
| 1881-85 | Virginia Water, Sanatorium Chapel |
| 1884 | Sunninghill, St Michael and All Angels Church, Holloway tomb |
| 1887 | Egham, head gardener's lodge, Royal Holloway College |
| 1887-89 | Sunninghill, St Michael and All Angels Church, memorial chapel and chancel (rebuilding) |
| 1887-93 | Egham, small alterations, improvements and additions for Royal Holloway College |
| 1889-90 | London, shops and residential chambers for Christie's, Bury Street |
| 1893 | Egham, swimming pool, Royal Holloway College |
| 1893 | London, 62 Regent Street and 9 Glasshouse Street, alteration plans |

## London office, 18 Great George Street

| 1898 | Egham, specifications for botanical laboratory, Royal Holloway College |

## London office, 25 Abchurch Lane

| 1900 | Egham, building survey for Royal Holloway College |

# Bibliography

*Published Works*

Akroyd, Edward, *On Improved Dwellings for the Working Class: A Plan for Building Them in Connection with Benefit Building Societies,* Shaw and Sons, London, 1862. Available at Weaver to Web, the online visual archive of Calderdale history, www.calderdale.gov.uk/wtw/search/controlservlet?PageId=Detail&DocId=100923) (accessed 1 February 2010 and later)

Akroyd, George Jackson, *Saint Thomas's Church, Bradley: One Hundred Years of History, 1863-1963,* St Thomas Church, Bradley, 1963

Banks, W.S., *Walks in Yorkshire: Wakefield and its Neighbourhood*, Longman, Green, Reader and Dyer, London and B.W. Allen, Fielding and McInnes, Wakefield, 1871

Bingham, Caroline, *The History of Royal Holloway College 1886-1896*, Constable & Company Limited, London, 1987

Bingham, Caroline, 'The Founder and the Founding of Royal Holloway College' in *Centenary Lectures, 1886-1986*, ed. Moreton Moore, Egham, Surrey, 1988

Blythman, Guy, *The Holloway Sanatorium*, Egham-by-Runnymede Historical Society, Egham, 2014

Brereton, Revd E.W., *History of the Ancient and Historic Church of St Andrew, Kildwick-in-Craven*, Crosshills, Yorkshire, 1909. Available at http://kildwick.org.uk/wp-content/uploads/2014/09/History-of-Kildwick-Church.pdf (accessed 7 August 2016)

Brookes, Laurie, *(Revised) Brief Notes on the Church of St James the Great, Flockton*, Lamp Publications, 2009

Calderdale Metropolitan Borough Council, *Akroydon Heritage Trail*, Halifax, undated

Calderdale Metropolitan Borough Council, *Akroydon – its Past and Present*, Halifax, undated

Chapel, Jeannie, *Victorian Taste: The Complete Catalogue of Paintings at the Royal Holloway College*, A. Zwemmer Ltd, London,1982, second impression 1993

Cleeves, Revd David, *St. Mary's Church, Masham*, Masham, undated

Crook, J. Mordaunt, 'Mr Holloway's Architect and Mr Holloway's Château' in *Centenary Lectures 1886-1986*, ed. Moreton Moore, Ch. 2, Royal Holloway and Bedford New College, Egham, Surrey, 1988

Cunningham, Colin, *Victorian and Edwardian Town Halls,* Routledge and Kegan Paul, London, Boston and Henley, 1981

Dennis, Graham and Richard Williams, *The Englefield Green Picture Book*, Egham-by-Runnymede Historical Society, Egham, 1992

Elliott, John, *Palaces, Patronage and Pills: Thomas Holloway, His Sanatorium, College and Picture Gallery*, Royal Holloway, University of London, Egham, 1996, redesigned and reprinted 2006

Ferriday, Peter, *Lord Grimthorpe, 1816-1905,* John Murray, London, 1957

Gibson, Keith and Albert Booth, *The Buildings of Huddersfield: An Illustrated Architectural History*, The History Press, Stroud, Gloucestershire, 2005, reprinted 2009

Gillard, D., *Education in England: A Brief History,* 2011. Available at www.educationengland.org.uk/history (accessed 25 January 2016)

Goodman, Ruth, *How to Be a Victorian*, Viking 2013, Penguin Books London, 2014

Harman, Ruth and Nikolaus Pevsner, *The Buildings of England, Yorkshire West Riding, Sheffield and the South,* Yale University Press, New Haven and London, 2017

Harrison-Barbet, Anthony, *Thomas Holloway: Victorian Philanthropist.* Lyfrow Trelyspen, Cornwall, 1990. Revised 1993. Royal Holloway, University of London, Egham, Surrey, 1994

Hartwell, Clare, Matthew Hyde and Nikolaus Pevsner, *The Buildings of England, Lancashire: Manchester and the South-East,* Yale University Press, New Haven and London, 2004

Howell, Peter, *St Stephen's Church, Copley, West Yorkshire*, The Churches Conservation Trust, undated

Jones, Revd Gareth T., *A History of the Chapel of the Hospital of St Mary Magdalen, Ripon*, St Mary Magdalen Ripon, revised 2016

Law, Edward, *William Henry Crossland, Architect, 1835-1908*, 1992. Available at http://homepage.eircom.net/ (accessed 13 January 11) (no page numbers)

Leach, Peter and Nikolaus Pevsner, *The Buildings of England, Yorkshire West Riding, Leeds, Bradford and the North,* Yale University Press, New Haven and London, 2009

Linstrum, Derek, *West Yorkshire: Architects and Architecture*, Lund Humphries, London, 1978

Makings, Rosemary, *St John the Evangelist, Hoylandswaine*, Hoylandswaine, undated

Pevsner, Nikolaus, *The Buildings of England: Yorkshire West Riding*, Penguin Books, Harmondsworth, 1959, revised edition (by E. Radcliffe), 1979

Powell, M.J., ed., *The Royal Holloway College 1887-1937*, Royal Holloway College, 1937

Robertson, William, *Rochdale Past & Present, a History and Guide*, Rochdale, 1876. Available at http://freepages.genealogy.rootsweb.ancestry.com/~todmordenandwalsden/St.Chads.htm (accessed 5 January 2016)

Scott, George Gilbert, *Personal and Professional Recollections*, London, 1879, new edition, G. Stamp (ed.), Stamford, 1995

Sharples, Joseph, *Rochdale Town Hall: An Illustrated Guide,* Rochdale Metropolitan Borough Council, undated

Stamp, Gavin, *Gothic for the Steam Age: An Illustrated Biography of George Gilbert Scott*, Aurum Press, London, 2015

Swires, Muriel and Revd Darryl Hall, ed., *A History of St Chad's Church, Middlesmoor*, The Diocese of West Yorkshire and the Dales, 2015

Wearing, J.P., *The London Stage 1890-1899: A Calendar of Productions, Performers, and Personnel*. Available at https://books.google.co.uk/

Williams, Richard, *Thomas Holloway's College, The First 125 Years*, Royal Holloway, University of London, 2012

Wood, Alec, *History and Description of the Parish Church of St Andrew, Kildwick-in-Craven*, St Andrew Kildwick, updated 1996

Wrathmell, Susan, *Leeds: Pevsner Architectural Guide*, Yale University Press, New Haven and London, 2005

## *Journals and Journal Articles*

Anonymous, 'Hidden painting revealed' in *Country Life*, 17 October 2012, p. 40

Bretton, R., 'Colonel Edward Akroyd' in *Transactions of the Halifax Antiquarian Society*, Halifax, 1948, pp. 61-96

*The Builder* (many editions, all referenced in text)

*Building News* (many editions, all referenced in text)

Crooke, J. Mordaunt, 'Mr Holloway's Château' in *Country Life*, 9 October 1986, pp. 1122-1124

Crossland, W.H., 'The Royal Holloway College' in *R.I.B.A. Transactions, Second series, Vol 3, 1886-7*, pp. 141-48

*The Ecclesiologist* (many editions, all referenced in text)

Gill, Annabel, 'Who'd Have Thought It, Pills Have Bought It!' in *Higher* (the magazine for the alumni of Royal Holloway and Bedford New College), issue 17, Autumn 2012, pp. 22-23

Grime, William, 'An Architect with Genius Leaves behind a Mystery', in *Rochdale Observer*, 21 August 1971, p. 10

Hall, Michael, 'A Thames Valley Château: Royal Holloway College, Egham, Surrey' in *Country Life*, 21 May 2014, pp. 120-23

*Huddersfield Daily Examiner*, 10 May 1985

Saint, Andrew and Richard Holder, 'Holloway Sanatorium: A Conservation Nightmare' in *The Victorian Society Annual*, 1993

*The Victorian*, July 2015

The Victorian Society, *Leeds and Saltaire*, Notes for AGM, 25-27 July 2005

Webster, E., 'Edward Akroyd' in *Transactions of the Halifax Antiquarian Society*, Halifax, 1987, pp.19-45

Whelan, A., 'The Victoria Cross in Akroydon' in *Transactions of the Halifax Antiquarian Society*, new series, 2004, p. 110

Williams, Elizabeth, 'An Architectural History of Royal Holloway College in Egham, 1874-87' in *Surrey Archaeological Collections*, vol 77, 1986, pp. 95-125

## *Unpublished Works*

Chapel, Jeannie, *Notes for Visit to Royal Holloway Picture Gallery by the Victorian Society*, Victorian Society, 1980

Douglas, Janet, *William Henry Crossland,* unpublished notes of lecture delivered at
     Cannon Hall, Cawthorne, South Yorkshire, 21 April 2012
Douglas, Janet, correspondence, 2 August 2017
Poë, Simon, *Stanhope Country,* unpublished notes from lecture delivered at Cannon
     Hall, Cawthorne, South Yorkshire, 21 April 2012
R.I.B.A., W.H. Crossland biographical file
Whitaker, L.J., *W.H. Crossland* (unpublished MA thesis), University of Manchester,
     1984
Wilkinson, J., typescript text of *Edward Akroyd Talk,* Halifax, undated
Correspondence between author and R.I.B.A., 3 June 16 regarding status of R.I.B.A.
     in nineteenth century

## Online Newspaper Resources

*The Times Digital Archive*
*The Times*


*19th Century British Library Newspapers, Part I: 1800-1900 and*

*19th Century British Library Newspapers, Part II: 1800-1900*
*Aberdeen Weekly Journal*
*Birmingham Daily Post*
*Hampshire Telegraph and Sussex Chronicle*
*North Wales Chronicle*
*The Bradford Observer*
*The Era*
*The Graphic*
*The Huddersfield Chronicle and West Yorkshire Advertiser*
*The Huddersfield Daily Chronicle*
*The Huddersfield Weekly News*
*The Leeds Mercury*
*The Morning Post*
*The North-Eastern Daily Gazette*
*The Pall Mall Gazette*
*The Sheffield & Rotherham Independent*
*The Standard*
*The York Herald*

## Other websites

https://ancestryinstitution.com
https://www.thegenealogist.co.uk
http://gbnames.publicprofiler.org/ (accessed 30 November 2015)
https://historicengland.org.uk/listing/
http://homepage.eircom.net/~lawedd/MEDALS%20HUDDERSFIELD%20
     COLLEGE.htm (accessed 25 November 2014)
http://www.visitchurches.org.uk

http://kildwick.org.uk/history/church-history-timeline (accessed 3 August 2016)
http://hidden-london.com/gazetteer/park-village/ (accessed 23 January 2017)
https://www.britishlistedbuildings.co.uk
http://archiveswiki.wyjs.org.uk/
http://www.wdco.org/site/Trinity-Church-Ossett/ (accessed 18 June 2013)
http://www.utopia-britannica.org.uk/pages/YORKS.htm
http://www.yorkshireindexers.info/wiki/index
http://www.bmtparish.co.uk/welcome/ (accessed 3 December 2015)
http://www.achurchnearyou.com/marsden-st-bartholomew/ (accessed 15 September 2015)
www.marsdenparishchurch.org.uk/history.htm (accessed 15 September 2015)
https://www.achurchnearyou.com/womersley-st-martin/ (accessed 19 December
    2016)
http://tyates.com/page2.htm (accessed 29 June 2016)
http://staincliffe.weebly.com/ (accessed 22 October 2015)
http://riponcathedral.info/the-chapels/ (accessed 29 February 2016)
http://www.shipoffools.com/ (accessed 29 February 2016)
www.rightmove.co.uk/property-for-sale/property-24399057.html (St Andrew's
    church, Leeds Road, Huddersfield)
https://londonstreetviews.wordpress.com/2015/02/13/carlton-chambers/ (accessed 25
    July 2016)
http://hidden-london.com/gazetteer/park-village/ (accessed 23 January 2017)
https://commons.wikimedia.org/
http://dictionaryofarchitectsincanada.org/node/179
https://www.myheritage.com/research/record-90100-441655148/notices-and-
    critiques-on-the-paintings-in-the-royal-academy (accessed 20 November 2016)
http://www.ucl.ac.uk/bloomsbury-project/streets/upper_bedford_place.htm (accessed
    9 January 2017)
http://www.british-history.ac.uk/survey-london/vols29-30/pt1/pp295-307#h3-0007
https://www.calderdale.gov.uk/wtw/*From Weaver to Web*, Online Visual Archive of
    Calderdale History (accessed 1 February 2010)
https://www.measuringworth.com/ (accessed 18 March 2018)
www.educationengland.org.uk/history (accessed 25 January 2016)

## Documents

*Centre for Buckinghamshire Studies*
D-RA/5/41 Correspondence including letters from Charles Dorman, 1890-1894

*Egham Museum*
The Joy Whitfield Collection, Box 476b, Holloway Sanatorium, Annual Report
    1886, cited by Andrew Saint in 'The Holloway Sanatorium, Virginia Water,
    Draft Report', October 1993

*North Yorkshire County Record Office*
PR/BGT 6/1 All Saints, Broughton, Broughton in Craven parish records: restoration
    of the chancel; elevation and plans for restoration of the chancel, 1866
PR/BGT 6/2 All Saints, Broughton, Broughton in Craven parish records, ground

plan of part of the church, undated

PR/BGT 6/5 All Saints, Broughton, Broughton in Craven parish records: balance sheet and subscription list for the restoration of the church, 1873

*West Yorkshire Archive*

CMT4/MU:21/23 Plan of two houses at the top of Westgate, Elland (demolished)

CMT4/MU:21/24 Plan of four houses and shop at Northgate, Elland (demolished)

CMT4/MU:21/29 Plan of two houses and shop in Westgate, Elland (demolished)

CMT4/MU:21/31 Plan of a house in Westgate, Elland (demolished)

DD/RA/C/26/2 Ramsden Estate correspondence

DD/RE/C/10/32 Ramsden Estate papers

DD/RA/C/box 36 Report of the Proposed Restoration of the Parish Church, Almondbury, 1872, copy

DD/RE/468 (part) Ramsden Estate papers

DD/RE/48 Ramsden Estate papers, 1876

WDP5 Birstall St Peter Parish Records

WDP9/244 Letters concerning plans for St Peter, Birstall

WDP12/275 Almondbury Parish Church and Schools: a sixth biennial report

WDP/59 Copley St Stephen Parish Records

WDP59/21 Letters about the Copley commission, 1861

WYL555/36 Plans, elevations, specifications and related papers for a parsonage house, Methley, 1865-66

*West Yorkshire Archaeology Advisory Service*

WYHER/10258 The Akroydon Workers Village

WYHER/12845 (regarding Fucigna's designs for Huddersfield buildings including Waverley Chambers)

*Royal Holloway Archive*

GB/131/1/3 Letter dated 24 August 1874 (Crossland to Holloway)

GB131/1/4 Letter dated 30 October 1874 (Crossland to Holloway)

GB131/1/5 Letter dated 18 October 1876 (Crossland to Holloway)

GB131/1/6 Letter dated 3 August 1877 (Crossland to Holloway)

GB131/1/7 Letter dated 4 August 1877 (Crossland to Holloway)

GB131/1/8 Letter dated 4 May 1878 (Crossland to Holloway)

GB131/1/9 Letter dated 17 June 1878 (Crossland to Holloway)

GB131/1/11 Letter dated 23 August 1878 (Crossland to Holloway)

GB131/1/12 Letter dated 26 August 1878 (Crossland to Holloway)

GB131/1/13 Letter dated 30 November 1878 (Crossland to Holloway)

GB131/1/19 Letter dated 25 September 1883 (Crossland to Holloway)

GB131/52/2 Letter dated 16 November 1883, (Crossland to Holloway)

RF/126/1 Press cuttings book, 1876-1900 (regarding Holloway's buildings)

RHC AR/511/1 Ground Plan of Cottages, 1883

RHC AR/511/3 Plans of alterations to domestic offices at College, 1887

RHC AR/511/4-7 Plans of alterations to heating system at College, 1888

RHC AR/511/10-11 Plan to support the bank behind the Engineer's shop at the College, 1892-93

RHC AR/511/12 Designs to improve ventilation at the College, 1893

RHC PH/101/48/1 Photograph of Crossland's bungalow c. 1895

RHC PH/100/1/20 Photograph of the north wing shortly after completion

RHC A43 Photograph of William Henry Crossland

RHC RF/146/1 Cartoon: design by W.H. Crossland

RHC RF/120/3 Engraving from 'The Graphic', 10 July 1886

Original design for Holloway College, published in *Building News*, 21 December
　　1877, uncatalogued copy in Royal Holloway Archive


*Surrey History Centre*

2620/9/5 Thomas Holloway, *Letterbook*, 4.8.169-19.2.1872

2620/6/1 *Suggestions for a Proposed Lunatic Asylum at St Ann's Heath, Near Virginia
　　Water Station*, 1872

2620/7/ Building purchase ledger for St Ann's Heath asylum, 1872

2620/6/22 *Holloway Sanatorium, St Ann's Heath, Virginia Water*, pamphlet,
　　unattributed and undated, apparently written just before the opening of the
　　Sanatorium

PX/56/74 Obituary of Thomas Holloway in *Illustrated London News*, 5 January 1884,
　　p. 24


*The National Archive*

LRRO1/2484 Land Revenue Records and Enrolments, Subject maps and plans,
　　(plans and elevations for 62 Regent Street and 9 Glasshouse Street, London),
　　1893

## Lectures

Douglas, Janet, *William Henry Crossland*, Cannon Hall, Cawthorne, South Yorkshire,
　　21 April 2012

White, William, *Scenes from Student Life, BBC Radio 4,* 25 April 2016 (regarding
　　student accommodation)

Williams, Richard, Royal Holloway College, Thorpe Village Hall, Surrey, 24 October
　　2016

# Index

Page numbers in italics refer to illustrations.

BV - #0047 - 220221 - C23 - 234/156/16 - PB - 9780718895488 - Gloss Lamination